eating together

First published in 2009 by ACP Books, Sydney
Reprinted 2011.

ACP Books are published by ACP Magazines
a division of PBL Media Pty Limited

ACP BOOKS
General manager Christine Whiston
Associate publisher Seymour Cohen
Editor-in-chief Susan Tomnay
Creative director Hieu Chi Nguyen
Art director & designer Hannah Blackmore
Senior editor Stephanie Kistner
Food writer Xanthe Roberts
Food director Pamela Clark
Food editor Cathie Lonnie
Sales & rights director Brian Cearnes
Marketing manager Bridget Cody
Senior business analyst Rebecca Varela
Operations manager David Scotto
Production manager Victoria Jefferys

Published by ACP Books, a division of ACP Magazines Ltd.
54 Park St, Sydney NSW Australia 2000.
GPO Box 4088, Sydney, NSW 2001.
Phone +61 2 9282 8618 Fax +61 2 9267 9438
acpbooks@acpmagazines.com.au www.acpbooks.com.au

Printed by Toppan Printing Co, China.

Australia Distributed by Network Services, GPO Box 4088, Sydney, NSW 2001.
Phone +61 2 9282 8777 Fax +61 2 9264 3278
networkweb@networkservicescompany.com.au
New Zealand Distributed by Southern Publishers Group, 21 Newton Road, Auckland, NZ.
Phone +64 9 360 0692 Fax +64 9 360 0695 hub@spg.co.nz
South Africa Distributed by PSD Promotions, 30 Diesel Road Isando, Gauteng
Johannesburg. PO Box 1175, Isando 1600, Gauteng Johannesburg.
Phone +27 11 392 6065/6/7 Fax +27 11 392 6079/80 orders@psdprom.co.za

Title: Eating together / food director Pamela Clark.
ISBN: 978-1-74245-005-6
Notes: Includes index.
Subjects: Dinners and dining. Cookery.
Other authors: Clark, Pamela.
Dewey number: 641.5

Special features and chapter openers
Photographers Maree Homer, Louise Lister
Stylists Louise Bickle, Kate Nixon

The publishers would like to thank the following for props used in photography:
The Bay Tree, Woollahra; Prop Stop, St Peters; Victoria's Basement, Alexandria;
No Chintz, Woollahra; Chef's Warehouse, Surry Hills; Rhubarb, Richmond (Vic);
Vicino, Waterloo; ici et la, Surry Hills; Butterfield Tate Gallery, Waterloo.

To order books, phone 136 116 (within Australia) or **order online** www.acpbooks.com.au
Send recipe enquiries to: recipeenquiries@acpmagazines.com.au

THE AUSTRALIAN
Women's Weekly

eating together

Bringing families back to the table

acp
books

contents

bringing families

Our lives have changed a lot over the past few decades. We're busier and more stressed than ever before, so it's easy to see how the family meal has fallen by the wayside. With both parents often working long hours and juggling kids' music, sporting and social commitments, it can be tough to get the whole family together for a meal. It's all too easy when everyone is hungry and tired at the end of the day to eat at different times or to collapse in front of the television balancing a plate on your lap. But eating together is an important part of family life. Mealtimes provide the perfect opportunity for families to bond and connect with each other. It's a chance to share what's going on in our lives, talk about what happened in our day and to discuss the news and current affairs. Mealtimes should be an exchange of ideas, conversation and feelings. They are a unifying experience for the family, fostering warmth, love and a sense of belonging. Eating family meals together is also associated with eating more healthfully. Home-cooked meals are usually far more nutritious and healthy than takeaway alternatives. They tend to contain more fruits and vegetables and essential nutrients that are vital to our health and wellbeing. Cooking and serving meals at home also means you have more control over the

back to the table

quality and quantity of what your family is eating. Children learn their eating habits from their parents, so by cooking and eating good nutritious food you are setting your kids up for a lifetime of healthy food choices. It is also the perfect opportunity for young children to learn table manners and social skills in a relaxed and loving environment.

The recipes in this book are designed to entice your family back to the table. Every mealtime is covered, from breakfasts to barbecues to the foods we've come to love from Grandma's kitchen. There are midweek meals, specifically designed so that you can make tasty and simple family meals after work. And there's Sunday lunch, with recipes for all those classic, comforting old favourites to help you leave behind a busy week – a traditional Sunday roast or chicken and leek pie, for example. There's a chapter for the kids, with easy-to-make recipes that will have your aspiring chefs pleading to make tonight's dinner. And let's not forget family celebrations when the food needs to be impressive.

This book is a celebration of food to share with those we love. By sharing mealtimes we strengthen family ties, establish family traditions and create memories that last a lifetime. It's time to bring familes back to the table.

all-day breakfast

Let a late-morning breakfast drift into lunch, there's no rush.

This twist on the classic bacon, lettuce and tomato sandwich is deliciously decadent when made with croissants.

blt on croissant

12 slices rindless shortcut bacon (420g)

4 large croissants (320g)

2 small tomatoes (180g), sliced thinly

8 large butter lettuce leaves

aïoli

½ cup (150g) mayonnaise

1 clove garlic, crushed

1 tablespoon finely chopped fresh flat-leaf parsley

1 Preheat grill.

2 Cook bacon in large frying pan until crisp.

3 Meanwhile, make aïoli.

4 Toast croissants under grill about 30 seconds. Split croissants in half; spread aïoli over one half of each croissant then top with bacon, tomato, lettuce and remaining croissant half.

aïoli Combine ingredients in small bowl.

prep & cook time 20 minutes **serves** 4
nutritional count per serving 36.8g total fat (13.9g saturated fat); 2592kJ (620 cal); 39.5g carbohydrate; 31.4g protein; 3.8g fibre

If you like canned baked beans then just wait till you taste these homemade ones. It takes a little more time, but is well worth it.

breakfast beans on toast

2 cups (400g) dried cannellini beans
1 tablespoon olive oil
1 large brown onion (200g), chopped coarsely
2 cloves garlic, sliced thinly
2 rindless bacon rashers (130g), chopped coarsely
2 tablespoons brown sugar
¼ cup (60ml) maple syrup
1 tablespoon dijon mustard
400g can chopped tomatoes
1 litre (4 cups) water
6 x 1cm-thick slices sourdough bread
2 tablespoons coarsely chopped
    fresh flat-leaf parsley

1 Place beans in large bowl, cover with water; stand overnight, drain. Rinse under cold water, drain.
2 Heat oil in large saucepan, add onion, garlic and bacon; cook, stirring, until onion softens. Stir in beans, sugar, syrup and mustard. Add undrained tomatoes and the water; bring to the boil. Reduce heat; simmer, covered, about 2 hours or until beans are tender.
3 Uncover; cook, stirring occasionally, 30 minutes or until mixture thickens. Serve beans on toasted sourdough bread; sprinkle with parsley.

prep & cook time 2 hours 50 minutes (+ standing)
serves 6
nutritional count per serving 6.3g total fat (1.1g saturated fat); 1626kJ (389 cal); 53.1g carbohydrate; 22.2g protein; 14.5g fibre

Put the kettle on and get the
china teacups — relax and settle
in for a leisurely breakfast.

huevos rancheros

herb omelette with sautéed mushrooms

Huevos rancheros, or 'ranch-style eggs', is a Mexican breakfast traditionally served on farms at a large mid-morning breakfast, or *almuerzo*.

huevos rancheros

3 chorizo sausages (500g), sliced thickly
8 eggs
½ cup (125ml) cream
20g butter
4 x 15cm flour tortillas
1 cup (120g) coarsely grated cheddar cheese
fresh tomato salsa
2 small tomatoes (180g), chopped finely
½ small red onion (50g), chopped finely
1 tablespoon red wine vinegar
1 tablespoon olive oil
¼ cup coarsely chopped fresh coriander

1 Preheat oven to 160°C/140°C fan-forced.
2 Make fresh tomato salsa.
3 Cook chorizo on heated oiled grill plate (or grill or barbecue) until well browned. Drain on absorbent paper; cover to keep warm.
4 Whisk eggs and cream in medium bowl. Melt butter in medium frying pan; cook egg mixture over low heat, stirring gently, until creamy.
5 Meanwhile, place tortillas on oven tray, sprinkle with cheese; warm in oven until cheese melts.
6 Divide tortillas among serving plates; top with egg, chorizo and salsa.
fresh tomato salsa Combine tomatoes, onion, vinegar and oil in small bowl; cover, stand 15 minutes. Stir in coriander just before serving.

prep & cook time 30 minutes (+ standing) **serves** 4
nutritional count per serving 81.7g total fat (35.8g saturated fat); 4126kJ (987 cal); 16.2g carbohydrate; 48.2g protein; 1.9g fibre

herb omelette with sautéed mushrooms

2 tablespoons finely chopped fresh flat-leaf parsley
2 tablespoons finely chopped fresh chervil
2 tablespoons finely chopped fresh chives
2 tablespoons finely chopped fresh tarragon
50g butter
2 tablespoons olive oil
250g swiss brown mushrooms, halved
½ cup (125ml) water
2 teaspoons finely grated lemon rind
1 tablespoon lemon juice
12 eggs

1 Combine herbs in small bowl.
2 Heat 30g of the butter and 1 tablespoon of the oil in large deep frying pan. Add mushrooms; cook, stirring, 5 minutes. Stir in 2 tablespoons of the water; cook, stirring, until water evaporates and mushrooms are tender. Remove pan from heat; stir in rind, juice and 2 tablespoons of the herb mixture. Cover to keep warm.
3 Gently whisk eggs and remaining water in a large bowl; whisk in remaining herb mixture.
4 Heat a quarter of the remaining butter and 1 teaspoon of the remaining oil in medium frying pan. When butter mixture bubbles, pour a quarter of the egg mixture into pan; cook over medium heat, tilting pan, until egg is almost set. Tilt pan backwards; fold omelette in half. Cook 30 seconds then slide onto serving plate.
5 Repeat process with remaining butter, oil and egg mixture, wiping out pan before each addition to make a total of 4 omelettes. Serve omelettes topped with sautéed mushrooms.

prep & cook time 30 minutes **serves** 4
nutritional count per serving 35.3g total fat (12.9g saturated fat); 1714kJ (410 cal); 1g carbohydrate; 22.4g protein; 1.8g fibre

The classic bacon and egg roll gets a sophisticated makeover in this grown-up Italian version.

italian egg, prosciutto and cheese roll

4 eggs
4 focaccia rolls (440g), split
120g taleggio or fontina cheese, sliced thinly
4 slices (60g) prosciutto
8 large fresh basil leaves
tomato sauce
400g can crushed tomatoes
¼ cup (60ml) red wine vinegar
2 tablespoons brown sugar

1 Make tomato sauce.
2 Preheat grill.
3 Fry eggs in heated oiled medium frying pan until cooked as you like.
4 Spread bottom half of each roll with about one tablespoon of the tomato sauce; place on oven tray. Layer cheese and prosciutto on rolls; grill until cheese starts to melt. Top each with 2 basil leaves, an egg and remaining tomato sauce; top with remaining roll half.

tomato sauce Place undrained tomatoes with remaining ingredients in medium saucepan; bring to the boil. Reduce heat; simmer 15 minutes

prep & cook time 20 minutes **serves** 4
nutritional count per serving 20.3g total fat (9g saturated fat); 2245kJ (537 cal); 58.8g carbohydrate; 27.5g protein; 4.1g fibre

eggs and smoked salmon on blini

8 eggs
200g sliced smoked salmon
2 tablespoons sour cream
1 tablespoon coarsely chopped fresh chives
blini
⅓ cup (50g) buckwheat flour
2 tablespoons plain flour
1 teaspoon baking powder
1 egg
½ cup (125ml) buttermilk
30g butter, melted

1 Make blini.

2 Half-fill a large frying pan with water; bring to the boil. Break 1 egg into cup then slide into pan. Working quickly, repeat process with 3 more eggs. When all 4 eggs are in pan, return water to the boil. Cover pan, turn off heat; stand about 4 minutes or until a light film of white sets over each yolk. Using a slotted spoon, remove eggs one at a time from pan; place spoon on absorbent-paper-lined saucer to blot up poaching liquid. Repeat process to poach remaining 4 eggs.

3 Serve blini topped with eggs, salmon, sour cream and chives.

blini Sift flours and baking powder into medium bowl; gradually whisk in combined egg and buttermilk until mixture is smooth. Stir in butter. Cook blini, in batches, by dropping 1 tablespoon of the batter into heated oiled large frying pan. Cook blini until browned both sides; you will have 12 blini. Cover to keep warm.

prep & cook time 40 minutes **serves** 4
nutritional count per serving 25.9g total fat (11.3g saturated fat); 1731kJ (414 cal); 14.1g carbohydrate; 31.5g protein; 1.6g fibre

creamy scrambled eggs

8 eggs
½ cup (125ml) cream
2 tablespoons finely chopped fresh chives
30g butter

1 Place eggs, cream and chives in medium bowl; beat lightly with fork.

2 Heat butter in large frying pan over medium heat. Add egg mixture, wait a few seconds, then use a wide spatula to gently scrape the set egg mixture along the base of the pan; cook until creamy and barely set. Serve immediately, with toast.

prep & cook time 20 minutes **serves** 4
nutritional count per serving 30.2g total fat (16.2g saturated fat); 1375kJ (329 cal); 1.3g carbohydrate; 14g protein; 0g fibre

cooked english breakfast

50g butter
300g button mushrooms, halved
8 chipolata sausages (240g)
4 rindless bacon rashers (260g)
2 medium tomatoes (300g), halved
1 tablespoon vegetable oil
8 eggs

1 Melt butter in medium saucepan; cook mushrooms, stirring, about 5 minutes or until tender.
2 Cook sausages and bacon in heated oiled large frying pan. Remove from pan; cover to keep warm. Drain fat from pan.
3 Preheat grill. Place tomato, cut-side up, on oven tray; grill tomato until browned lightly.
4 Meanwhile, heat oil in same large frying pan, add eggs; cook eggs until done to your liking.
5 Serve mushrooms, sausages, bacon, tomato and eggs with toast.

prep & cook time 20 minutes **serves** 4
nutritional count per serving 47.7g total fat (20.2g saturated fat); 2424kJ (580 cal); 3.5g carbohydrate; 34.6g protein; 2.4g fibre

serving idea Accompany these baked eggs with some fresh cherry tomatoes and toast.

These may be small but they pack a flavour punch. Don't be tempted to add salt — the prosciutto and fetta are quite salty enough.

prosciutto and fetta baked eggs

12 slices prosciutto (180g)
¼ cup (35g) finely chopped drained semi-dried
  tomatoes in oil
50g fetta cheese, crumbled
2 tablespoons coarsely chopped fresh basil
2 tablespoons coarsely chopped fresh chives
6 eggs

1 Preheat oven to 200°C/180°C fan-forced. Oil six-hole (⅓-cup/80ml) muffin pan.
2 Wrap one prosciutto slice around edge of each pan hole, lay another slice to cover bases; press firmly to seal edges to form a cup.
3 Combine tomato, cheese and herbs in medium bowl; divide half the mixture between prosciutto cups. Break an egg into each cup. Sprinkle with remaining cheese mixture.
4 Bake about 12 minutes or until eggs are cooked. Remove carefully from pan. Serve top-side up.

prep & cook time 30 minutes **makes** 6
nutritional count per baked egg 9.4g total fat (3.6g saturated fat); 635kJ (152 cal); 2.3g carbohydrate; 14.3g protein; 0.9g fibre

serving idea Serve these fritters with tomato chutney and fresh coriander leaves.

For the sweetest and most delicious corn, select cobs with fresh, green husks and bright, plump kernels.

corn fritters

1 cup (150g) self-raising flour
½ teaspoon bicarbonate of soda
1 teaspoon ground cumin
¾ cup (180ml) milk
2 eggs, separated
2 cups (330g) fresh corn kernels
2 green onions, sliced finely
2 tablespoons finely chopped fresh coriander

1 Sift flour, soda and cumin into medium bowl. Gradually whisk in milk and egg yolks until batter is smooth.
2 Beat egg whites in small bowl with electric mixer until soft peaks form.
3 Stir corn, onion and coriander into batter; fold in egg whites.
4 Pour 2 tablespoons of the batter for each fritter into heated oiled large frying pan; spread batter into round shape. Cook fritters about 2 minutes each side. Remove from pan; cover to keep warm. Repeat with remaining batter to make a total of 18 fritters.

prep & cook time 40 minutes **makes** 18
nutritional count per fritter 1.3g total fat (0.5g saturated fat); 263kJ (63 cal); 9.9g carbohydrate; 2.7g protein; 1.2g fibre

cranberry cooler

1⅓ cups (150g) frozen cranberries, thawed
1kg watermelon, peeled, chopped coarsely
2 lebanese cucumbers (260g), chopped coarsely
2 medium pears (460g), chopped coarsely

1 Push ingredients through juice extractor into glass;
stir to combine.

prep time 10 minutes **makes** 1 litre (4 cups)
nutritional count per 250ml 0.2g total fat (0g
saturated fat); 134kJ (32 cal); 6.6g carbohydrate;
0.3g protein; 1.2g fibre

zesty beetroot juice

*You need 2kg of silver beet to get the required
amount of trimmed leaves.*

3 medium beetroots (525g), chopped coarsely
4 medium oranges (960g), peeled, quartered
500g trimmed silver beet
1 cup (250ml) water
1 fresh small red thai chilli, chopped finely

1 Push beetroot, orange and silver beet through
juice extractor into glass. Stir in the water.
2 Add chilli; stand 5 minutes. Strain mixture through
fine sieve into large jug.

prep time 10 minutes **makes** 1 litre (4 cups)
nutritional count per 250ml 0.5g total fat (0g
saturated fat); 617kJ (147 cal); 24.5g carbohydrate;
5.8g protein; 10.4g fibre

ruby red citrus juice

2 medium ruby red grapefruits (700g),
    peeled, quartered
3 large oranges (900g), peeled, quartered
1 medium lemon (140g), peeled, quartered
1 cup (250ml) water
2 tablespoons honey

1 Push fruit through juice extractor into glass.
Add the water and honey; stir to combine.

prep time 10 minutes **makes** 1 litre (4 cups)
nutritional count per 250ml 0.4g total fat (0g
saturated fat); 579kJ (138 cal); 28.3g carbohydrate;
2.8g protein; 4.4g fibre

honeydew, papaya and orange juice

1 medium honeydew melon (1.5 kg), peeled,
    chopped coarsely
1 small papaya (650g), peeled, chopped coarsely
3 medium oranges (720g), peeled, quartered

1 Push fruit through juice extractor into glass;
stir to combine

prep time 10 minutes **makes** 1 litre (4 cups)
nutritional count per 250ml 0.2g total fat (0g
saturated fat); 150kJ (36 cal); 6.9g carbohydrate;
0.7g protein; 1.5g fibre

Hollandaise sauce can be made in advance and reheated gently (and very carefully) over simmering water, stirring constantly.

eggs benedict

8 eggs
4 english muffins
200g shaved leg ham
¼ cup finely chopped fresh chives
hollandaise sauce
1½ tablespoons white wine vinegar
1 tablespoon lemon juice
½ teaspoon black peppercorns
2 egg yolks
125g unsalted butter, melted

1 Make hollandaise sauce.
2 To poach eggs, half-fill a large shallow frying pan with water; bring to the boil. Break 1 egg into a cup, then slide into pan; repeat with three more eggs. When all eggs are in pan, allow water to return to the boil. Cover pan, turn off heat; stand about 4 minutes or until a light film of egg white sets over yolks. Remove the egg with a slotted spoon and drain on absorbent paper; cover to keep warm. Repeat with remaining eggs.
3 Meanwhile, split muffins in half and toast.
4 Serve muffins topped with ham, poached eggs, sauce and chives.

hollandaise sauce Combine vinegar, juice and peppercorns in small saucepan; bring to the boil. Reduce heat; simmer, uncovered, until liquid is reduced by half. Strain through a fine sieve into small heatproof bowl; cool 10 minutes. Whisk egg yolks into vinegar mixture. Set bowl over small saucepan of simmering water; do not allow water to touch base of bowl. Whisk mixture over heat until thickened. Remove bowl from heat; gradually whisk in melted butter in a thin steady stream, whisking constantly until sauce is thick and creamy.

prep & cook time 50 minutes **serves** 4
nutritional count per serving 40.6g total fat (21.2g saturated fat); 2450kJ (586 cal); 24.2g carbohydrate; 30.8g protein; 2g fibre

strawberries and cream on brioche

ricotta and banana toasts

strawberries and cream on brioche

3 eggs
⅓ cup (80ml) milk
1 teaspoon vanilla extract
1 tablespoon caster sugar
6 small brioche (600g), halved
40g unsalted butter
250g strawberries, sliced thinly
⅔ cup (160ml) thickened cream

1 Combine eggs, milk, extract and sugar in large shallow bowl. Submerge brioche in egg mixture.
2 Melt half the butter in large frying pan; cook half the brioche until browned both sides. Remove from pan; cover to keep warm. Repeat with remaining butter and brioche. Serve brioche with strawberries and cream.

prep & cook time 25 minutes **serves** 6
nutritional count per serving 30.5g total fat (16.5g saturated fat); 2286kJ (547 cal); 53.5g carbohydrate; 13.4g protein; 2.8g fibre

ricotta and banana toasts

8 x 1cm-thick slices fruit bread, toasted
1 cup (240g) ricotta cheese
2 large bananas (460g), sliced thickly
2 tablespoons honey

1 Top toast with cheese and banana; drizzle with honey.

prep & cook time 10 minutes **serves** 4
nutritional count per serving 10.7g total fat (5g saturated fat); 2199kJ (526 cal); 87.1g carbohydrate; 15.8g protein; 6.6g fibre

pancakes with three toppings

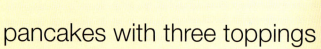

pancakes

1 cup (150g) self-raising flour
¼ cup (55g) caster sugar
2 eggs
1 cup (250ml) milk

1 Sift flour and sugar into medium bowl; gradually whisk in combined eggs and milk until batter is smooth.
2 Pour ¼ cup batter into heated oiled medium frying pan; cook pancake until bubbles begin to appear on surface. Turn pancake; cook until browned lightly. Cover to keep warm.
3 Repeat with remaining batter.
4 Serve pancakes with your choice of topping.

prep & cook time 25 minutes **serves** 4
nutritional count per pancake 1.4g total fat (0.8g saturated fat); 502kJ (120 cal); 21.7g carbohydrate; 4.4g protein; 0.7g fibre

toppings

rhubarb and pear
Combine 2 cups coarsely chopped rhubarb, 1 coarsely chopped medium pear, ¼ cup caster sugar, 2 tablespoons water and 1 teaspoon mixed spice in medium saucepan; bring to the boil. Reduce heat; simmer, stirring occasionally, about 5 minutes or until fruit softens slightly.

nutritional count per serving 0.2g total fat (0g saturated fat); 380kJ (91 cal); 19.8g carbohydrate; 1g protein; 2.7g fibre

orange-glazed strawberries
Combine ¼ cup water and ¼ cup caster sugar in small saucepan; stir over low heat until sugar dissolves. Bring to the boil; boil, uncovered, about 3 minutes or until syrup thickens slightly. Stir in 2 teaspoons finely grated orange rind and 1 tablespoon orange juice; cool. Stir in 250g quartered strawberries and ¼ cup coarsely chopped fresh mint.

nutritional count per serving 0.1g total fat (0g saturated fat); 301kJ (72 cal); 15.5g carbohydrate; 1.2g protein; 1.7g fibre

chocolate, banana and hazelnut
Combine 100g coarsely chopped milk eating chocolate, 10g butter and ½ cup cream in small saucepan; stir over low heat until smooth. Drizzle chocolate sauce over pancakes; top with 2 thinly sliced medium bananas and ¼ cup coarsely chopped roasted hazelnuts.

nutritional count per serving 27.8g total fat (14.7g saturated fat); 1588kJ (380 cal); 29.9g carbohydrate; 4.9g protein; 2.3g fibre

berry yogurt muffins

banana bread

berry yogurt muffins

*We used a mixture of raspberries and blueberries
in these muffins.*

1½ cups (225g) self-raising flour
⅓ cup (30g) rolled oats
3 eggs
¾ cup (165g) firmly packed brown sugar
¾ cup (200g) yogurt
⅓ cup (80ml) vegetable oil
180g fresh or frozen berries

1 Preheat oven to 200°C/180°C fan-forced.
Grease six-hole (¾-cup/180ml) texas muffin pan.
2 Combine sifted flour with oats in medium bowl.
Stir in eggs, sugar, yogurt and oil; add berries, stir
gently into muffin mixture.
3 Spoon mixture into pan holes; bake about 20 minutes.
Stand 5 minutes before turning, top-side up, onto
wire rack to cool.

prep & cook time 30 minutes **serves** 6
nutritional count per muffin 16.9g total fat (3.2g
saturated fat); 1806kJ (432 cal); 58.8g carbohydrate;
9.7g protein; 2.5g fibre

banana bread

*You need two large overripe bananas (460g)
for this recipe.*

90g unsalted butter, softened
1 teaspoon vanilla extract
1 cup (220g) firmly packed brown sugar
2 eggs
1 cup mashed banana
1 cup (150g) plain flour
1 cup (150g) self-raising flour

1 Preheat oven to 180°C/160°C fan-forced. Grease
14cm x 21cm loaf pan; line base and long sides with
baking paper, extending paper 5cm above long sides.
2 Beat butter, extract and sugar in small bowl with
electric mixer until light and fluffy. Beat in eggs, one at
a time. Transfer mixture to large bowl; stir in banana
then sifted flours, in two batches.
3 Spread mixture into pan; cover with a strip of
pleated foil. Bake 40 minutes; uncover, bake about
30 minutes. Stand 5 minutes; lift onto wire rack to
cool. Serve toasted or warm, with butter.

prep & cook time 1 hour 20 minutes **makes** 12 slices
nutritional count per slice 7.8g total fat (5.0g
saturated fat); 1296kJ (309 cal); 49.7g carbohydrate;
5.1g protein; 1.7g fibre

blueberry buttermilk hotcakes with bacon

2 cups (300g) self-raising flour
¼ cup (55g) caster sugar
2 eggs
600ml buttermilk
50g butter, melted
1 cup (150g) fresh blueberries
cooking-oil spray
12 thin rindless bacon rashers (360g)
½ cup (125ml) maple syrup

1 Sift flour and sugar into large bowl. Whisk eggs, buttermilk and butter in large jug. Gradually whisk egg mixture into flour mixture until smooth. Stir in berries, pour batter into large jug.

2 Spray large heavy-based frying pan with cooking oil. Pour ¼-cup batter for each pancake into heated pan (you can cook four at a time). Cook pancakes until bubbles appear on the surface; turn, brown other side. Cover to keep warm.

3 Repeat process using cooking oil and remaining batter, wiping out pan between batches, to make 14 more pancakes.

4 Meanwhile, heat oiled large frying pan; cook bacon until crisp.

5 Drizzle pancakes with syrup, serve with bacon.

prep & cook time 35 minutes **serves** 6
nutritional count per serving 15.4g total fat (7.7g saturated fat); 2224kJ (532 cal); 71.8g carbohydrate; 24.5g protein; 2.4g fibre

Make sure you use real maple syrup here. It is very different from 'maple-flavoured' syrup, and well worth the extra cost.

french toast

bircher muesli

french toast

4 eggs
½ cup (125ml) cream
¼ cup (60ml) milk
1 teaspoon ground cinnamon
¼ cup (55g) caster sugar
100g butter, melted
8 thick slices white bread (360g)
2 tablespoons icing sugar
⅓ cup (80ml) maple syrup

1 Whisk eggs in medium bowl, then whisk in cream, milk, cinnamon and sugar.
2 Heat a quarter of the butter in medium frying pan. Dip two bread slices into egg mixture, one at a time; cook bread until browned both sides. Remove french toast from pan; keep warm.
3 Repeat step 2 to make a total of 8 french toasts.
4 Serve toasts dusted with sifted icing sugar and drizzled with maple syrup. Serve, topped with sliced strawberries.

prep & cook time 20 minutes **serves** 4
nutritional count per serving 42.2g total fat (24.8g saturated fat); 3194kJ (764 cal); 79.4g carbohydrate; 15.5g protein; 2.0g fibre

bircher muesli

2 cups (180g) rolled oats
1¼ cups (310ml) apple juice
1 cup (280g) yogurt
2 medium green-skinned apples (300g)
¼ cup (35g) roasted slivered almonds
¼ cup (40g) dried currants
¼ cup (20g) toasted shredded coconut
1 teaspoon ground cinnamon
½ cup (140g) yogurt, extra

1 Combine oats, juice and yogurt in medium bowl. Cover; refrigerate overnight.
2 Peel, core and coarsely grate one apple; stir into oat mixture with nuts, currants, coconut and cinnamon.
3 Core and thinly slice remaining apple. Serve muesli topped with extra yogurt and apple slices.

prep time 10 minutes (+ refrigeration) **serves** 6
nutritional count per serving 9.2g total fat (3g saturated fat); 1120kJ (268 cal); 36.1g carbohydrate; 8.1g protein; 3.9g fibre

Dr Bircher-Benner, a physician and pioneer in nutritional research, introduced his now famous muesli to the patients at his clinic in Zurich, Switzerland in the early 20th Century.

serving idea These muffins are delicious eaten still warm with a good slab of butter. Serve them alongside a fresh fruit platter and a pot of piping hot coffee or tea.

The beauty of these muffins is that you prepare the mixture the night before, then all you have to do in the morning is pop them in the oven.

overnight bran muffins

1 egg
1¼ cups (185g) plain flour
1 teaspoon ground cinnamon
1 teaspoon bicarbonate of soda
½ cup (110g) firmly packed brown sugar
1¾ cups (105g) unprocessed bran
¾ cup (105g) coarsely chopped seedless
   fresh or dried dates
1½ cups (375ml) buttermilk
½ cup (125ml) vegetable oil

1 Whisk egg in medium bowl, stir in remaining ingredients. (Do not over-mix; mixture should be lumpy.) Cover mixture, refrigerate overnight.
2 Preheat oven to 200°C/180°C fan-forced. Grease 12-hole (⅓-cup/80ml) muffin pan.
3 Spoon muffin mixture into pan holes; bake about 20 minutes. Stand muffins in pan 5 minutes before turning, top-side up, onto wire rack to cool. Serve with butter.

prep & cook time 30 minutes (+ refrigeration)
makes 12
nutritional count per muffin 11.3g total fat (1.9g saturated fat); 1037kJ (248 cal); 28.7g carbohydrate; 5.2g protein; 5.3g fibre

indian chai

vanilla caffé latte

5 cardamom pods, bruised
10 cloves
1 cinnamon stick
1cm piece fresh ginger (5g), sliced thickly
2 teaspoons fennel seeds
1 teaspoon vanilla extract
3 cups (750ml) water
4 darjeeling teabags
2 cups (500ml) milk
⅓ cup (90g) grated palm sugar

1 Combine cardamom, cloves, cinnamon, ginger, fennel, extract and the water in medium saucepan; bring to the boil. Cover; simmer 5 minutes. Remove from heat; stand, covered, 10 minutes.
2 Return spice mixture to the boil, add teabags; remove from heat. Stand 5 minutes.
3 Meanwhile, heat milk in medium saucepan without boiling. Add milk to tea mixture; add sugar, stir until dissolved.

prep & cook time 15 minutes (+ standing)
makes 1 litre (4 cups)
nutritional count per 250ml 4.9g total fat (3.2g saturated fat); 727kJ (174 cal); 27.9g carbohydrate; 4.3g protein; 0g fibre

⅔ cup (60g) coarsely ground coffee beans
1 litre (4 cups) milk
2 teaspoons vanilla extract

1 Combine ingredients in medium saucepan, stir, over low heat until heated through, but not boiling.
2 Pour mixture through fine strainer into heatproof serving glasses.

prep & cook time 10 minutes **serves** 4
nutritional count per 250ml 9.8g total fat (6.4g saturated); 702kJ (168 cal); 12.1g carbohydrate; 8.5g protein; 0g fibre

spiced chocolate milk

60g dark eating chocolate, melted
1 litre (4 cups) milk
2 cinnamon sticks

1 Using a teaspoon, drizzle melted chocolate onto the insides of heatproof glasses.
2 Stir milk and cinnamon stick in medium saucepan, over low heat until heated through, but not boiling. Remove cinnamon. Pour milk into glasses.

prep & cook time 10 minutes **serves** 4
nutritional count per 250ml 14.1g total fat (9g saturated); 1024kJ (245 cal), 21.5g carbohydrate, 9.3g protein; 0.2g fibre

hot mocha

2 cups (500ml) milk
100g dark eating chocolate, chopped coarsely
2 cups (500ml) hot black coffee
1 teaspoon cocoa powder

1 Heat milk in medium saucepan, without boiling.
2 Meanwhile, divide chocolate among four 1¼-cup (310ml) glasses.
3 Stir coffee into milk then pour mixture into glasses. Dust with sifted cocoa powder before serving.

prep & cook time 10 minutes **serves** 4
nutritional count per 250ml 10.1g total fat (7.5g saturated fat); 920kJ (220 cal); 21.9g carbohydrate, 5.7g protein; 0.4g fibre

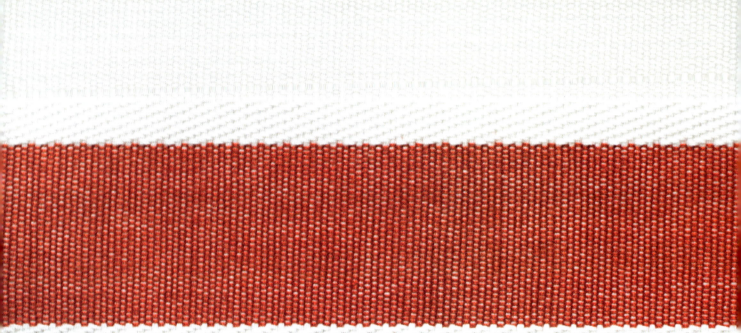

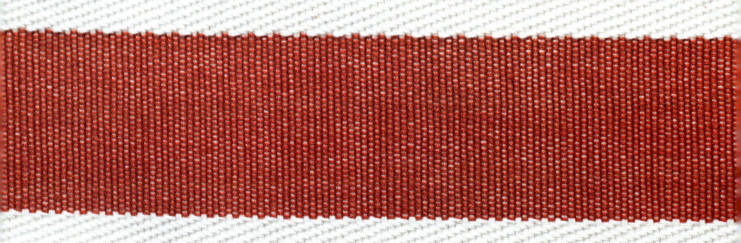

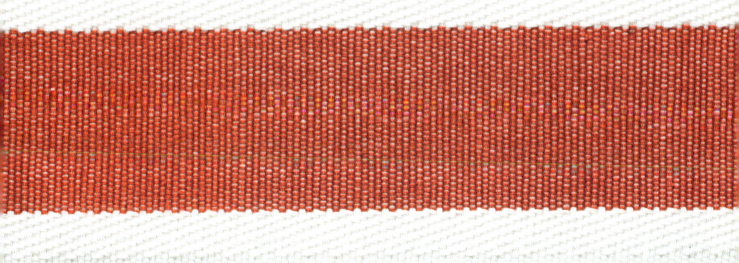

midweek meals

These meals are perfect after a long day, when time is of the essence.

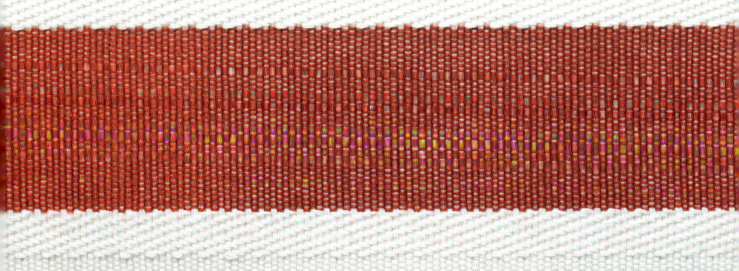

Don't be afraid of poaching fish
— it's quick, easy, and produces
a wonderfully tender, moist result.

poached trout and potato salad

800g kipfler potatoes, unpeeled, halved

1 litre (4 cups) water

4 x 5cm strips lemon rind

2 sprigs fresh dill

600g ocean trout fillets

1 small red onion (100g), sliced thinly

1 lebanese cucumber (130g),
    seeded, sliced thinly

50g rocket leaves

lemon and dill dressing

⅓ cup (80ml) olive oil

¼ cup (60ml) lemon juice

1 clove garlic, crushed

1 tablespoon finely chopped fresh dill

1 tablespoon drained, rinsed baby capers

1 Boil, steam or microwave potato until tender; drain.

2 Place the water, rind and dill in medium saucepan; bring to the boil. Add fish; simmer, covered, about 10 minutes or until cooked as desired. Drain fish; discard cooking liquid. Flake fish coarsely into large bowl; discard skin.

3 Meanwhile, make lemon and dill dressing.

4 Add potato, dressing and remaining ingredients to bowl of fish; toss gently to combine.

lemon and dill dressing Place ingredients in screw-top jar; shake well.

prep & cook time 25 minutes **serves** 4

nutritional count per serving 24.3g total fat (3.9g saturated fat); 2031kJ (486 cal); 29.3g carbohydrate; 34.9g protein; 5.1g fibre

garlic seafood stir-fry

snapper fillets with ginger soy syrup

garlic seafood stir-fry

1kg uncooked medium king prawns
500g cleaned baby squid hoods
¼ cup (60ml) peanut oil
1 tablespoon finely chopped coriander
   root and stem mixture
2 fresh small red thai chillies
½ teaspoon coarsely ground black pepper
4 cloves garlic, crushed
170g asparagus, trimmed, chopped coarsely
175g broccolini, chopped coarsely
1 cup (80g) bean sprouts
2 green onions, sliced thinly
2 tablespoons coarsely chopped fresh coriander
1 lime, cut into wedges

1 Shell and devein prawns, leaving tails intact.
2 Cut squid down centre to open out; score inside
in diagonal pattern then cut into thick strips.
3 Heat half the oil in wok; cook seafood, in batches,
until prawns change in colour.
4 Heat remaining oil in wok; stir-fry coriander mixture,
chilli, pepper and garlic until fragrant. Add asparagus
and broccolini; cook, stirring, until vegetables are
almost tender. Return seafood to wok with sprouts;
stir-fry until hot.
5 Serve stir-fry sprinkled with green onion and
coriander, accompanied with lime.

prep & cook time 40 minutes **serves** 4
nutritional count per serving 16.2g total fat (3.1g
saturated fat); 1509kJ (361 cal); 1.6g carbohydrate;
50.3g protein; 3.7g fibre

snapper fillets with ginger soy syrup

2 medium carrots (240g), cut into matchsticks
2 medium zucchini (240g), cut into matchsticks
4 x 275g snapper fillets, skin on
1 cup (250ml) bottled sweet chilli, ginger and
   soy marinade

1 Boil, steam or microwave carrot and zucchini,
separately, until tender.
2 Meanwhile, score fish skin. Cook fish, skin-side
down, in heated oiled large frying pan about 5 minutes.
Turn fish; cook about 3 minutes. Remove from pan.
3 Add ⅓ cup (80ml) water and marinade to same
pan; stir until hot.
4 Serve fish with sauce and vegetables. Serve with
steamed jasmine rice.

prep & cook time 20 minutes **serves** 4
nutritional count per serving 4.6g total fat (1.7g
saturated fat); 1304kJ (312 cal); 5.4g carbohydrate;
60.4g protein; 2.4g fibre

cranberry and pine nut pilaf with chicken

30g butter
1 tablespoon olive oil
1 medium brown onion (150g), chopped finely
1 stalk celery (150g), trimmed, chopped finely
1½ cups (300g) basmati rice, rinsed, drained
1 bay leaf
1 cinnamon stick
1 litre (4 cups) chicken stock
⅔ cup (160ml) water
400g chicken breast fillets
1 cup (250ml) dry white wine
⅓ cup (45g) dried cranberries
30g butter, extra
⅓ cup (50g) roasted pine nuts
1 tablespoon lemon juice

1 Melt butter with half the oil in medium saucepan; cook onion and celery, stirring, until celery softens. Add rice, bay leaf and cinnamon stick; cook, stirring, 2 minutes. Add stock and the water; bring to the boil. Reduce heat; simmer, covered, about 15 minutes or until rice is tender and liquid is absorbed.
2 Meanwhile, heat remaining oil in a large frying pan. Cook chicken until browned and cooked through. Remove from heat. Cover to keep warm.
3 Pour wine into same pan; bring to the boil. Reduce heat; simmer, uncovered, until liquid is reduced by half. Stir in cranberries and extra butter; add to rice mixture, stir until combined.
4 Fluff pilaf with fork; stir in nuts and juice. Serve with sliced chicken.

prep & cook time 40 minutes **serves** 4
nutritional count per serving 29.5g total fat (10.5g saturated fat); 3068kJ (734 cal); 72.2g carbohydrate; 33.2g protein; 2.7g fibre

gorgonzola and sage-stuffed chicken

ginger-plum chicken and noodle stir-fry

gorgonzola and sage-stuffed chicken

⅓ cup (50g) semi-dried tomatoes in oil
4 chicken breast fillets (800g)
100g gorgonzola cheese, cut into four even slices
12 fresh sage leaves
8 slices pancetta (120g)
80g baby rocket leaves

1 Drain tomatoes; reserve 2 tablespoons of the oil.
2 Cut horizontal slits into chicken fillets, three-quarters of the way through, to make pockets.
3 Divide cheese, sage and tomatoes among pockets in chicken. Wrap two pancetta slices around each chicken breast; cook chicken in heated oiled large frying pan until cooked through. Slice chicken thickly.
4 Toss rocket with reserved oil; serve with chicken.

prep & cook time 30 minutes **serves** 4
nutritional count per serving 24.3g total fat (10.3g saturated fat); 1940kJ (464 cal); 4.8g carbohydrate; 55.5g protein; 2.1g fibre

ginger-plum chicken and noodle stir-fry

We used a 400g packet of prepared asian stir-fry vegetables for this recipe, available from supermarkets.

2 tablespoons vegetable oil
600g chicken breast fillets, sliced thinly
450g hokkien noodles
1 medium brown onion (150g), sliced thinly
1 clove garlic, crushed
3cm piece fresh ginger (15g), grated
400g packaged fresh asian stir-fry vegetables
2 tablespoons sweet chilli sauce
2 tablespoons plum sauce

1 Heat half the oil in wok; stir-fry chicken, in batches, until browned.
2 Meanwhile, place noodles in medium heatproof bowl, cover with boiling water; separate with fork, drain.
3 Heat remaining oil in wok; stir-fry onion, garlic and ginger until onion softens. Add vegetables; stir-fry until just tender. Return chicken to wok with noodles and sauces; stir-fry until hot.

prep & cook time 25 minutes **serves** 4
nutritional count per serving 19.4g total fat (4.6g saturated fat); 2784kJ (666 cal); 73.3g carbohydrate; 45.6g protein; 6.2g fibre

serving idea Steamed beans are delicious with a drizzle of extra virgin olive oil, a squeeze of lemon and a sprinkle of sea salt.

This bistro-style meal is robust, simple and perfect for casual dining.

peppered fillet steaks with creamy bourbon sauce

4 x 125g beef fillet steaks
2 teaspoons cracked black pepper
2 tablespoons olive oil
6 shallots (150g), sliced thinly
1 clove garlic, crushed
⅓ cup (80ml) bourbon
¼ cup (60ml) beef stock
2 teaspoons dijon mustard
300ml cream

1 Rub beef all over with pepper. Heat half the oil in large frying pan; cook beef, uncovered, until cooked as desired. Remove from pan; cover to keep warm.
2 Heat remaining oil in same pan; cook shallot and garlic, stirring, until shallot softens. Add bourbon; stir until mixture simmers and starts to thicken. Add remaining ingredients; bring to the boil. Reduce heat; simmer, uncovered, about 5 minutes or until sauce thickens slightly.
3 Place beef on serving plates, drizzle with sauce; serve with fried potatoes and steamed green beans.

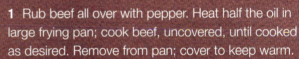

prep & cook time 20 minutes **serves** 4
nutritional count per serving 49.3g total fat (25.9g saturated fat); 2742kJ (656 cal); 13.2g carbohydrate; 28.7g protein; 0.7g fibre

chilli-garlic mince with snake beans

2 cloves garlic, quartered

2 long green chillies, chopped coarsely

2 fresh small red thai chillies, chopped coarsely

1 tablespoon peanut oil

600g beef mince

150g snake beans, chopped coarsely

1 medium red capsicum (200g), sliced thinly

2 tablespoons kecap asin

¼ cup (60ml) hoisin sauce

4 green onions, sliced thickly

2 tablespoons crushed peanuts

1 Blend or process garlic and chillies until mixture is finely chopped.

2 Heat half the oil in wok; stir-fry garlic mixture until fragrant. Add beef; stir-fry, in batches, until cooked through.

3 Heat remaining oil in cleaned wok; stir-fry beans and capsicum until tender.

4 Return beef to wok with sauces and onion; stir-fry until hot. Sprinkle over nuts; serve with lime wedges.

prep & cook time 25 minutes **serves** 4
nutritional count per serving 18.6g total fat (5.6g saturated fat); 1476kJ (353 cal); 9.6g carbohydrate; 34.8g protein; 4.2g fibre

tip Try roasting your own red capsicums for this meal. Place capsicum halves, cut-side down, on an oven tray and roast under the grill or in a very hot oven until the skins are black and have blistered. Put them in a paper bag until they've cooled enough to handle and then gently peel the skins off. They are also delicious when added on sandwiches or salads so it's worth making a big batch.

italian braised sausages with white beans

We used semi-dried tomatoes, marinated artichokes, grilled eggplant and red capsicum for the antipasto mix; however, any combination of vegetables can be used.

8 thick beef sausages (1.2kg)
2 x 400g can diced tomatoes
200g drained marinated antipasto vegetables
400g can cannellini beans, rinsed, drained
½ cup loosely packed fresh baby basil leaves

1 Cook sausages in heated oiled large saucepan until browned. Remove from pan; cut in half lengthways.
2 Add undrained tomatoes and ⅓ cup (80ml) water to same pan; bring to the boil. Return sausages to pan with antipasto vegetables; simmer, covered, 15 minutes.
3 Add beans to pan; simmer, uncovered, about 10 minutes or until thickened slightly.
4 Remove from heat, stir in half the basil; serve topped with remaining basil.

prep & cook time 25 minutes **serves** 4
nutritional count per serving 78.1g total fat (36.9g saturated fat); 4113kJ (983 cal); 23g carbohydrate; 41.9g protein; 16g fibre

spicy veal pizzaiola

lamb cutlets niçoise

spicy veal pizzaiola

2 tablespoons olive oil
2 cloves garlic, crushed
4 slices pancetta (60g), chopped finely
¼ cup (60ml) dry white wine
700g bottled tomato pasta sauce
1 teaspoon dried chilli flakes
4 x 170g veal cutlets
75g baby spinach leaves

1 Heat 2 teaspoons of the oil in large saucepan;
cook garlic and pancetta, stirring, about 5 minutes.
Add wine; cook, stirring, until wine is reduced by half.
Add sauce and chilli; simmer, uncovered, about
15 minutes or until sauce thickens.
2 Meanwhile, heat remaining oil in large frying pan.
Cook veal, uncovered, until cooked as desired.
3 Remove sauce from heat; stir in spinach. Top veal
with sauce.

prep & cook time 30 minutes **serves** 4
nutritional count per serving 14.6g total fat (2.8g
saturated fat); 1555kJ (372 cal); 18.8g carbohydrate;
36.3g protein; 4.3g fibre

lamb cutlets niçoise

12 french-trimmed lamb cutlets (600g)
1 large cos lettuce, chopped coarsely
420g can white beans, rinsed, drained
3 medium tomatoes (450g), cut into wedges
lemon anchovy dressing
4 drained anchovy fillets, chopped finely
3 cloves garlic, crushed
3 teaspoons finely grated lemon rind
⅓ cup (80ml) lemon juice
⅓ cup (80ml) olive oil

1 Make lemon anchovy dressing.
2 Combine lamb and 2 tablespoons of the dressing
in large bowl.
3 Cook lamb in heated oiled large frying pan,
uncovered, in batches, until cooked as desired.
Remove from heat; drizzle with 1 tablespoon of the
dressing, cover to keep warm.
4 Combine remaining dressing, lettuce, beans and
tomato in large bowl. Serve lamb with salad.
lemon anchovy dressing Place ingredients in
screw-top jar; shake well.

prep & cook time 30 minutes **serves** 4
nutritional count per serving 33g total fat (8.8g
saturated fat); 1852kJ (443 cal); 9.9g carbohydrate;
24.8g protein; 5.2g fibre

These flavourful skewers, made smaller, are also perfect as party nibbles. You can make them ahead of time and gently reheat them in the oven before serving.

rosemary lamb skewers

8 sprigs fresh rosemary
600g lamb mince
1 egg yolk
2 cloves garlic, crushed
1 tablespoon tomato paste
⅓ cup (25g) stale breadcrumbs
¼ cup (60ml) olive oil
1 large brown onion (200g), sliced thinly
1 tablespoon plain flour
1 cup (250ml) beef stock
2 medium tomatoes (300g), chopped coarsely

1 Remove two-thirds of the leaves from the bottom part of each rosemary sprig to make skewers. Finely chop 2 teaspoons of the leaves and reserve.
2 Combine mince, egg yolk, garlic, paste, breadcrumbs and reserved rosemary in medium bowl. Shape lamb mixture into sausage shapes on rosemary skewers.
3 Heat 1 tablespoon of the oil in large frying pan; cook skewers until browned and cooked through. Cover to keep warm.
4 Heat remaining oil in same pan; cook onion, stirring, until soft. Add flour; cook, stirring, until mixture bubbles and thickens. Gradually stir in stock until smooth. Add tomato; cook, stirring, until gravy boils and thickens.
5 Serve rosemary lamb skewers with gravy.

prep & cook time 35 minutes **serves** 4
nutritional count per serving 26g total fat (7.1g saturated fat); 1781kJ (426 cal); 11.9g carbohydrate; 35.1g protein; 2.5g fibre

herb-crumbed lamb racks

pork cutlets with caramelised pear sauce

herb-crumbed lamb racks

1 cup (70g) stale breadcrumbs
1 tablespoon finely chopped fresh flat-leaf parsley
2 tablespoons finely chopped fresh mint
2 teaspoons finely grated lemon rind
40g butter
2 shallots (50g), chopped finely
4 x 4 french-trimmed lamb cutlet racks (720g)
250g baby vine-ripened truss tomatoes
cooking-oil spray

1 Preheat oven to 220°C/200°C fan-forced.
2 Combine breadcrumbs, herbs and rind in small bowl.
3 Melt butter in small frying pan; pour half the butter into breadcrumb mixture.
4 Cook shallot in remaining butter, stirring, until soft; stir into breadcrumb mixture.
5 Place lamb and tomatoes in oiled large baking dish; spray tomatoes with oil. Press breadcrumb mixture onto lamb. Roast, uncovered, about 15 minutes or until cooked as desired. Serve lamb with roasted tomatoes.

prep & cook time 40 minutes **serves** 4
nutritional count per serving 25g total fat (12.6g saturated fat); 1538kJ (368 cal); 13.7g carbohydrate; 21.4g protein; 1.9g fibre

pork cutlets with caramelised pear sauce

1 tablespoon olive oil
20g butter
6 x 180g french-trimmed pork cutlets
2 tablespoons brown sugar
3 medium pears (700g), cut crossways
   into 1.5cm-thick slices
¾ cup (180ml) dry white wine
1 cup (250ml) chicken stock
¼ cup coarsely chopped fresh sage

1 Heat oil and half the butter in large heavy-based frying pan; cook pork, in batches, until browned and cooked as desired. Cover to keep warm.
2 Stir sugar and remaining butter into pan; add pear. Cook about 5 minutes; remove from pan.
3 Add wine to pan; simmer, stirring, 2 minutes. Add stock to pan; simmer, uncovered, 10 minutes or until liquid has reduced by half. Return pear to pan with sage; simmer until heated through.
4 Serve pork with pear sauce.

prep & cook time 35 minutes **serves** 6
nutritional count per serving 18.6g total fat (6.6g saturated fat); 1488kJ (356 cal); 18.8g carbohydrate; 22.3g protein; 2.6g fibre

char siu pork with spicy fried noodles

600g pork fillets
½ cup (125ml) char siu sauce
450g fresh wide rice noodles
2 tablespoons peanut oil
350g broccolini, chopped coarsely
2 fresh long red chillies, sliced thinly

1 Combine pork and ⅓ cup of the sauce in medium bowl; refrigerate 10 minutes.
2 Cook pork on heated oiled grill plate (or grill or barbecue) until cooked through.
3 Meanwhile, place noodles in large heatproof bowl, cover with boiling water; separate with fork, drain.
4 Heat oil in wok; stir-fry broccolini and chilli until tender. Add noodles, remaining sauce and about a tablespoon of water to wok; stir-fry until hot.
5 Slice pork; serve with noodle mixture.

prep & cook time 25 minutes **serves** 4
nutritional count per serving 15.1g total fat (3.1g saturated fat); 1927kJ (461 cal); 37.2g carbohydrate; 38.8g protein; 7.7g fibre

Pork fillet is an incredibly lean cut of meat, making this simple, delicious meal healthy as well as easy.

The combination of pork and veal mince gives these meatballs a deliciously rich quality that you won't get with beef mince.

serving idea This hearty Italian-American classic needs nothing more than a simple green salad to follow.

spaghetti and meatballs

500g pork and veal mince

½ cup (35g) stale breadcrumbs

1 egg

¼ cup (20g) finely grated parmesan cheese

1 tablespoon olive oil

1 medium brown onion (150g), chopped coarsely

2 cloves garlic, quartered

1 fresh small red thai chilli

6 anchovy fillets

1 cup (150g) drained sun-dried tomatoes

¼ cup (70g) tomato paste

1 cup (250ml) chicken stock

12 pimiento-stuffed olives, sliced thinly

375g spaghetti

⅓ cup coarsely chopped fresh flat-leaf parsley

1 Combine mince, breadcrumbs, egg and cheese in medium bowl; roll level tablespoons of mixture into balls.

2 Heat oil in medium frying pan; cook meatballs, uncovered, until browned.

3 Blend or process onion, garlic, chilli, anchovy, tomatoes and paste until smooth. Combine tomato mixture with stock in medium saucepan; bring to the boil. Add meatballs and olives; simmer, uncovered, 15 minutes.

4 Meanwhile, cook spaghetti in large saucepan of boiling water until tender; drain.

5 Serve spaghetti topped with meatballs and sauce; sprinkle with parsley.

prep & cook time 50 minutes **serves** 4

nutritional count per serving 20.6g total fat (6.3g saturated fat); 2964kJ (709 cal); 78.8g carbohydrate; 47.5g protein; 7.9g fibre

macaroni cheese with olives

375g elbow macaroni
60g butter
1 small red onion (100g), sliced thinly
1 clove garlic, crushed
1 medium red capsicum (200g), sliced thinly
150g mushrooms, sliced thinly
⅓ cup (50g) plain flour
3 cups (750ml) milk
⅓ cup (95g) tomato paste
⅓ cup (40g) seeded black olives, halved
½ cup finely chopped fresh basil
1½ cups (150g) coarsely grated pizza cheese

1 Cook pasta in large saucepan of boiling water until just tender; drain.
2 Meanwhile, melt butter in large saucepan; cook onion, garlic, capsicum and mushrooms, stirring, until vegetables soften. Add flour; cook, stirring, until mixture bubbles and thickens. Gradually stir in milk. Add paste; cook, stirring, until sauce boils and thickens.
3 Preheat grill.
4 Stir pasta, olives, basil and half the cheese into sauce. Place mixture in deep 2-litre (8-cup) ovenproof dish; sprinkle with remaining cheese. Grill until cheese melts and is browned lightly.

prep & cook time 35 minutes **serves** 4
nutritional count per serving 29.5g total fat (18.4g saturated fat); 3223kJ (771 cal); 90.1g carbohydrate; 32.4g protein; 6.7g fibre

spinach and beetroot tart

1 sheet puff pasty
250g frozen spinach, thawed, drained
1 cup (200g) fetta cheese, crumbled
½ x 850g can drained baby beetroot, sliced thinly

1 Preheat oven to 220°C/200°C fan-forced.
2 Place pastry on an oiled oven tray. Fold edges of pastry over to make a 0.5cm border all the way around pastry. Prick pastry base with fork. Place another oven tray on top of pastry; bake 10 minutes. Remove top tray from pastry; reduce temperature to 200°C/180°C fan-forced.
3 Meanwhile, combine spinach with half the cheese in medium bowl.
4 Top tart with spinach mixture, beetroot and remaining cheese. Bake about 10 minutes.

prep & cook time 30 minutes **serves** 4
nutritional count per serving 21.4g total fat (12.8g saturated fat); 1421kJ (340 cal); 22.1g carbohydrate; 13.4g protein; 4g fibre

macaroni cheese with olives

spinach and beetroot tart

when friends drop by

it's worth having these very impressive recipes at your fingertips.

turkish beetroot dip

3 medium beetroot (500g), trimmed
1 teaspoon caraway seeds
1 teaspoon ground cumin
¼ teaspoon hot paprika
¾ cup (200g) yogurt
½ cup loosely packed fresh mint leaves
2 cloves garlic, crushed
1 tablespoon lemon juice

1 Cook beetroot in medium saucepan of boiling water, uncovered, about 45 minutes or until tender; drain. When cool enough to handle, peel beetroot then chop coarsely.
2 Meanwhile, dry-fry spices in a small frying pan until fragrant; cool.
3 Blend or process beetroot with spices and remaining ingredients until smooth.

prep & cook time 50 minutes **makes** 2 cups
nutritional count per tablespoon 0.3g total fat (0.2g saturated fat); 67kJ (16 cal); 2g carbohydrate; 0.8g protein; 0.7g fibre

warm orange and fennel olives

1 large orange (300g)

400g mixed marinated seeded olives

½ cup (125ml) dry red wine

1 teaspoon coarsely ground black pepper

½ teaspoon fennel seeds

1 Peel thin strips of rind from orange. Combine rind with remaining ingredients in medium saucepan; bring to a simmer. Stand 10 minutes before serving warm.

prep & cook time 10 minutes **serves** 6
nutritional count per serving 2.1g total fat (0.3g saturated fat); 360kJ (86 cal); 12g carbohydrate; 0.6g protein; 1.8g fibre

eggplant, haloumi and rocket pizza

1½ cups (225g) plain flour
1 teaspoon dried yeast
½ teaspoon salt
¾ cup (180ml) warm water
2 tablespoons olive oil
2 cloves garlic, crushed
¾ cup (195g) bottled tomato pasta sauce
2 small red onions (200g), cut into wedges
1 small eggplant (230g), sliced thinly
250g haloumi cheese, sliced thinly
¼ cup firmly packed fresh oregano leaves
60g rocket leaves

1 Combine flour, yeast and salt in medium bowl; gradually stir in the water and half the oil. Mix to a soft, sticky dough; turn onto floured surface, knead about 10 minutes or until smooth and elastic. Shape dough into ball; place in large oiled bowl. Cover bowl; stand in warm place about 1 hour or until dough doubles in size.

2 Preheat oven to 230°C/210°C fan-forced. Oil two oven trays.

3 Punch down dough; knead until smooth. Divide dough in half; roll each half on floured surface into two 23cm x 33cm rectangles. Place dough on trays; prick with fork, spread with combined garlic and pasta sauce. Stand in warm place 10 minutes.

4 Meanwhile, combine onion, eggplant and remaining oil in large bowl. Cook, in batches, on heated grill plate (or grill or barbecue) until browned on both sides.

5 Top pizza bases with onion and eggplant mixture, cheese and oregano. Bake, in oven, about 15 minutes or until crust is golden brown. Serve pizzas topped with rocket.

prep & cook time 40 minutes (+ standing) **serves** 4
nutritional count per serving 21.2g total fat (8.3g saturated fat); 2065kJ (494 cal); 50.9g carbohydrate; 22.1g protein; 5.6g fibre

witlof, pear and blue cheese salad

2 red witlof (250g), trimmed, leaves separated
2 yellow witlof (250g), trimmed, leaves separated
1 medium pear (230g), sliced thinly
¾ cup (90g) roasted pecans, chopped coarsely
blue cheese dressing
⅓ cup (80ml) buttermilk
100g blue cheese, crumbled
1 tablespoon lemon juice

1 Make blue cheese dressing.
2 Combine salad ingredients in large bowl.
3 Serve salad drizzled with blue cheese dressing.
blue cheese dressing Whisk ingredients in small jug until smooth.

prep time 20 minutes **serves** 4
nutritional count per serving 24.9g total fat (6.5g saturated fat); 1295kJ (309 cal); 9.9g carbohydrate; 9.5g protein; 5.3g fibre

prawn, crab and avocado salad

Crab meat is available from fishmongers or supermarkets. If frozen, thaw then drain well before use.

16 cooked medium king prawns (800g)
4 large butter lettuce leaves
250g crab meat, shredded coarsely
1 large avocado (320g), sliced thinly
thousand island dressing
½ cup (150g) mayonnaise
1 tablespoon tomato sauce
½ small red capsicum (75g), chopped finely
½ small white onion (40g), grated finely
8 pimiento-stuffed green olives, chopped finely
1 teaspoon lemon juice

1 Make thousand island dressing.
2 Shell and devein prawns, leaving tails intact.
3 Divide lettuce leaves among serving plates; divide prawns, crab and avocado among lettuce leaves. Drizzle with dressing.
thousand island dressing Combine ingredients in small bowl.

prep time 25 minutes **serves** 4
nutritional count per serving 26.5g total fat (4.4g saturated fat); 1718kJ (411 cal); 11.5g carbohydrate; 30.7g protein; 2.8g fibre

witlof, pear and blue cheese salad

prawn, crab and avocado salad

Put some music on, pour everyone a glass of wine and pull out the nibbles for some casual entertaining.

steamed mussels in tomato garlic broth

1 tablespoon olive oil

2 shallots (50g), chopped finely

4 cloves garlic, crushed

410g can crushed tomatoes

1 cup (250ml) dry white wine

1 teaspoon caster sugar

2kg small black mussels

½ cup coarsely chopped fresh flat-leaf parsley

1 Heat oil in large saucepan; cook shallot and garlic, stirring, until shallot softens.

2 Add undrained tomatoes, wine and sugar; bring to the boil. Reduce heat; simmer, uncovered, about 10 minutes or until sauce thickens slightly.

3 Meanwhile, scrub mussels; remove beards. Add mussels to pan; simmer, covered, about 5 minutes, shaking pan occasionally, until mussels open (discard any that do not). Remove mussels from pan, divide among serving bowls; cover with foil to keep warm.

4 Bring tomato mixture to the boil; boil, uncovered, about 5 minutes or until sauce thickens slightly. Pour tomato mixture over mussels; sprinkle with parsley.

prep & cook time 55 minutes **serves** 4
nutritional count per serving 6.7g total fat (1.2g saturated fat); 828kJ (198 cal); 9.9g carbohydrate; 13.3g protein; 2.2g fibre

italian sausage and three-cheese lasagne

500g italian sausages
250g frozen chopped spinach, thawed, drained
250g ricotta cheese
¼ teaspoon ground nutmeg
½ cup (40g) finely grated parmesan cheese
1 egg
6 sheets fresh lasagne
250g mozzarella cheese, sliced thinly

tomato sauce

1 tablespoon olive oil
1 medium onion (150g), chopped finely
1 medium carrot (120g), chopped finely
1 stalk celery (150g), trimmed, chopped finely
5 x 8cm long parsley stalks, crushed
2 cloves garlic, crushed
½ cup (125ml) dry red wine
¼ cup (70g) tomato paste
700g bottled tomato pasta sauce

cheese sauce

50g butter
⅓ cup (50g) plain flour
2 cups (500ml) milk
1½ cups (120g) finely grated parmesan cheese

1 Make tomato sauce. Make cheese sauce.
2 Preheat oven to 200°C/180°C fan-forced.
3 Cook sausages in oiled large frying pan until browned all over; drain then slice thinly.
4 Combine spinach, ricotta, nutmeg, parmesan and egg in medium bowl.

5 Spread ½ cup of the cheese sauce over base of 20cm x 30cm ovenproof dish. Top with two pasta sheets then spread with half the spinach mixture. Sprinkle with half the sausage; cover with 1 cup of the tomato sauce then half the remaining cheese sauce.
6 Top with two pasta sheets. Spread remaining spinach mixture over pasta; sprinkle with remaining sausage. Spread with 1 cup tomato sauce, then remaining cheese sauce.
7 Top with remaining pasta, then half the remaining tomato sauce. Top with mozzarella; spread with remaining tomato sauce.
8 Bake lasagne, covered, 30 minutes. Uncover, bake about 10 minutes or until browned lightly. Stand 10 minutes before serving.

tomato sauce Heat oil in large saucepan, add onion, carrot, celery and parsley; cook, stirring occasionally, until vegetables soften. Add garlic; cook, stirring, 1 minute. Add wine; cook, stirring, until almost evaporated. Discard parsley stalks. Add paste; cook, stirring, 3 minutes. Add sauce; simmer, uncovered, about 15 minutes.

cheese sauce Melt butter in medium saucepan, add flour; cook, stirring, until mixture thickens and bubbles. Gradually add milk; stir until mixture boils and thickens. Reduce heat; cook, stirring, 1 minute, remove from heat. Add cheese, stir until melted.

prep & cook time 2 hours 40 minutes **serves** 8
nutritional count per serving 46.8g total fat (23.1g saturated fat); 3227kJ (772 cal); 44g carbohydrate; 39.3g protein; 5.4g fibre

This hearty lasagne can be assembled
ahead of time and baked at the
last minute, giving you more precious
time with your guests.

seafood chowder

eggplant parmigiana

seafood chowder

1 tablespoon olive oil
3 rindless bacon rashers (195g), sliced thinly
1 medium brown onion (150g), chopped finely
1 small fennel bulb (200g), sliced thinly
3 cloves garlic, sliced thinly
2 medium tomatoes (300g), seeded,
   chopped coarsely
2 tablespoons tomato paste
1 teaspoon hot paprika
½ cup (125ml) dry white wine
2 x 400g cans whole tomatoes
3 cups (750ml) fish stock
1 litre (4 cups) water
500g kipfler potatoes, cut into 3cm pieces
1.2kg marinara mix
½ cup coarsely chopped fresh flat-leaf parsley

1 Heat oil in large saucepan, add bacon; cook until crisp. Drain on absorbent paper.
2 Add onion, fennel and garlic to pan; cook until vegetables soften. Add fresh tomato; cook until soft. Add tomato paste and paprika; cook, stirring, 2 minutes. Return bacon to pan with wine; cook, stirring, 2 minutes.
3 Slice canned tomatoes thickly. Add slices with juice from can, stock, the water and potato to pan; bring to the boil. Reduce heat; simmer, covered, about 20 minutes or until potato is soft.
4 Add marinara mix; cook, covered, about 3 minutes. Stir in parsley.

prep & cook time 50 minutes **serves** 6
nutritional count per serving 8.8g total fat (2.2g saturated fat); 1781kJ (426 cal); 24.5g carbohydrate; 50.5g protein; 5.7g fibre

eggplant parmigiana

2 large eggplants (1kg)
vegetable oil, for shallow-frying
½ cup (75g) plain flour
4 eggs, beaten lightly
2 cups (200g) packaged breadcrumbs
750ml bottled tomato pasta sauce
1 cup (100g) coarsely grated mozzarella cheese
¼ cup (20g) finely grated parmesan cheese
⅓ cup loosely packed fresh oregano leaves

1 Using vegetable peeler, peel random strips of skin from eggplants; discard skins. Slice eggplants thinly.
2 Heat oil in large frying pan. Coat eggplant in flour; shake off excess. Dip in egg, then in breadcrumbs. Shallow-fry eggplant, in batches, until browned lightly. Drain on absorbent paper.
3 Preheat oven to 200°C/180°C fan-forced.
4 Spread about one-third of the pasta sauce over base of greased 2.5-litre (10-cup) ovenproof dish. Top with about one-third of the eggplant, one-third of the cheeses and one-third of the oregano. Repeat layering.
5 Bake, covered, 20 minutes. Uncover; bake about 10 minutes or until browned lightly.

prep & cook time 1 hour **serves** 6
nutritional count per serving 27.7g total fat (6.6g saturated fat); 2266kJ (542 cal); 49.4g carbohydrate; 19.9g protein, 8.3g fibre

To get that wonderfully crispy skin on your fish, place the fillets skin-side down in the pan then weigh them down with a plate for a few minutes before turning them over.

caraway salmon with beetroot and fennel salad

1 small fennel bulb (200g), trimmed
1 medium beetroot (175g), peeled
1 small radicchio (150g), trimmed, shredded finely
½ cup loosely packed fresh flat-leaf parsley leaves
1 tablespoon rice wine vinegar
¼ cup (60ml) olive oil
4 salmon fillets (880g)
1½ teaspoons caraway seeds
1 clove garlic, crushed
1 lime, cut into wedges

1 Using mandolin, V-slicer or very sharp knife, slice fennel and beetroot finely. Place in large bowl with radicchio, parsley, vinegar and 2 tablespoons of the oil.
2 Combine fish, remaining oil, seeds and garlic in large bowl. Cook fish in heated large frying pan until cooked as desired.
3 Divide salad and fish among serving plates; serve with lime.

prep & cook time 30 minutes **serves** 4
nutritional count per serving 29.5g total fat (5.5g saturated fat); 1960kJ (469 cal); 4.8g carbohydrate; 44.7g protein; 3.6g fibre

grilled steaks with anchovy butter

crab cakes with avocado salsa

grilled steaks with anchovy butter

6 x 220g new-york cut steaks
2 tablespoons olive oil
lemony potato wedges
1.5kg potatoes
¼ cup (60ml) olive oil
2 cloves garlic, crushed
1 tablespoon finely grated lemon rind
2 teaspoons sea salt flakes
anchovy butter
80g butter, softened
6 drained anchovy fillets, chopped coarsely
2 cloves garlic, crushed
2 tablespoons finely chopped fresh flat-leaf parsley

1 Make lemony potato wedges and anchovy butter.
2 About 10 minutes before wedges are cooked, brush beef all over with oil; cook on heated grill plate (or grill or barbecue) until cooked as desired. Cover beef; stand 5 minutes.
3 Serve beef topped with sliced anchovy butter and potato wedges.
lemony potato wedges Preheat oven to 220°C/200°C fan-forced. Line oven tray with baking paper. Slice potatoes lengthways into 8 wedges; boil, steam or microwave until slightly softened. Drain; pat dry with absorbent paper. Combine potato in large bowl with oil, garlic, rind and salt. Place wedges, in single layer, on tray; roast 50 minutes or until browned lightly.
anchovy butter Mash ingredients in small bowl with fork until well combined. Roll mixture tightly in plastic wrap to make a log; refrigerate until firm.

prep & cook time 1 hour **serves** 6
nutritional count per serving 39.8g total fat (14.9g saturated fat); 2989kJ (715 cal); 33.1g carbohydrate; 53.7g protein; 5.5g fibre

crab cakes with avocado salsa

Crab meat is available from fishmongers or supermarkets. If frozen, thaw then drain well before use.

600g cooked crab meat
1 cup (70g) stale white breadcrumbs
1 egg
1 clove garlic, crushed
2 tablespoons mayonnaise
¼ cup finely chopped fresh coriander
½ teaspoon cayenne pepper
15g butter
1 tablespoon olive oil
avocado salsa
2 small avocados (400g), chopped coarsely
1 medium tomato (150g), chopped coarsely
¾ cup loosely packed fresh coriander leaves
2 teaspoons Tabasco
1 tablespoon lime juice
1 tablespoon olive oil

1 Combine crab meat, breadcrumbs, egg, garlic, mayonnaise, coriander and pepper in medium bowl. Shape mixture into eight patties; place on tray. Cover; refrigerate 1 hour.
2 Meanwhile, make avocado salsa.
3 Heat butter and oil in large frying pan; cook crab cakes, in batches, until browned both sides and heated through. Serve crab cakes topped with salsa.
avocado salsa Combine ingredients in medium bowl.

prep & cook time 35 minutes (+ refrigeration)
serves 4
nutritional count per serving 34.1g total fat (7.8g saturated fat); 2011kJ (481 cal); 17.6g carbohydrate; 25.3g protein; 2.8g fibre

berry frangipane tart

1 sheet sweet puff pastry
300g frozen mixed berries
frangipane
80g butter, softened
½ teaspoon vanilla extract
⅓ cup (75g) caster sugar
2 egg yolks
1 tablespoon plain flour
1 cup (120g) almond meal

1 Preheat oven to 220°C/200°C fan-forced. Grease 20cm x 30cm lamington pan.
2 Roll pastry until large enough to cover base and sides of pan; line pan with pastry, press into sides. Prick pastry all over with fork; freeze 5 minutes.
3 Place another lamington pan on top of pastry; bake 5 minutes. Remove top pan; bake about 5 minutes or until pastry is browned lightly. Cool 5 minutes. Reduce temperature to 180°C/160°C fan-forced.
4 Meanwhile, make frangipane.
5 Spread frangipane over pastry base. Sprinkle with berries, press into frangipane. Bake about 30 minutes or until browned lightly.
frangipane Beat butter, extract, sugar and egg yolks in small bowl with electric mixer until light and fluffy. Stir in flour and almond meal.

prep & cook time 50 minutes **serves** 6
nutritional count per serving 30.2g total fat (11.9g saturated fat); 1722kJ (412 cal); 26.4g carbohydrate; 7.7g protein; 3.3g fibre

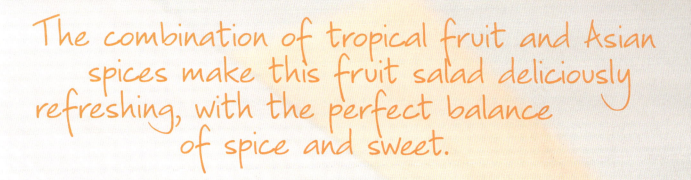

The combination of tropical fruit and Asian spices make this fruit salad deliciously refreshing, with the perfect balance of spice and sweet.

serving idea If lychees are in season, try buying fresh instead of canned ones. Don't be put off by their tough-looking skin – they are easy to peel and are silky and sweet on the inside.

asian-spiced fruit salad

1 tablespoon grated palm sugar

2cm piece fresh ginger (10g), grated

1 star anise

1 cup (250ml) water

1 small pineapple (900g), chopped coarsely

1 small honeydew melon (1.3kg), chopped coarsely

1 small papaya (650g), chopped coarsely

2 small mangoes (600g), chopped coarsely

3 medium kiwifruits (255g), chopped coarsely

565g can lychees, drained, halved

¼ cup (60ml) lime juice

2 tablespoons passionfruit pulp

1 teaspoon finely grated whole nutmeg

1 Stir sugar, ginger, star anise and the water in small saucepan over heat, without boiling, until sugar dissolves; bring to the boil. Reduce heat; simmer, uncovered, without stirring, about 10 minutes or until syrup thickens slightly. Cool.

2 Meanwhile, combine pineapple, melon, papaya, mango, kiwifruit and lychees in large bowl.

3 Combine juice, pulp and nutmeg in medium jug; stir in syrup. Pour syrup mixture over fruit. Cover; refrigerate 20 minutes before serving.

prep & cook time 30 minutes (+ refrigeration)
serves 6
nutritional count per serving 0.9g total fat (0g saturated fat); 920kJ (220 cal); 44.3g carbohydrate; 3.9g protein; 8.7g fibre

strawberries in rosewater syrup

¼ cup (55g) caster sugar
⅓ cup (80ml) water
2 teaspoons rosewater
750g strawberries, hulled, sliced thickly
⅓ cup (45g) coarsely chopped roasted pistachios

1 Stir sugar and the water in small saucepan over heat until sugar dissolves.
2 Remove pan from heat; stir in rosewater. Add strawberries; stir to coat in syrup.
3 Divide strawberry mixture among serving dishes; sprinkle with nuts. Serve with mini meringues or vanilla ice-cream.

prep & cook time 10 minutes **serves** 6
nutritional count per serving 3.7g total fat (0.4g saturated fat); 456kJ (109 cal); 13.8g carbohydrate; 3.7g protein; 3.5g fibre

sticky banana puddings with butterscotch sauce

125g butter, softencd
⅔ cup (150g) firmly packed brown sugar
2 eggs
1½ cups (225g) self-raising flour
1 teaspoon mixed spice
1 cup mashed banana
¼ cup (60g) sour cream
¼ cup (60ml) milk
2 tablespoons brown sugar, extra
1 large banana (230g), sliced thinly
butterscotch sauce
½ cup (110g) firmly packed brown sugar
⅔ cup (160ml) cream
50g butter

1 Preheat oven to 180°C/160°C fan-forced. Grease eight holes of two six-hole (¾-cup/180ml) texas muffin pans.
2 Beat butter and sugar in small bowl with electric mixer until light and fluffy. Beat in eggs, one at a time; transfer mixture to large bowl. Stir in sifted flour and mixed spice, mashed banana, sour cream and milk in two batches.
3 Sprinkle extra sugar in pan holes; cover bases of pan holes with sliced banana. Divide cake mixture between pan holes. Bake 30 minutes.
4 Meanwhile, make butterscotch sauce.
5 Turn puddings, top-side down, onto serving plates; serve warm with butterscotch sauce.
butterscotch sauce Stir ingredients in small saucepan over heat, without boiling, until sugar dissolves. Simmer, stirring, about 3 minutes or until sauce thickens slightly.

prep & cook time 45 minutes **makes** 8
nutritional count per pudding 31.6g total fat (20.1g saturated fat); 2404kJ (575 cal); 65.5g carbohydrate; 6.3g protein; 2.1g fibre

strawberries in rosewater syrup

sticky banana puddings with butterscotch sauce

affogato with frangelico

⅓ cup (30g) ground espresso coffee beans
1½ cups (375ml) boiling water
12 small scoops of vanilla ice-cream
½ cup (125ml) Frangelico

1 Place coffee in coffee plunger; add boiling water, stand 4 minutes before plunging.

2 Place 2 small scoops of ice-cream in each of 6 small heatproof glasses or coffee cups; pour 1 tablespoon of the Frangelico over each.

3 Give the hot coffee to the guests to pour over the ice-cream.

prep time 10 minutes **serves** 6
nutritional count per serving 6.4g total fat (4.2g saturated fat); 723kJ (173 cal); 20.2g carbohydrate; 2.1g protein; 0g fibre

sunday lunch

Let your long, leisurely Sunday lunch go on all afternoon.

Pumpkin soup is one of those comforting old classics that is loved by everyone.

creamy pumpkin and potato soup

1 tablespoon olive oil

1 medium brown onion (150g), chopped coarsely

1 clove garlic, crushed

600g pumpkin, chopped coarsely

2 medium potatoes (400g), chopped coarsely

2 cups (500ml) water

1½ cups (375ml) vegetable stock

½ cup (125ml) cream

1 tablespoon lemon juice

garlic and chive croûtons

⅓ loaf ciabatta (150g)

2 tablespoons olive oil

1 clove garlic, crushed

1 tablespoon finely chopped fresh chives

1 Heat oil in large saucepan; cook onion and garlic, stirring, until onion softens. Add pumpkin, potato, the water and stock; bring to the boil. Reduce heat; simmer, covered, about 20 minutes or until vegetables are tender.

2 Meanwhile, make garlic and chive croûtons.

3 Blend or process soup, in batches, until smooth. Return soup to same pan; add cream and juice. Reheat, stirring, without boiling, until hot.

4 Serve bowls of soup topped with croûtons.

garlic and chive croûtons Preheat oven to 180°C/160°C fan-forced. Cut bread into 2cm cubes; combine bread in large bowl with oil, garlic and chives. Place bread on oven tray; toast bread in oven until croûtons are brown.

prep & cook time 35 minutes **serves** 4
nutritional count per serving 29.3g total fat (11.7g saturated fat); 2006kJ (480 cal); 41.4g carbohydrate; 10.7g protein; 5g fibre

tip There are several varieties of pumpkin readily available and any can be used in this soup, but to get that velvety smooth texture and sweet nutty flavour, butternut is the best.

black-eyed bean and ham soup

french onion soup with gruyère croûtons

black-eyed bean
and ham soup

1 cup (200g) black-eyed beans
1 tablespoon olive oil
1 stalk celery (150g), trimmed, chopped coarsely
1 small brown onion (80g), chopped coarsely
1 medium carrot (120g), chopped coarsely
1 bay leaf
2 cloves garlic
1.2kg ham hock
1 litre (4 cups) chicken stock
2 litres (8 cups) water
½ bunch trimmed silver beet (125g),
   shredded finely
2 tablespoons cider vinegar

1 Place beans in medium bowl, cover with water; stand overnight, rinse, drain.
2 Heat oil in large saucepan, add celery, onion and carrot; cook until vegetables are soft. Add bay leaf, garlic, ham hock, stock and the water; bring to the boil. Reduce heat; simmer, uncovered, 1 hour.
3 Add beans to soup; simmer, uncovered, 1 hour or until beans are tender.
4 Remove hock from soup. When cool enough to handle, remove meat from hock. Discard bone; shred meat coarsely, return to soup.
5 Add silver beet to soup; cook, stirring, until wilted. Remove from heat; stir in vinegar.

prep & cook time 2 hours 50 minutes (+ standing)
serves 6
nutritional count per serving 7.2g total fat (1.8g saturated fat); 945kJ (226 cal); 16.1g carbohydrate; 21.2g protein; 6.3g fibre

french onion soup
with gruyère croûtons

50g butter
4 large brown onions (800g), sliced thinly
¾ cup (180ml) dry white wine
3 cups (750ml) water
1 litre (4 cups) beef stock
1 bay leaf
1 tablespoon plain flour
1 teaspoon fresh thyme leaves
gruyère croûtons
1 small french bread (150g), cut in 1.5cm slices
½ cup (60g) coarsely grated gruyère cheese

1 Melt butter in large saucepan, add onion; cook, stirring occasionally, about 30 minutes or until caramelised.
2 Meanwhile, bring wine to the boil in large saucepan; boil 1 minute then stir in the water, stock and bay leaf; return to the boil. Remove from heat.
3 Stir flour into onion mixture; cook, stirring, 2 minutes. Gradually add hot broth mixture to onion mixture, stirring, until mixture boils and thickens slightly. Reduce heat; simmer, uncovered, stirring occasionally, 20 minutes. Discard bay leaf; stir in thyme.
4 Meanwhile, make gruyère croûtons.
5 Serve bowls of soup topped with croûtons. Sprinkle with extra thyme leaves, if you like.
gruyère croûtons Preheat grill. Toast bread on one side then turn and sprinkle with cheese; grill croûtons until cheese browns lightly.

prep & cook time 1 hour 10 minutes **serves** 4
nutritional count per serving 16.7g total fat (10g saturated fat); 1522kJ (364 cal); 31.1g carbohydrate; 13.4g protein; 3.9g fibre

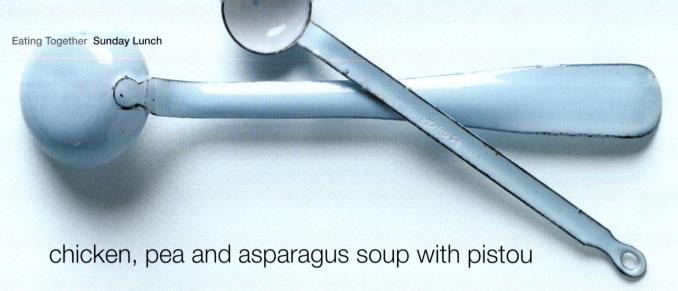

chicken, pea and asparagus soup with pistou

*You need 450g of fresh peas in the pod or
2 cups (240g) frozen peas for this recipe.*

3 cups (750ml) chicken stock
3 cups (750ml) water
1 clove garlic, crushed
¼ teaspoon coarsely ground black pepper
400g chicken breast fillets
170g asparagus, trimmed, chopped coarsely
1½ cups (240g) shelled fresh peas
1 tablespoon lemon juice
pistou
½ cup coarsely chopped fresh flat-leaf parsley
½ cup coarsely chopped fresh mint
¼ cup coarsely chopped fresh garlic chives
2 teaspoons finely grated lemon rind
1 clove garlic, crushed
2 teaspoons olive oil

1 Bring stock, the water, garlic and pepper to the boil in large saucepan. Add chicken; return to boil. Reduce heat; simmer, covered, about 10 minutes or until chicken is cooked through. Cool in poaching liquid 10 minutes. Remove chicken from pan; slice thinly.
2 Meanwhile, make pistou.
3 Add remaining ingredients to soup; bring to the boil. Return chicken to pan; simmer, uncovered, about 3 minutes or until vegetables are just tender.
4 Divide soup among serving bowls; top with pistou.
pistou Using mortar and pestle, pound ingredients until smooth.

prep & cook time 30 minutes **serves** 4
nutritional count per serving 5.7g total fat (1.3g saturated fat); 861kJ (206 cal); 7.3g carbohydrate; 28.9g protein; 4.4g fibre

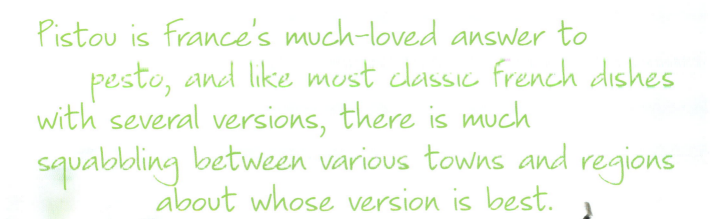

Pistou is France's much-loved answer to pesto, and like most classic french dishes with several versions, there is much squabbling between various towns and regions about whose version is best.

note Pistou is most commonly associated with a Provençal summer vegetable soup, but is also delicious served on pasta dishes or spread on thick slices of crusty bread.

chicken and leek pie

veal goulash and potato pies

chicken and leek pie

2 cups (500ml) chicken stock
600g chicken breast fillets
1 tablespoon olive oil
40g butter
1 large leek (500g), sliced thinly
2 stalks celery (300g), trimmed, chopped finely
2 tablespoons plain flour
2 teaspoons fresh thyme leaves
½ cup (125ml) milk
1 cup (250ml) cream
2 teaspoons wholegrain mustard
2 sheets shortcrust pastry
1 sheet puff pastry
1 egg yolk

1 Bring stock to the boil in medium saucepan.
Add chicken; return to the boil. Reduce heat;
simmer, covered, about 10 minutes or until chicken
is cooked. Remove from heat; stand chicken in
poaching liquid 10 minutes. Remove chicken; chop
coarsely. Reserve ⅓ cup of the poaching liquid;
keep remainder for another use, or discard.
2 Heat oil and butter in medium saucepan; cook
leek and celery, stirring, until leek softens. Add flour
and thyme; cook, stirring, 1 minute. Gradually stir
in reserved poaching liquid, milk and cream; cook,
stirring, until mixture boils and thickens. Stir in
chicken and mustard. Cool 10 minutes.
3 Preheat oven to 200°C/180°C fan-forced.
Oil 1.5-litre (6-cup) ovenproof dish.
4 Line base and side of dish with shortcrust pastry,
trim to fit; prick well all over with fork. Bake 10 minutes.
Cool 5 minutes. Spoon chicken mixture into pastry
case; place puff pastry over filling, trim to fit dish.
Brush pastry with egg yolk; cut two small slits in top
of pastry. Bake 20 minutes or until browned lightly.

prep & cook time 1 hour 35 minutes **serves** 6
nutritional count per serving 56g total fat (30.1g
saturated fat); 3344kJ (800 cal); 42.5g carbohydrate;
31.1g protein; 3.6g fibre

veal goulash and potato pies

¼ cup (60ml) olive oil
1kg boneless veal shoulder, cut into 2cm pieces
1 large brown onion (200g), chopped coarsely
1 clove garlic, crushed
1 large red capsicum (350g), chopped coarsely
1 tablespoon plain flour
2 teaspoons hot paprika
2 teaspoons sweet paprika
2 teaspoons caraway seeds
2 cups (500ml) beef stock
400g can diced tomatoes
1 tablespoon tomato paste
4 medium potatoes (800g), chopped coarsely
1 cup (120g) coarsely grated cheddar cheese

1 Heat 1 tablespoon of the oil in large saucepan;
cook veal, in batches, until browned.
2 Heat remaining oil in same pan; cook onion, garlic
and capsicum, stirring, until onion softens. Add flour,
spices and seeds; cook, stirring, 2 minutes.
3 Return veal to pan with stock, undrained tomatoes
and paste; bring to the boil. Reduce heat; simmer,
covered, 1 hour. Uncover; simmer about 30 minutes
or until veal is tender and sauce thickens slightly.
4 Meanwhile, boil, steam or microwave potato
until tender; drain. Mash potato in medium bowl
until smooth.
5 Preheat grill.
6 Divide goulash mixture among six oiled 1¼-cup
(310ml) ovenproof dishes; top with potato, sprinkle
with cheese. Grill until browned.

prep & cook time 2 hours 25 minutes **serves** 6
nutritional count per serving 20.6g total fat (6.8g
saturated fat); 2011kJ (481 cal); 23g carbohydrate;
48.8g protein; 3.9g fibre

tip If you're short on time, use sheets of ready-made frozen pastry. Use shortcrust to line the tins and top the pie with puff pastry. Brushing the top of the pastry with egg gives it a lovely golden brown finish.

meat pies

1½ cups (225g) plain flour
100g cold butter, chopped coarsely
1 egg
1 tablespoon iced water, approximately
2 sheets puff pastry
1 egg, extra
beef filling
1 tablespoon vegetable oil
1 small brown onion (80g), chopped finely
600g beef mince
415g can crushed tomatoes
2 tablespoons tomato paste
2 tablespoons worcestershire sauce
¾ cup (180ml) beef stock

1 Process flour and butter until crumbly. Add egg and enough of the water to make ingredients cling together. Knead pastry on lightly floured surface until smooth. Cover; refrigerate 30 minutes.
2 Meanwhile, make beef filling.
3 Oil six ⅔-cup (160ml) pie tins. Divide pastry into six portions; roll each between sheets of baking paper until large enough to line tins. Lift pastry into tins; gently press over base and sides; trim. Refrigerate 30 minutes.
4 Cut six 11cm rounds from puff pastry. Refrigerate until required.
5 Preheat oven to 200°C/180°C fan-forced.
6 Place pastry cases on oven tray; line pastry with baking paper then fill with dried beans or uncooked rice. Bake 10 minutes; remove paper and beans. Bake a further 5 minutes; cool.
7 Fill pastry cases with beef filling; brush edges of pastry with extra egg. Top with puff pastry rounds; press edges to seal. Brush tops with egg. Cut steam holes in top of pies. Bake about 20 minutes or until pastry is golden. Serve pies with tomato sauce.
beef filling Heat oil in large saucepan, add onion and beef; cook, stirring, until beef is well browned. Stir in undrained tomatoes, paste, sauce and stock; bring to the boil. Reduce heat, simmer, uncovered, about 20 minutes or until thick. Cool.

prep & cook time 1 hour 35 minutes (+ refrigeration)
makes 6
nutritional count per pie 38.7g total fat (13.8g saturated fat); 2876kJ (688 cal); 52.4g carbohydrate; 31.2g protein; 3.5g fibre

What could be more quintessentially Australian than a meat pie?

There is no better time for a traditional roast and vegies than Sunday lunch.

roast chicken with tomato-braised beans

roast chicken with herb stuffing

Roast chicken is one of those foods that everyone loves but few actually make themselves. Try either of these recipes and you'll see how easy and satisfying it is to make.

roast chicken with tomato-braised beans

2kg chicken
1 medium lemon (140g), quartered
6 sprigs fresh thyme
6 cloves garlic, unpeeled
60g butter, softened
2 tablespoons lemon juice
2 cloves garlic, crushed
2 teaspoons finely chopped fresh thyme
1 cup (250ml) water
1 tablespoon olive oil
1 medium brown onion (150g), chopped coarsely
1kg green beans, trimmed
4 medium tomatoes (600g), chopped coarsely

1 Preheat oven to 200°C/180°C fan-forced.
2 Tuck wing tips under chicken. Fill cavity with lemon, thyme sprigs and garlic, fold skin over to enclose filling; secure with toothpicks. Tie legs together with kitchen string.
3 Combine butter, juice, crushed garlic and chopped thyme in small bowl; rub mixture all over chicken.
4 Place chicken on oiled rack in large baking dish; pour the water into dish. Roast about 2 hours, basting occasionally with pan juices.
5 Meanwhile, heat oil in large saucepan; cook onion, stirring, until onion softens. Add beans and tomato; cook, covered, stirring occasionally, about 20 minutes or until vegetables soften slightly.
6 Serve chicken with beans.

prep & cook time 2 hours 40 minutes **serves** 6
nutritional count per serving 33.5g total fat (12.7g saturated fat); 2123kJ (508 cal); 8.3g carbohydrate; 40.3g protein; 7.3g fibre

roast chicken with herb stuffing

1.5kg chicken
20g butter, melted
herb stuffing
1½ cups (105g) stale breadcrumbs
1 stalk celery (150g), trimmed, chopped finely
1 small white onion (100g), chopped finely
1 teaspoon dried mixed herbs
1 egg, beaten lightly
50g butter, melted

1 Preheat oven to 200°C/180°C fan-forced.
2 Make herb stuffing. Fill chicken cavity with stuffing, fold over skin to enclose; secure with toothpicks. Tie legs together with kitchen string.
3 Place chicken on rack over baking dish half-filled with water (water should not touch chicken). Brush chicken with melted butter; roast 15 minutes. Reduce oven to 180°C/160°C fan-forced; roast chicken about 1½ hours or until cooked through.
4 Stand chicken 10 minutes before serving. Serve chicken with steamed asparagus and roasted baby new potatoes.
herb stuffing Combine ingredients in medium bowl.

prep & cook time 2 hours 15 minutes **serves** 4
nutritional count per serving 46.8g total fat (19.4g saturated fat); 2817kJ (674 cal); 19.7g carbohydrate; 43.4g protein; 1.9g fibre

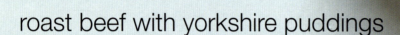

roast beef with yorkshire puddings

2kg corner piece beef topside roast
2 cups (500ml) dry red wine
2 bay leaves
6 black peppercorns
¼ cup (70g) wholegrain mustard
4 cloves garlic, sliced
4 sprigs fresh thyme
1 medium brown onion (150g), chopped coarsely
2 medium carrots (240g), chopped coarsely
1 large leek (500g), chopped coarsely
2 stalks celery (300g), trimmed, chopped coarsely
2 tablespoons olive oil
yorkshire puddings
1 cup (150g) plain flour
2 eggs
½ cup (125ml) milk
½ cup (125ml) water
gravy
2 tablespoons plain flour
1½ cups (375ml) beef stock

1 Combine beef, wine, bay leaves, peppercorns, mustard, garlic, thyme and onion in large bowl; cover, refrigerate 3 hours or overnight.
2 Preheat oven to 180°C/160°C fan-forced.
3 Drain beef over medium bowl; reserve 1 cup (250ml) of marinade. Combine carrot, leek and celery in large baking dish, top with beef; brush beef with oil.
4 Roast beef, uncovered, about 1½ hours. Remove beef from dish, wrap in foil; stand beef 20 minutes before serving.
5 Increase oven to 220°C/200°C fan-forced.
6 Remove vegetables with slotted spoon; discard vegetables. Pour pan juices into jug; stand 2 minutes. Reserve 1½ tablespoons oil for yorkshire puddings, pour off excess oil; reserve 2 tablespoons of pan juices for gravy.
7 Make yorkshire puddings and gravy.
8 Serve beef with yorkshire puddings and gravy; accompany with roasted potatoes and steamed baby carrots.

yorkshire puddings Sift flour into medium bowl; whisk in combined eggs, milk and water all at once until smooth. Stand batter 30 minutes. Divide reserved oil between eight holes of 12-hole (⅓-cup/80ml) muffin pan; heat in oven 2 minutes. Divide batter among pan holes. Bake about 20 minutes or until puddings are puffed and golden.

gravy Heat reserved pan juices in same baking dish, add flour; cook, stirring, until browned. Gradually add stock and reserved marinade; cook, stirring, until mixture boils and thickens. Strain gravy into heatproof jug.

prep & cook time 2 hours 35 minutes (+ refrigeration & standing) **serves** 8
nutritional count per serving 15.4g total fat (4.8g saturated fat); 2169kJ (519 cal); 21.1g carbohydrate; 61.2g protein; 4g fibre

This Sunday roast with Yorkshire puddings and gravy is a tradition well worth keeping.

tip Parmesan is the perfect cheese to use in stuffing because it doesn't go stringy when heated. If you ever end up with too much stuffing to fill the meat just bake the remainder in a greased muffin pan and serve the stuffing muffins as a side dish.

sirloin roast

2.5kg boneless beef sirloin roast
2 large kumara (1kg)
1kg potatoes, cut into wedges
2 tablespoons olive oil
2 tablespoons lemon juice
2 teaspoons sweet paprika
1 clove garlic, crushed
2 tablespoons plain flour
⅓ cup (80ml) dry red wine
1½ cups (375ml) beef stock
cheese and herb stuffing
50g butter
2 rindless bacon rashers (130g), chopped finely
1 medium brown onion (150g), chopped finely
1 clove garlic, crushed
1½ cups (105g) stale breadcrumbs
½ cup (40g) coarsely grated parmesan cheese
1 egg
1 tablespoon wholegrain mustard
2 tablespoons finely chopped fresh oregano
2 tablespoons finely chopped fresh flat-leaf parsley
2 teaspoons finely grated lemon rind

1 Make cheese and herb stuffing.
2 Preheat oven to 220°C/200°C fan-forced.
3 Cut between fat and meat of beef, making a pocket for stuffing; trim and discard a little of the fat. Spoon stuffing into pocket; lay fat over stuffing to enclose. Tie beef with kitchen string at 2cm intervals; place beef on wire rack over shallow large baking dish.
4 Roast beef, uncovered, about 1½ hours.
5 Meanwhile, cut kumara into thirds crossways; cut each piece into wedges. Combine kumara with potato, oil, juice, paprika and garlic in shallow large baking dish; roast about 1 hour.
6 Remove beef from dish; cover, stand 10 minutes. Slice beef thinly.
7 Reserve 2 tablespoons of beef juices in baking dish; place over heat. Add flour; cook, stirring, until mixture thickens and bubbles. Gradually add wine and stock, stirring, until gravy boils and thickens slightly.
8 Serve beef with potato and kumara wedges and gravy.
cheese and herb stuffing Melt butter in medium frying pan; cook bacon, onion and garlic, stirring, until onion softens. Cool. Combine bacon mixture with remaining ingredients in medium bowl.

prep & cook time 2 hours 25 minutes **serves** 8
nutritional count per serving 43.5g total fat (19g saturated fat); 3716kJ (889 cal); 41.6g carbohydrate; 78.7g protein; 4.8g fibre

chilli and lemon-baked veal rack

1 large kumara (500g), sliced thickly
4 medium potatoes (800g), sliced thickly
1 large brown onion (200g), sliced thickly
2 tablespoons olive oil
1 tablespoon lemon juice
3 cloves garlic, crushed
1.6kg veal rack (8 chops), trimmed
2 cups (140g) stale breadcrumbs
1 tablespoon finely grated lemon rind
1 fresh long red chilli, sliced thinly
1 fresh long red chilli, chopped finely
60g butter, melted

1 Preheat oven to 220°C/200°C fan-forced.
2 Combine kumara, potato, onion, oil, juice and two-thirds of the garlic in large ovenproof dish. Place veal on wire rack over potato mixture in dish.
3 Combine remaining garlic, breadcrumbs, rind, chillies and butter in small bowl; press breadcrumb mixture over veal.
4 Roast, uncovered, about 40 minutes or until cooked as desired. Stand, covered, 10 minutes before serving.

prep & cook time 50 minutes **serves** 8
nutritional count per serving 15.2g total fat (5.9g saturated fat); 1852kJ (443 cal); 32.2g carbohydrate; 42g protein; 3.7g fibre

pot-roasted pork with apple and sage

1 tablespoon olive oil
1.5kg piece pork neck
600g spring onions, stems trimmed
    to 10cm lengths
6 large sprigs fresh sage
6 large sprigs fresh thyme
1 cup (250ml) dry white wine
2 tablespoons boiling water
40g butter
3 large apples (600g), unpeeled, cored,
    cut into thick wedges

1 Cook pork with 2 teaspoons of the oil in large heavy-based saucepan, turning, until browned all over. Add onions, herbs and wine to pan; bring to the boil. Reduce heat; simmer, covered tightly, about 1½ hours or until pork is cooked, turning pork twice during cooking time. Transfer pork and onions to serving platter; cover to keep warm.
2 Strain pan juices into serving jug; discard solids. Stir the water into jug; cover to keep sauce warm.
3 Meanwhile, heat butter and remaining oil in large frying pan; cook apple, stirring, about 10 minutes or until tender and golden.
4 Serve sliced pork with sauce, apple and onions.

prep & cook time 2 hours **serves** 6
nutritional count per serving 28.8g total fat (16.8g saturated fat); 2391kJ (572 cal); 14.7g carbohydrate; 55.1g protein; 3.8g fibre

roast loin of pork with apple sauce

Ask your butcher to roll and tie the pork at 2cm intervals for you, and to score the rind, if it isn't already done so.

2 sprigs rosemary
2.5kg boneless loin of pork, rind on
1 tablespoon olive oil
1 tablespoon coarse cooking salt
apple sauce
3 large apples (600g)
¼ cup (60ml) water
1 teaspoon white sugar
pinch ground cinnamon

1 Preheat oven to 250°C/230°C fan-forced.
2 Tuck the rosemary into the string under the pork. Place pork in large baking dish; rub rind with oil then salt. Roast about 40 minutes or until rind blisters. Drain excess fat from dish.
3 Reduce oven to 180°C/160°C fan-forced. Roast pork about 1 hour.
4 Meanwhile, make apple sauce.
5 Transfer pork to plate; cover loosely, stand 15 minutes before carving. Serve pork with apple sauce.
apple sauce Peel and core apples; slice thickly. Place apple and the water in medium saucepan; simmer, covered, 5 minutes. Uncover; simmer, further 5 minutes or until apple is soft. Remove from heat, stir in sugar and cinnamon.

prep & cook time 2 hours **serves** 8
nutritional count per serving 72g total fat (24.1g saturated fat); 3762kJ (900 cal); 7.7g carbohydrate; 56.7g protein; 1.1g fibre

pot-roasted pork with apple and sage

roast loin of pork with apple sauce

tip Broad beans can be bought ready-peeled and frozen just about as easily as peas and in this mash you won't be able to tell the difference between frozen and fresh ones. They also get the thumbs up from nutritionists as they are high in fibre and a good source of vitamin C and folate.

Lamb and mint is one of the ultimate taste combinations – the tangy mint sauce brings out the distinct flavour of the meat.

lamb leg roast with broad bean mash

2kg lamb leg
2 tablespoons olive oil
2 cloves garlic, crushed
1 tablespoon wholegrain mustard
2 teaspoons finely grated lemon rind
1 tablespoon lemon juice
1.5kg potatoes, chopped coarsely
2 cups (240g) peeled broad beans
40g butter
¾ cup (180ml) hot milk

mint sauce
2 cups firmly packed fresh mint leaves
2 cloves garlic, quartered
½ cup (125ml) olive oil
¼ cup (60ml) white wine vinegar
1 tablespoon caster sugar

1 Using sharp knife, score lamb skin at 2cm intervals. Combine lamb, oil, garlic, mustard, rind and juice in large bowl. Cover; refrigerate 3 hours or overnight.
2 Preheat oven to 200°C/180°C fan-forced.
3 Place lamb on oiled wire rack over large baking dish; roast about 45 minutes. Cover lamb; stand 10 minutes, slice thinly.
4 Meanwhile, boil, steam or microwave potato and beans, separately, until tender; drain. Push potato through fine sieve into large bowl; stir in butter and milk until smooth. Place beans in small bowl; crush coarsely with fork. Fold beans into potato mixture.
5 Make mint sauce.
6 Serve lamb with mint sauce and broad bean mash.
mint sauce Blend or process mint and garlic until smooth; with motor operating, gradually add oil, in a thin steady stream, until mixture is smooth. Stir in vinegar and sugar.

prep & cook time 1 hour 50 minutes (+ refrigeration)
serves 6
nutritional count per serving 45.7g total fat (13.9g saturated fat); 3373kJ (807 cal); 32.6g carbohydrate; 60.6g protein; 6.1g fibre

tomato braised lamb shanks

2 tablespoons olive oil
16 french-trimmed lamb shanks (4kg)
1 large red onion (300g), sliced thinly
1 clove garlic, crushed
2 tablespoons tomato paste
1 cup (250ml) dry red wine
2 cups (500ml) chicken stock
1 cup (250ml) water
400g can diced tomatoes
2 tablespoons coarsely chopped fresh rosemary
creamy polenta
3 cups (750ml) water
2 cups (500ml) milk
1 cup (250ml) chicken stock
1½ cups (250g) polenta
½ cup (40g) coarsely grated parmesan cheese
1 cup (250ml) cream

1 Preheat oven to 200°C/180°C fan-forced.

2 Heat half the oil in large baking dish, brown lamb, in batches.

3 Heat remaining oil in same dish; cook onion and garlic, stirring, until onion softens. Add paste; cook, stirring, 2 minutes. Add wine; bring to the boil. Boil, uncovered, until liquid reduces by about half.

4 Return lamb to dish with stock, the water, undrained tomatoes and rosemary; cover, cook in oven, turning lamb occasionally, about 3 hours.

5 Remove lamb from dish; cover to keep warm. Reserve pan juices.

6 Meanwhile, make creamy polenta.

7 Divide polenta among serving plates; top with lamb drizzle with juices.

creamy polenta Bring the water, milk and stock to the boil in medium saucepan; gradually stir in polenta. Cook, stirring, about 5 minutes or until polenta thickens slightly. Stir in cheese and cream.

prep & cook time 4 hours **serves** 8
nutritional count per serving 28g total fat (14.8g saturated fat); 2826kJ (676 cal); 30.3g carbohydrate; 69.1g protein; 2.3g fibre

note Skordalia is a traditional Greek garlic and potato sauce that can also be used on fish, vegetables or as a dip.

greek roast lamb with skordalia and potatoes

2kg leg of lamb
2 cloves garlic, crushed
½ cup (125ml) lemon juice
2 tablespoons olive oil
1 tablespoon fresh oregano leaves
1 teaspoon fresh lemon thyme leaves
5 large potatoes (1.5kg), cut into 3cm cubes
1 tablespoon finely grated lemon rind
2 tablespoons lemon juice, extra
2 tablespoons olive oil, extra
1 teaspoon fresh lemon thyme leaves, extra
skordalia
1 medium potato (200g), quartered
3 cloves garlic, crushed
1 tablespoon lemon juice
1 tablespoon white wine vinegar
2 tablespoons water
⅓ cup (80ml) olive oil

1 Combine lamb with garlic, juice, oil, oregano and thyme in large bowl. Cover; refrigerate 3 hours or overnight.
2 Preheat oven to 160°C/140°C fan-forced.
3 Place lamb in large baking dish; roast, uncovered, 4 hours.
4 Meanwhile, make skordalia.
5 Combine potatoes in large bowl with rind and extra juice, oil and thyme. Place potatoes, in single layer, on oven tray. Roast potatoes for last 30 minutes of lamb cooking time.
6 Remove lamb from oven; cover to keep warm.
7 Increase oven to 220°C/200°C fan-forced; roast potatoes a further 20 minutes or until browned lightly and cooked through. Serve potatoes and lamb with skordalia; sprinkle with extra lemon thyme leaves.
skordalia Boil, steam or microwave potato until tender; drain. Push potato through food mill or fine sieve into medium bowl; cool 10 minutes. Whisk combined garlic, juice, vinegar and the water into potato. Gradually whisk in oil in a thin, steady stream; continue whisking until skordalia thickens. Stir in about a tablespoon of warm water if skordalia is too thick.

prep & cook time 4 hours 50 minutes (+ refrigeration)
serves 4
nutritional count per serving 57g total fat (14g saturated fat); 4556kJ (1090 cal); 51.5g carbohydrate; 91.2g protein; 6.7g fibre

hasselback potatoes

4 medium desiree potatoes (800g),
  halved horizontally
40g butter, melted
2 tablespoons olive oil
¼ cup (25g) packaged breadcrumbs
½ cup (60g) finely grated cheddar cheese

1 Preheat oven to 180°C/160°C fan-forced.
2 Place one potato half, cut-side down, on chopping board; place a chopstick on board along each side of potato. Slice potato thinly, cutting through to chopsticks to prevent cutting all the way through. Repeat with remaining potato halves.
3 Coat potatoes in combined butter and oil in medium baking dish; place, rounded-side up, in single layer. Roast 1 hour, brushing frequently with oil mixture.
4 Sprinkle combined breadcrumbs and cheese over potatoes; roast about 10 minutes or until browned.

prep & cook time 1 hour 30 minutes **serves** 4
nutritional count per serving 22.8g total fat (10g saturated fat); 1463kJ (350 cal); 24.5g carbohydrate; 8.8g protein; 3g fibre

creamed spinach

20g butter
600g spinach, trimmed
½ cup (125ml) cream

1 Melt butter in large frying pan; cook spinach, stirring, until wilted.
2 Add cream to pan; bring to the boil. Reduce heat; simmer, uncovered, until liquid reduces by half.

prep & cook time 15 minutes **serves** 4
nutritional count per serving 38.7g total fat (25.4g saturated fat); 1555kJ (372 cal); 2.8g carbohydrate; 3.5g protein; 2.1g fibre

cauliflower gratin

6 baby cauliflowers (750g), trimmed
50g butter
¼ cup (35g) plain flour
1½ cups (375ml) hot milk
½ cup (60g) coarsely grated cheddar cheese
¼ cup (20g) finely grated parmesan cheese
1 tablespoon packaged breadcrumbs

1 Preheat oven to 220°C/200°C fan-forced.
2 Boil, steam or microwave cauliflowers until tender; drain. Place in medium shallow ovenproof dish.
3 Meanwhile, melt butter in medium saucepan, add flour; cook, stirring, until mixture bubbles and thickens. Gradually stir in milk until smooth; cook, stirring, until mixture boils and thickens. Remove from heat, stir in cheeses.
4 Pour cheese sauce over cauliflower in dish; sprinkle with breadcrumbs. Bake about 15 minutes or until browned lightly.

prep & cook time 30 minutes **serves** 6
nutritional count per serving 14.1g total fat (9g saturated fat); 865kJ (207 cal); 10.2g carbohydrate; 9.1g protein; 2.2g fibre

peas with mint butter

You need approximately 1kg fresh pea pods to get the required amount of shelled peas needed for this recipe.

2¼ cups (350g) fresh shelled peas
40g butter, softened
1 tablespoon finely chopped fresh mint
1 teaspoon finely grated lemon rind

1 Boil, steam or microwave peas until tender; drain.
2 Meanwhile, combine remaining ingredients in small bowl.
3 Serve peas topped with butter mixture.

prep & cook time 10 minutes **serves** 4
nutritional count per serving 8.6g total fat (5.4g saturated fat); 589kJ (141 cal); 8.6g carbohydrate; 5.2g protein; 5g fibre

rhubarb and pear sponge pudding

lemon delicious pudding

rhubarb and pear sponge pudding

825g can pear slices in natural juice
800g rhubarb, trimmed, cut into 4cm pieces
2 tablespoons caster sugar
2 eggs
⅓ cup (75g) caster sugar, extra
2 tablespoons plain flour
2 tablespoons self-raising flour
2 tablespoons cornflour

1 Preheat oven to 180°C/160°C fan-forced.
2 Drain pears; reserve ¾ cup (180ml) of the juice.
3 Place reserved juice, rhubarb and sugar in large saucepan; cook, stirring occasionally, about 5 minutes or until rhubarb is just tender. Stir in pears. Pour mixture into deep 1.75-litre (7-cup) ovenproof dish.
4 Meanwhile, beat eggs in small bowl with electric mixer until thick and creamy. Gradually add extra sugar, 1 tablespoon at a time, beating until sugar dissolves between additions. Gently fold in combined sifted flours.
5 Spread sponge mixture over hot rhubarb mixture. Bake about 45 minutes or until browned lightly and cooked through.

prep & cook time 1 hour 10 minutes **serves** 6
nutritional count per serving 2.1g total fat (0.6g saturated fat); 823kJ (197 cal); 35.7g carbohydrate; 5.4g protein; 5.9g fibre

lemon delicious pudding

125g butter, melted
2 teaspoons finely grated lemon rind
1½ cups (330g) caster sugar
3 eggs, separated
½ cup (75g) self-raising flour
⅓ cup (80ml) lemon juice
1⅓ cups (330ml) milk

1 Preheat oven to 180°C/160°C fan-forced. Grease six 1-cup (250ml) ovenproof dishes; place in large baking dish.
2 Combine butter, rind, sugar and yolks in large bowl. Whisk in sifted flour then juice. Gradually whisk in milk; mixture should be smooth and runny.
3 Beat egg whites in small bowl with electric mixer until soft peaks form; fold into lemon mixture in two batches.
4 Divide lemon mixture among dishes. Add enough boiling water to baking dish to come halfway up side of ovenproof dishes. Bake about 30 minutes or until puddings have risen and are a light golden colour.

prep & cook time 1 hour **serves** 6
nutritional count per serving 22g total fat (13.5g saturated fat); 2069kJ (495 cal); 67.1g carbohydrate; 6.7g protein; 0.5g fibre

apple, date and orange pie

8 medium Granny Smith apples (1.2kg),
    peeled, cored, sliced thickly
½ cup (125ml) water
1½ cups (210g) coarsely chopped dried dates
¼ cup (55g) caster sugar
2 teaspoons finely grated orange rind
1 tablespoon demerara sugar
pastry
1 cup (150g) plain flour
½ cup (75g) self-raising flour
¼ cup (35g) cornflour
¼ cup (30g) custard powder
1 tablespoon caster sugar
100g cold butter, chopped
1 egg, separated
¼ cup (60ml) cold water

1 Make pastry.
2 Place apples with the water in large saucepan; bring to the boil. Reduce heat; simmer, covered, 5 minutes. Add dates; simmer a further 5 minutes. Drain; stir in caster sugar and rind. Cool.
3 Preheat oven to 220°C/200°C fan-forced. Grease deep 25cm pie dish.
4 Divide pastry in half. Roll one half between sheets of baking paper until large enough to line dish. Spoon apple mixture into dish; brush pastry edges with egg white.
5 Roll remaining pastry large enough to cover filling. Press edges together. Brush pastry with egg white; sprinkle with demerara sugar. Bake 20 minutes. Reduce oven to 180°C/160°C fan-forced; bake a further 25 minutes.

pastry Process dry ingredients and butter until crumbly. Add egg yolk and the water; process until combined. Knead on floured surface until smooth. Cover; refrigerate 30 minutes.

prep & cook time 1 hour 50 minutes (+ refrigeration)
serves 8
nutritional count per serving 11.5g total fat (7g saturated fat); 1680kJ (402 cal); 68.5g carbohydrate; 4.9g protein; 5.7g fibre

The addition of dates and orange rind gives this otherwise traditional apple pie a wonderful distinct flavour.

friday night

Unwind with friends and effortless food at the end of the week.

turkish chicken club

⅓ cup (80ml) lime juice
2 tablespoons olive oil
2 teaspoons sumac
2 chicken thigh fillets (400g)
1 large turkish bread (430g)
1 lebanese cucumber (130g), sliced thinly
1 medium tomato (150g), sliced thinly
24 small butter lettuce leaves
coriander aïoli
½ cup (150g) mayonnaise
1 tablespoon lime juice
1 clove garlic, crushed
2 tablespoons finely chopped fresh coriander

1 Combine juice, oil, sumac and chicken in medium bowl; cover, refrigerate 30 minutes.
2 Meanwhile, make coriander aïoli.
3 Drain chicken; reserve marinade. Cook chicken on heated oiled grill plate (or grill or barbecue) until cooked through, brushing with reserved marinade after turning. Cover; stand 5 minutes then slice thinly.
4 Halve bread horizontally; cut each piece into 6 slices. Toast slices lightly.
5 Spread each toast slice with aïoli. Layer 4 toast slices with half the chicken, cucumber, tomato and lettuce, then top with toasts; layer with remaining chicken, cucumber, tomato and lettuce then top with remaining toast. Cut in half to serve.
coriander aïoli Combine ingredients in small bowl.

prep & cook time 30 minutes (+ refrigeration)
serves 4
nutritional count per sandwich 32.1g total fat (5.4g saturated fat); 2700kJ (646 cal); 57.5g carbohydrate; 29.6g protein; 4.6g fibre

This double-decker feast is the king of sandwiches — filling, delicious and satisfying.

croque-monsieur

8 slices wholemeal bread (360g)
8 slices leg ham (180g)
40g butter
cheese sauce
20g butter
1 tablespoon plain flour
¾ cup (180ml) milk
¾ cup (90g) coarsely grated cheddar cheese
1 tablespoon finely chopped fresh flat-leaf parsley

1 Make cheese sauce.
2 Spread sauce over bread slices; top four slices with ham then top with remaining bread.
3 Melt butter in large frying pan. Add sandwiches; cook, in batches, until browned both sides. Cut into triangles to serve.
cheese sauce Melt butter in small saucepan, add flour; cook, stirring, until mixture bubbles and thickens. Gradually add milk; cook, stirring, until sauce boils and thickens. Remove from heat; stir in cheese and parsley.

prep & cook time 30 minutes **serves** 4
nutritional count per serving 25.9g total fat (15g saturated fat); 2077kJ (497 cal); 38.4g carbohydrate; 24.8g protein; 5.8g fibre

pepperoni pizzetta

1 small (112g) pizza base
2 tablespoons tomato paste
40g pepperoni, sliced thinly
1 fresh small red thai chilli, sliced thinly
¼ cup (20g) flaked parmesan cheese
15g wild rocket leaves
2 teaspoons lemon juice

1 Preheat oven to 220°C/200°C fan-forced. Place pizza base on oven tray.
2 Spread pizza base with paste; top with pepperoni then sprinkle with chilli.
3 Bake pizzetta about 8 minutes.
4 Combine cheese, rocket and juice in small bowl. Serve pizzetta topped with rocket salad.

prep & cook time 15 minutes **serves** 1
nutritional count per serving 25.4g total fat (9.9g saturated fat); 2592kJ (620 cal); 65.5g carbohydrate; 29g protein; 6.2g fibre

steak sandwich

blt

steak sandwich

2 cloves garlic, crushed
2 tablespoons olive oil
4 thin beef scotch fillet steaks (500g)
2 medium brown onions (200g), sliced thinly
1 tablespoon brown sugar
1 tablespoon balsamic vinegar
8 thick slices white bread (560g)
1 baby cos lettuce (180g), leaves separated
2 dill pickles (40g) sliced thinly
¼ cup (80g) tomato chutney

1 Combine garlic and half the oil in medium bowl; add steaks, rub both sides with mixture.
2 Heat remaining oil in medium frying pan; cook onion over low heat, stirring occasionally, about 10 minutes or until soft. Add sugar and vinegar; cook, stirring, about 5 minutes or until caramelised. Remove from pan.
3 Meanwhile, cook steaks in heated oiled large frying pan.
4 Toast bread both sides. Sandwich lettuce, steaks, onion, pickle and chutney between toast slices.

prep & cook time 30 minutes **serves** 4
nutritional count per serving 20.5g total fat (5g saturated fat); 2809kJ (672 cal); 78.1g carbohydrate; 39.7g protein; 6.4g fibre

blt

8 rindless bacon rashers (520g)
⅓ cup (100g) mayonnaise
8 thick slices white bread (560g)
8 large butter lettuce leaves
2 small tomatoes (180g), sliced thinly

1 Cook bacon in heated oiled large frying pan until crisp.
2 Spread mayonnaise over half the bread slices; top with lettuce, tomato and bacon. Top with remaining bread.

prep & cook time 15 minutes **serves** 4
nutritional count per serving 29.1g total fat (7.8g saturated fat); 2934kJ (702 cal); 69.2g carbohydrate; 37.8g protein; 5.2g fibre

It's Friday night. Put a DVD on, sink into the couch and put your feet up.

classic fish and chips

lamb and tomato pide

classic fish and chips

1 cup (150g) self-raising flour
1 cup (250ml) dry ale
1 tablespoon sea salt
1kg potatoes, peeled
peanut oil, for deep-frying
4 x 150g blue-eye fillets, halved lengthways
tartare sauce
⅔ cup (200g) whole-egg mayonnaise
½ small brown onion (40g), chopped finely
2 tablespoons finely chopped cornichons
1 tablespoon drained, rinsed capers,
   chopped finely
1 tablespoon finely chopped fresh flat-leaf parsley
1 tablespoon lemon juice

1 Make tartare sauce.
2 Sift flour into medium bowl; whisk in beer and salt until smooth.
3 Cut potatoes lengthways into 1cm slices; cut each slice lengthways into 1cm-chips; dry with absorbent paper.
4 Heat oil in large saucepan. Cook chips, in three batches, about 2 minutes or until tender but not brown. Drain on absorbent paper.
5 Dip fish in batter; drain away excess. Deep-fry fish, in batches, until cooked. Drain on absorbent paper.
6 Deep-fry chips, in three batches, until crisp and golden brown; drain on absorbent paper.
7 Serve fish and chips with sauce and lemon wedges.
tartare sauce Combine ingredients in medium bowl.

prep & cook time 30 minutes **serves** 4
nutritional count per serving 38.3g total fat (6.2g saturated fat); 3340kJ (799 cal); 66.1g carbohydrate; 40.3g protein; 5.4g fibre

lamb and tomato pide

1 tablespoon olive oil
1 medium brown onion (150g), chopped finely
1 clove garlic, crushed
300g lamb mince
1 teaspoon ground cinnamon
1 teaspoon cumin
1 teaspoon smoked paprika
½ teaspoon cayenne pepper
1 tablespoon chopped fresh coriander
1 large tomato (220g), chopped coarsely
pizza dough
7g yeast
1 teaspoon sugar
⅔ cup (160ml) warm water
2 tablespoons warm milk
2 cups (300g) plain flour
1 teaspoon salt
1 tablespoon olive oil

1 Make pizza dough.
2 Preheat oven to 240°C/220°C fan-forced.
3 Heat oil in pan; cook onion and garlic until soft. Add lamb mince and spices; cook until lamb is browned. Stir in coriander; cool.
4 Divide dough into three; roll each piece to 12cm x 30cm. Spread filling across centre of each piece, leaving 2cm border. Brush edges with water; fold and press around dough. Fold corners to make oval shape.
5 Heat oven trays 3 minutes, place pide on trays; bake 10 minutes. Sprinkle with tomato; bake 5 minutes.
pizza dough Combine yeast, sugar, warm water and warm milk in jug. Stand in warm place until frothy. Place ½ cup of the flour in bowl; whisk in yeast mixture. Cover; stand in warm place 1 hour. Stir remaining flour, salt and oil into yeast mixture. Knead dough on floured surface until smooth. Place in oiled bowl, cover; stand in warm place 1 hour.

prep & cook time 1 hour (+ standing) **serves** 8
nutritional count per serving 10.5g total fat (2.4g saturated fat); 1087kJ (260 cal); 27.5g carbohydrate; 12.6g protein; 2.2g fibre

tip You could easily turn these patties into burgers if you wanted to. When you shape them into patties just make them a little wider and flatter than if you were serving them on their own.

These chicken patties are packed full of flavour and effortless to make.

chicken, tomato and fetta patties with spinach salad

750g chicken mince
⅓ cup (50g) drained semi-dried tomatoes, chopped coarsely
1 egg
½ cup (35g) stale breadcrumbs
200g fetta cheese, crumbled
1 small white onion (80g), sliced thinly
100g baby spinach leaves
1 tablespoon olive oil
1 tablespoon balsamic vinegar

1 Combine chicken, tomato, egg, breadcrumbs and half the cheese in large bowl; shape mixture into 12 patties.
2 Cook patties in heated oiled large frying pan, in batches, until cooked through. Drain on absorbent paper.
3 Meanwhile, combine onion, spinach, oil, vinegar and remaining cheese in medium bowl.
4 Serve patties with spinach salad.

prep & cook time 30 minutes **serves** 4
nutritional count per serving 33.7g total fat (13.3g saturated fat); 2320kJ (555 cal); 11.8g carbohydrate; 50.1g protein; 3.2g fibre

lamb skewers with chilli jam

tandoori chicken wings

lamb skewers with chilli jam

800g lamb backstrap, cut into 3cm pieces
24 fresh bay leaves
chilli jam
⅓ cup (80ml) sweet chilli sauce
1 tablespoon brown sugar
1 tablespoon lemon juice
1 clove garlic, crushed

1 Thread lamb and bay leaves equally onto eight bamboo skewers. Cook skewers on heated oiled grill plate (or grill or barbecue) until cooked through.
2 Meanwhile, make chilli jam.
3 Serve skewers with jam and mixed salad leaves.
chilli jam Stir ingredients in small saucepan over low heat until sugar dissolves. Bring to the boil. Reduce heat; simmer, uncovered, 5 minutes or until thickened slightly.

prep & cook time 30 minutes **serves** 4
nutritional count per serving 7.8g total fat (3.3g saturated fat); 1116kJ (267 cal); 7.3g carbohydrate; 41.3g protein; 1g fibre

tandoori chicken wings

16 small chicken wings (1.3kg)
½ cup (150g) tandoori paste
½ cup (140g) yogurt
1 medium brown onion (150g), grated

1 Preheat oven to 220°C/200°C fan-forced.
2 Cut wings into three pieces at joints; discard tips.
3 Combine remaining ingredients in large bowl, add chicken; toss chicken to coat in mixture. Cover; refrigerate 3 hours or overnight.
4 Place chicken, in single layer, on oiled wire rack set inside large shallow baking dish. Roast, uncovered, about 30 minutes or until chicken is well browned and cooked through. Serve with lime wedges.

prep & cook time 40 minutes (+ refrigeration)
makes 32
nutritional count per wing 3g total fat (0.7g saturated fat); 234kJ (56 cal); 0.8g carbohydrate; 6.4g protein; 0.5g fibre

nacho stacks

1 tablespoon olive oil
1 small brown onion (80g), chopped finely
1 clove garlic, crushed
400g beef mince
1 fresh long red chilli, chopped finely
35g packet taco seasoning mix
400g can diced tomatoes
1 tablespoon tomato paste
⅓ cup (80ml) beef stock
420g can mexican chilli beans, rinsed, drained
¼ cup coarsely chopped fresh coriander
230g corn chips, chopped coarsely
1½ cups (180g) coarsely grated cheddar cheese
guacamole
1 large avocado (320g), chopped coarsely
1 medium tomato (150g), chopped finely
½ small red onion (50g), chopped finely
1 tablespoon lime juice
1 tablespoon finely chopped fresh coriander

1 Heat oil in large frying pan; cook onion and garlic, stirring, until onion softens. Add beef; cook, stirring, until beef changes colour. Add chilli and seasoning mix; cook, stirring, until fragrant.
2 Add undrained tomatoes, paste and stock; bring to the boil. Reduce heat; simmer, uncovered, 15 minutes. Add beans; cook, stirring, about 5 minutes or until thickened. Stir in coriander. Cool.
3 Preheat oven to 200°C/180°C fan-forced. Oil eight holes of two 6-hole (¾-cup/180ml) texas muffin pans; line greased pan holes with two criss-crossed 5cm x 20cm strips of baking paper.
4 Combine corn chips and 1 cup of the cheese in small bowl; divide half the corn chip mixture between pan holes, pressing down firmly. Divide beef mixture between pan holes; top with remaining corn chip mixture, pressing down firmly. Sprinkle with remaining cheese. Bake 15 minutes or until browned lightly.
5 Meanwhile, make guacamole by mashing avocado in medium bowl; stir in remaining ingredients.
6 Stand nachos in pan 5 minutes. Using baking paper strips as lifters, carefully remove nacho stacks from pan holes. Serve topped with guacamole; sprinkle with fresh coriander leaves.

prep & cook time 1 hour **makes** 8
nutritional count per stack 27.7g total fat (11g saturated fat); 1839kJ (440 cal); 23.1g carbohydrate; 21.9g protein; 6.9g fibre

Nachos are a popular Mexican snack food. For an extra tangy kick, add a squeeze of lime and some sour cream.

fajitas with guacamole

3 cloves garlic, crushed
¼ cup (60ml) lemon juice
2 teaspoons ground cumin
1 tablespoon olive oil
600g piece beef eye fillet, sliced thinly
1 large red capsicum (350g), sliced thinly
1 large green capsicum (350g), sliced thinly
1 medium yellow capsicum (200g), sliced thinly
1 large red onion (300g), sliced thinly
8 large flour tortillas
guacamole
1 large avocado (320g), mashed roughly
¼ cup finely chopped fresh coriander
1 tablespoon lime juice
1 small white onion (80g), chopped finely
salsa cruda
2 medium tomatoes (300g), seeded, chopped finely
1 fresh long red chilli, chopped finely
½ cup coarsely chopped fresh coriander
1 small white onion (80g), chopped finely
1 tablespoon lime juice

1 Combine garlic, juice, cumin, oil and beef in large bowl, cover; refrigerate.
2 Make guacamole. Make salsa cruda.
3 Cook beef, in batches, in heated oiled large frying pan until cooked as desired. Remove from pan; cover to keep warm.
4 Cook capsicums and onion in same pan until softened. Return beef to pan; stir until heated through.
5 Meanwhile, warm tortillas according to manufacturer's instructions.
6 Divide beef mixture among serving plates; serve with tortillas, guacamole and salsa.
guacamole Combine ingredients in small bowl.
salsa cruda Combine ingredients in small bowl.

prep & cook time 40 minutes **serves** 4
nutritional count per serving 31.5g total fat (7.6g saturated fat); 3089kJ (739 cal); 62.7g carbohydrate; 46.2g protein; 8.9g fibre

chinese barbecued spare ribs

¾ cup (180ml) barbecue sauce
2 tablespoons dark soy sauce
1 tablespoon honey
¼ cup (60ml) orange juice
2 tablespoons brown sugar
1 clove garlic, crushed
2cm piece fresh ginger (10g), grated
2kg slabs american-style pork spare ribs

1 Combine sauces, honey, juice, sugar, garlic and ginger in large shallow dish; add ribs, turn to coat in marinade. Cover; refrigerate 3 hours or overnight.
2 Preheat oven to 180°C/160°C fan-forced.
3 Brush ribs both sides with marinade; place, in single layer, in large shallow baking dish. Roast, covered, 45 minutes. Uncover; roast a further 15 minutes or until ribs are browned. Serve with fried rice.

prep & cook time 1 hour 15 minutes (+ refrigeration)
serves 4
nutritional count per serving 26.4g total fat (10.2g saturated fat); 2675kJ (640 cal); 35.2g carbohydrate; 64.7g protein; 0.8g fibre

tajitas with guacamole

chinese barbecued spare ribs

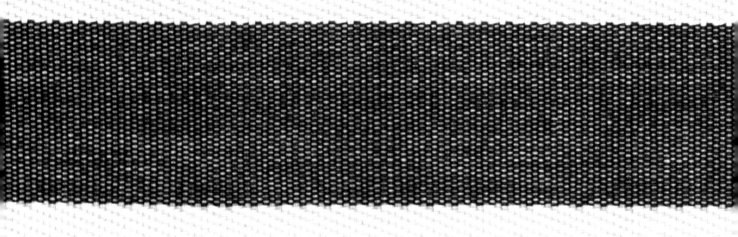

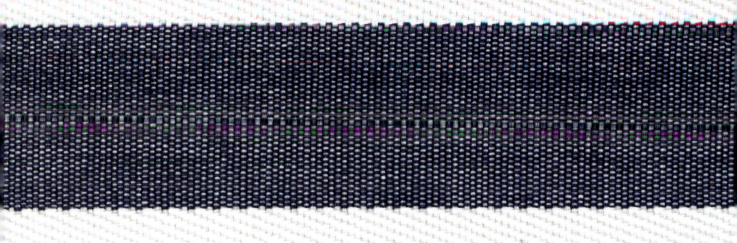

barbecues

Marinate the meat, toss the salad and turn up the heat.

You can't get much more traditionally Turkish than this combination of lamb, spinach and fetta, but for a diversion from tradition try cooking these in a sandwich press — it works beautifully.

gözleme

4 cups (600g) plain flour

1 teaspoon coarse cooking salt

1⅔ cups (410ml) warm water

2 tablespoons vegetable oil

lamb filling

1 tablespoon vegetable oil

2 teaspoons ground cumin

½ teaspoon hot paprika

3 cloves garlic, crushed

500g lamb mince

400g can diced tomatoes

½ cup coarsely chopped fresh flat-leaf parsley

spinach and cheese filling

300g spinach, trimmed, shredded finely

½ cup coarsely chopped fresh mint

1 small brown onion (80g), chopped finely

½ teaspoon ground allspice

250g fetta cheese, crumbled

1 cup (100g) coarsely grated mozzarella cheese

1 Combine flour and salt in large bowl. Gradually stir in the water; mix to a soft dough. Knead dough on floured surface about 5 minutes or until smooth and elastic. Return to bowl; cover.

2 Make lamb filling.

3 Make spinach and cheese filling.

4 Divide dough into six pieces; roll each piece into 30cm square. Divide spinach and cheese filling among dough squares, spreading filling across centre of squares; top each with equal amounts of lamb filling. Fold top and bottom edges of dough over filling; tuck in ends to enclose.

5 Cook gözleme, both sides, over low heat on oiled grill plate, brushing with oil, until browned lightly and heated through.

lamb filling Heat oil in large frying pan; cook spices and garlic until fragrant. Add lamb; cook, stirring, until browned. Add undrained tomatoes; simmer about 15 minutes or until liquid is almost evaporated. Stir in parsley.

spinach and cheese filling Combine ingredients in medium bowl.

prep & cook time 1 hour **serves** 6
nutritional count per serving 29.9g total fat (12.7g saturated fat); 3168kJ (758 cal); 75.8g carbohydrate; 41.8g protein; 7.1g fibre

barbecued lamb, shallot and mesclun salad

150g sugar snap peas, trimmed
600g lamb backstrap
8 large shallots (200g), peeled, quartered
60g mesclun
mint dressing
1 cup firmly packed fresh mint leaves
2 cloves garlic, quartered
¼ cup (60ml) olive oil
2 tablespoons white wine vinegar
2 teaspoons caster sugar

1 Boil, steam or microwave peas until tender; drain.
2 Meanwhile, cook lamb and shallots on heated oiled grill plate (or grill or barbecue) until lamb is cooked as desired and shallots are tender. Cover lamb; stand 5 minutes then slice thinly.
3 Make mint dressing.
4 Combine peas, lamb, shallot, dressing and mesclun in large bowl.
mint dressing Blend or process mint and garlic until smooth. With motor operating, gradually add oil in a thin, steady stream; blend until smooth. Stir in vinegar and sugar.

prep & cook time 25 minutes **serves** 4
nutritional count per serving 19.4g total fat (4.4g saturated fat); 1404kJ (336 cal); 6.2g carbohydrate; 33.2g protein; 2.7g fibre

lamb kebabs

Soak 12 bamboo skewers in water for at least an hour before using to prevent them from scorching during cooking.

500g lamb mince
1 egg
1 small brown onion (80g), chopped finely
2 tablespoons finely chopped fresh flat-leaf parsley
1 clove garlic, crushed
2 teaspoons ground cinnamon
2 teaspoons sweet paprika
½ teaspoon cayenne pepper
½ cup (120g) greek-style yogurt

1 Combine ingredients in large bowl.
2 Form lamb mixture into 16 sausage shapes, thread onto 16 small bamboo skewers or strong toothpicks; flatten slightly.
3 Cook skewers on heated oiled grill plate (or grill or barbecue) until browned and cooked as desired. Serve with yogurt, lemon wedges and pitta bread.

prep & cook time 30 minutes **serves** 4
nutritional count per serving 10.8g total fat (4.8g saturated fat); 1004kJ (240 cal); 5.6g carbohydrate; 29.2g protein; 0.4g fibre

barbecued lamb, shallot and mesclun salad

lamb kebabs

The barbecue is the perfect way to cook a butterflied leg of lamb. Have your butcher trim, split, and debone a whole leg for you.

barbecued soy and ginger lamb with coriander potatoes

1.5kg butterflied leg of lamb, trimmed
¾ cup (180ml) japanese soy sauce
½ cup (110g) firmly packed brown sugar
2 tablespoons olive oil
9cm piece fresh ginger (45g), grated
6 cloves garlic, crushed
⅓ cup (80ml) water
coriander potatoes
750g baby new potatoes, quartered
1 tablespoon olive oil
2 tablespoons finely chopped fresh coriander

1 Cut lamb into two even-sized pieces; combine in large shallow dish with sauce, sugar, oil, ginger and garlic. Cover; refrigerate 3 hours or overnight.
2 Drain lamb over small bowl; reserve marinade. Cook lamb on heated oiled barbecue over low heat, covered, about 30 minutes or until cooked as desired, turning halfway through cooking time. Cover, stand 10 minutes.
3 Meanwhile, make coriander potatoes.
4 Bring reserved marinade and the water to the boil in small saucepan. Reduce heat; simmer, uncovered, 5 minutes. Strain into small jug. Serve sliced lamb with potato; drizzle with sauce.
coriander potatoes Boil, steam or microwave potatoes until tender; drain. Drizzle with oil; sprinkle with coriander.

prep & cook time 40 minutes (+ refrigeration)
serves 6
nutritional count per serving 19.5g total fat (5.8g saturated fat); 2140kJ (512 cal); 35.7g carbohydrate; 46.5g protein; 3.3g fibre

barbecued lamb chops with mustard and thyme

grilled chicken with coriander and chilli

barbecued lamb chops
with mustard and thyme

2 tablespoons olive oil
2 cloves garlic, crushed
2 tablespoons wholegrain mustard
2 tablespoons lemon juice
2 teaspoons finely chopped fresh thyme
4 forequarter lamb chops (760g)

1 Combine oil, garlic, mustard, juice and thyme in large bowl; add chops, turn to coat in marinade. Cover; refrigerate 3 hours or overnight.
2 Cook drained chops on heated oiled grill plate (or grill or barbecue) until browned both sides and cooked as desired.
3 Serve chops with vegetables and extra mustard.

prep & cook time 30 minutes (+ refrigeration)
serves 4
nutritional count per serving 17.5g total fat (5.1g saturated fat); 1158kJ (277 cal); 0.8g carbohydrate; 29g protein; 0.5g fibre

grilled chicken with
coriander and chilli

8 chicken thigh cutlets (1.6kg)
coriander and chilli paste
2 teaspoons coriander seeds
4 fresh small red thai chillies, chopped coarsely
1 teaspoon ground cumin
2 whole cloves
2 cardamom pods, bruised
¼ teaspoon ground turmeric
10cm stick fresh lemon grass (20g),
    chopped coarsely
2 medium brown onions (300g), chopped coarsely
4 cloves garlic
⅓ cup (80ml) lime juice
2 teaspoons coarse cooking salt
2 tablespoons peanut oil

1 Make coriander and chilli paste.
2 Pierce chicken all over with sharp knife. Combine paste and chicken in large bowl, rubbing paste into cuts. Cover; refrigerate overnight.
3 Cook chicken, covered, on heated oiled grill plate (or grill or barbecue), 5 minutes. Uncover; cook, turning occasionally, about 20 minutes or until cooked. Serve with lime wedges.
coriander and chilli paste Blend or process ingredients until mixture forms a smooth paste.

prep & cook time 35 minutes (+ refrigeration)
serves 4
nutritional count per serving 29.5g total fat (7.8g saturated fat); 2094kJ (501 cal); 5.2g carbohydrate; 53.5g protein; 1.7g fibre

lemon and chilli chicken skewers

Soak 12 bamboo skewers in water for at least an hour before using to prevent them from scorching during cooking.

400g chicken breast fillets, cut into 2cm pieces
2 chorizo (340g), cut into 2cm pieces
1 medium yellow capsicum (200g),
  cut into 2cm pieces
12 bay leaves
1 tablespoon finely grated lemon rind
1 tablespoon lemon juice
¼ cup (60ml) olive oil
2 cloves garlic, crushed
1 teaspoon dried chilli flakes
¼ cup finely chopped fresh flat-leaf parsley

1 Combine ingredients in large bowl; cover, refrigerate 30 minutes.
2 Thread chicken, chorizo, capsicum and bay leaves, alternately, onto skewers.
3 Cook skewers on heated oiled grill plate (or grill or barbecue) until chicken is cooked through and chorizo is browned lightly.

prep & cook time 30 minutes (+ refrigeration)
makes 12
nutritional count per skewer 15.3g total fat (4.4g saturated fat); 832kJ (199 cal); 1.3g carbohydrate; 14.3g protein; 0.4g fibre

barbecued chicken with minted tomato salad

2 tablespoons lemon juice

1 tablespoon sumac

2 teaspoons finely chopped fresh oregano

2 tablespoons olive oil

6 x 200g chicken breast fillets

3 lemons, halved

3 large pitta bread (240g)

minted tomato salad

2 tablespoons lemon juice

2 tablespoons olive oil

500g grape tomatoes, halved

2 lebanese cucumbers (260g), cut into ribbons

1 cup firmly packed fresh flat-leaf parsley leaves

1 cup firmly packed fresh mint leaves

2 teaspoons finely chopped fresh oregano

8 green onions, sliced thinly

1 Combine juice, sumac, oregano and half the oil in large bowl with chicken. Cover; refrigerate 3 hours or overnight.

2 Make minted tomato salad.

3 Cook chicken on barbecue (or grill or grill plate) until browned both sides and cooked through. Stand 5 minutes then slice thickly.

4 Cook lemon, cut-side down, about 3 minutes or until browned lightly. Brush bread, both sides, with remaining oil; brown lightly on barbecue, break into coarse pieces.

5 Combine salad and bread; serve with chicken and lemon.

minted tomato salad Whisk juice and oil in large serving bowl, add remaining ingredients; toss gently to combine.

prep & cook time 35 minutes (+ refrigeration)
serves 6
nutritional count per serving 24.4g total fat (5.2g saturated fat); 2199kJ (526 cal); 25.6g carbohydrate; 48.2g protein; 5.4g fibre

A barbecue is the perfect solution for a summer get-together with friends.

grilled salmon with nam jim and herb salad

barbecued baby octopus

grilled salmon with nam jim and herb salad

4 x 220g salmon fillets, skin-on
nam jim
3 long green chillies, chopped coarsely
2 fresh small red thai chillies, chopped coarsely
2 cloves garlic, quartered
1 shallot (25g), quartered
2cm piece fresh ginger (10g), quartered
⅓ cup (80ml) lime juice
2 tablespoons fish sauce
1 tablespoon grated palm sugar
1 tablespoon peanut oil
¼ cup (35g) roasted unsalted cashews,
   chopped finely
herb salad
1½ cups loosely packed fresh mint leaves
1 cup loosely packed fresh coriander leaves
1 cup loosely packed fresh basil leaves, torn
1 medium red onion (170g), sliced thinly
2 lebanese cucumbers (260g), seeded, sliced thinly

1 Make nam jim.
2 Cook salmon, both sides, on heated oiled grill plate
(or grill or barbecue) until cooked as desired.
3 Meanwhile, make herb salad.
4 Serve salmon and herb salad topped with nam jim.
nam jim Blend or process chillies, garlic, shallot,
ginger, juice, sauce, sugar and oil until smooth;
stir in nuts.
herb salad Place ingredients in medium bowl; toss
gently to combine.

prep & cook time 40 minutes **serves** 4
nutritional count per serving 25g total fat (5.1g
saturated fat); 1948kJ (466 cal); 10.8g carbohydrate;
47.6g protein; 4.4g fibre

barbecued baby octopus

1kg baby octopus
⅓ cup (80ml) lemon juice
⅓ cup (80ml) olive oil
2 cloves garlic, crushed
2 teaspoons dried rigani
1 medium lemon, cut into wedges

1 Clean octopus, remove eyes and beaks. Combine
octopus with juice, oil, garlic and rigani in medium
bowl. Cover, refrigerate 3 hours or overnight.
2 Drain octopus; discard marinade. Cook octopus on
heated oiled barbecue (or grill or grill plate) until tender.
Serve with lemon wedges.

prep & cook time 25 minutes (+ refrigeration)
serves 6
nutritional count per serving 13.4g total fat (1.7g
saturated fat); 982kJ (235 cal); 1g carbohydrate;
27.6g protein; 0.2g fibre
tip Rigani is a Greek oregano; it is a stronger, sharper
version of the familiar herb we use in Italian cooking
and is available from good delicatessens and
Mediterranean food stores.

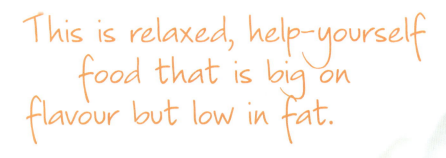

This is relaxed, help-yourself food that is big on flavour but low in fat.

barbecued seafood platter

16 uncooked medium king prawns (720g)
1 teaspoon finely grated lemon rind
½ teaspoon dried chilli flakes
1 clove garlic, crushed
1 tablespoon finely chopped fresh oregano
2 tablespoons olive oil
8 slices prosciutto (120g)
8 butterflied sardines (240g)
300g baby octopus, quartered
200g squid hoods, sliced into rings
2 tablespoons balsamic vinegar
¼ cup coarsely chopped fresh flat-leaf parsley
500g small black mussels
¼ cup (60ml) lemon juice
1 medium tomato (150g), seeded, chopped finely

1 Remove and discard prawn heads. Cut prawns lengthwise, three-quarters of the way through, (and down to 1cm before the tail) leaving shells intact; press down on prawns on board to flatten.
2 Combine prawns, rind, chilli, garlic, oregano and half the oil in medium bowl; cover, refrigerate 1 hour.
3 Wrap a prosciutto slice firmly around each sardine.
4 Cook octopus and squid on heated oiled grill plate (or grill or barbecue). Combine octopus and squid in medium heatproof bowl with remaining oil, vinegar and 2 tablespoons of the parsley. Cover to keep warm.
5 Cook prawns and sardines on heated oiled grill plate (or grill or barbecue).
6 Meanwhile, cook mussels, covered, on heated oiled flat plate about 5 minutes or until mussels open (discard any that do not). Place mussels in medium heatproof bowl; drizzle with juice, sprinkle with tomato and remaining parsley.
7 Serve seafood with lemon wedges.

prep & cook time 1 hour (+ refrigeration) **serves** 8
nutritional count per serving 8.7g total fat (1.7g saturated fat); 836kJ (200 cal); 1.3g carbohydrate; 28.5g protein; 0.4g fibre

grilled balmain bug salad

plum and star anise pork spare ribs

grilled balmain bug salad

2 baby eggplants (120g)

1 medium zucchini (120g)

1 medium red capsicum (200g), chopped finely

3 flat mushrooms (240g), quartered

2 tablespoons olive oil

6 uncooked balmain bug tails (1.5kg),
  halved lengthways

250g rocket, trimmed

chilli lime butter

60g butter, softened

2 teaspoons finely grated lime rind

2 tablespoons lime juice

1 fresh long red chilli, chopped finely

2 cloves garlic, crushed

1 Using vegetable peeler, cut eggplant and zucchini into long, thin strips. Combine eggplant, zucchini, capsicum, mushrooms and oil in large bowl.

2 Cook vegetables, in batches, on heated oiled grill plate (or grill or barbecue) until tender. Cover to keep warm.

3 Cook balmain bug on heated oiled grill plate until cooked.

4 Meanwhile, make chilli lime butter.

5 Combine vegetables, balmain bug and chilli lime butter in large bowl.

6 Divide rocket among serving plates; top with vegetable and balmain bug mixture.

chilli lime butter Combine ingredients in small bowl.

prep & cook time 40 minutes **serves** 4
nutritional count per serving 25.1g total fat (10g saturated fat); 2282kJ (456 cal); 5.4g carbohydrate; 72.4g protein; 4.6g fibre

plum and star anise pork spare ribs

2kg slabs american-style pork spare ribs

plum and star anise marinade

1 cup (250ml) plum sauce

5cm piece fresh ginger (25g), grated

⅓ cup (80ml) oyster sauce

2 star anise

1 teaspoon dried chilli flakes

pear, ginger and chilli salad

2 medium pears (460g), sliced thinly

2 fresh long red chillies, sliced thinly

2 green onions, sliced thinly

2 cups coarsely chopped fresh mint

2cm piece fresh ginger (10g), grated

2 tablespoons lime juice

1 Make plum and star anise marinade.

2 Place pork in large shallow baking dish; brush marinade all over pork. Pour remaining marinade over pork; cover, refrigerate 3 hours or overnight, turning pork occasionally.

3 Drain pork; reserve marinade. Cook pork on heated oiled grill plate (or grill or barbecue) about 30 minutes or until cooked through, turning and brushing frequently with some of the reserved marinade.

4 Meanwhile, make pear, ginger and chilli salad.

5 Boil remaining marinade, uncovered, in small saucepan about 5 minutes or until thickened slightly.

6 Slice slabs into portions; serve with hot marinade and salad.

plum and star anise marinade Bring ingredients to the boil in medium saucepan. Remove from heat; cool 10 minutes.

pear, ginger and chilli salad Combine ingredients in medium bowl.

prep & cook time 55 minutes (+ refrigeration) **serves** 4
nutritional count per serving 18.1g total fat (6.6g saturated fat); 2847kJ (681 cal); 56.3g carbohydrate; 69.6g protein; 5.2g fibre

grilled pork sausages with fruit relish

1 tablespoon olive oil
1 small red onion (100g), chopped finely
1 clove garlic, crushed
2 medium pears (460g), chopped finely
¼ cup (55g) finely chopped dried apricots
¼ cup (40g) sultanas, chopped finely
2 tablespoons cider vinegar
2 tablespoons brown sugar
½ teaspoon ground allspice
12 thick pork sausages (1.5kg)

1 Heat oil in medium saucepan; cook onion and garlic, stirring, until onions soften. Add fruit, vinegar, sugar and spice; cook, uncovered, stirring occasionally, about 10 minutes or until mixture is thick and pulpy.
2 Meanwhile, cook sausages on heated oiled grill plate (or grill or barbecue) until cooked through.
3 Serve sausages with fruit relish.

prep & cook time 30 minutes **serves** 6
nutritional count per serving 58.7g total fat (22.9g saturated fat); 3252kJ (778 cal); 29.9g carbohydrate; 31g protein; 6.2g fibre

spiced sliced rump with chilli peanut sauce

1 fresh small red thai chilli, chopped finely
1 shallot (25g), chopped finely
1 tablespoon peanut oil
800g beef rump steak
¼ cup (60ml) water
⅓ cup (75g) caster sugar
¼ cup (60ml) fish sauce
½ cup (125ml) lime juice
1 medium carrot (120g), chopped finely
1 medium red capsicum (200g), chopped finely
1 cup (140g) crushed roasted unsalted peanuts
20 peking duck pancakes (200g)

1 Combine chilli and shallot in medium bowl. Combine half the chilli mixture with oil in large bowl; add beef, turn to coat in mixture.
2 Cook beef on heated oiled flat plate (or grill or barbecue), turning once, until cooked. Cover; stand 5 minutes, slice thinly.
3 Meanwhile, stir the water, sugar, sauce, juice, carrot, capsicum and nuts into remaining chilli mixture.
4 Heat pancakes by folding each into quarters; place in steamer over large saucepan of simmering water until just pliable. Serve beef with chilli peanut sauce and pancakes.

prep & cook time 45 minutes **serves** 4
nutritional count per serving 35.6g total fat (9.4g saturated fat); 3047kJ (729 cal); 41.1g carbohydrate; 58.6g protein; 5.4g fibre

grilled pork sausages with fruit relish

spiced sliced rump with chilli peanut sauce

char-grilled t-bones with potato pancakes

3 fresh long red chillies, chopped finely
2cm piece fresh ginger (10g), grated
2 cloves garlic, crushed
2 tablespoons olive oil
4 x 300g beef t-bone steaks
4 trimmed corn cobs (1kg)
4 medium potatoes (800g), grated coarsely
50g butter

1 Combine chilli, ginger, garlic and oil in large bowl; add steaks, turn to coat in mixture.
2 Cook steaks on heated oiled grill plate (or grill or barbecue). Cover; stand 5 minutes.
3 Meanwhile, cook corn, turning occasionally, on heated flat plate until tender.
4 To make potato pancakes, squeeze excess moisture from potato; divide into four portions. Heat half the butter on flat plate; cook potato portions, flattening with spatula, until browned both sides.
5 Spread corn with remaining butter; serve with steaks and potato pancakes.

prep & cook time 50 minutes **serves** 4
nutritional count per serving 33.1g total fat (13g saturated fat); 3118kJ (746 cal); 53.4g carbohydrate; 52.8g protein; 11.4g fibre

"Let the crisp potato pancakes soak up some of the zesty chilli and ginger liquid from the steaks."

mixed grill

700g kipfler potatoes, halved lengthways
1 tablespoon olive oil
2 cloves garlic, crushed
2 teaspoons caraway seeds
½ small cabbage (600g), shredded coarsely
4 pork butterflied steaks (400g)
4 thick pork sausages (480g)
4 thin bacon rashers (120g), rind removed
⅓ cup (80ml) olive oil, extra
¼ cup (60ml) white wine vinegar
2 teaspoons dijon mustard

1 Preheat oven to 220°C/200°C fan-forced.
2 Combine potato, oil, garlic and seeds in large shallow baking dish. Roast about 30 minutes or until potato is browned lightly.

3 Remove potato mixture from oven; stir in cabbage. Return to oven; cook, uncovered, a further 15 minutes or until cabbage wilts.
4 Meanwhile, cook steaks, sausages and bacon, in batches, on heated oiled grill plate. Remove from heat; cover to keep warm.
5 Combine extra oil, vinegar and mustard in large bowl with potato mixture. Serve mixed grill with warm salad.

prep & cook time 55 minutes **serves** 4
nutritional count per serving 61g total fat (17.9g saturated fat); 2724kJ (891 cal); 31.2g carbohydrate; 49.7g protein; 10.1g fibre

grilled haloumi

Haloumi is best cooked just before serving as it becomes tough and rubbery on cooling.

500g haloumi cheese
2 tablespoons lemon juice
1 tablespoon coarsely chopped fresh
   flat-leaf parsley

1 Cut cheese into 1cm slices. Cook cheese on heated oiled flat plate until browned both sides
2 Transfer cheese to serving plate; drizzle with juice. Serve immediately, sprinkled with parsley.

prep & cook time 10 minutes **serves** 6
nutritional count per serving 14.3g total fat (9.2g saturated fat); 861kJ (206 cal); 1.7g carbohydrate; 17.8g protein; 0g fibre

horseradish and tarragon potato salad

1kg large kipfler potatoes
1¼ cups (300g) sour cream
¼ cup (60ml) lemon juice
2 tablespoons prepared horseradish
2 tablespoons coarsely chopped fresh tarragon
2 stalks celery (300g), trimmed, sliced thinly
40g baby rocket leaves

1 Scrub and peel potatoes; cut lengthways into 5mm slices. Boil, steam or microwave potato until tender; drain.
2 Meanwhile, combine sour cream, juice, horseradish and tarragon in large bowl. Add celery and hot potato; toss gently to combine.
3 Serve salad topped with rocket.

prep & cook time 20 minutes **serves** 8
nutritional count per serving 15.7g total fat (10.1g saturated fat); 995kJ (238 cal); 18.8g carbohydrate; 4.3g protein; 3.1g fibre

mixed cabbage coleslaw

⅓ cup (80ml) olive oil
2 tablespoons cider vinegar
2 teaspoons dijon mustard
2 cups (160g) finely shredded green cabbage
2 cups (160g) finely shredded red cabbage
2 cups (160g) finely shredded wombok
1 medium carrot (120g), grated coarsely
4 green onions, sliced thinly

1 Whisk oil, vinegar and mustard in large bowl, add remaining ingredients; toss gently to combine.

prep time 20 minutes **serves** 4
nutritional count per serving 18.4g total fat (2.6g saturated fat); 836kJ (200 cal); 4.5g carbohydrate; 2.4g protein; 4.7g fibre

four-bean salad

¼ cup (45g) dried lima beans
¼ cup (50g) dried borlotti beans
¼ cup (50g) dried kidney beans
¼ cup (50g) dried cannellini beans
125g cherry tomatoes, halved
½ small red onion (50g), sliced thinly
½ small green capsicum (75g), sliced thinly
½ cup loosely packed fresh flat-leaf parsley leaves
wholegrain mustard dressing
⅓ cup (80ml) olive oil
2 tablespoons red wine vinegar
2 teaspoons wholegrain mustard

1 Cover lima beans with cold water in medium bowl. Cover remaining beans with cold water in another medium bowl. Stand overnight; rinse, drain.
2 Cook beans, separately, in medium saucepans of boiling water until tender; drain.
3 Place ingredients for wholegrain mustard dressing in screw-top jar; shake well.
4 Place beans, dressing and remaining ingredients in medium bowl; toss gently to combine.

prep & cook time 1 hour (+ standing) **serves** 8
nutritional count per serving 9.6g total fat (1.4g saturated fat); 681kJ (163 cal); 11.4g carbohydrate; 5.6g protein; 4.5g fibre

mixed leaf salad with cranberry dressing

1 baby cos lettuce (180g), trimmed, leaves separated
250g rocket, trimmed
1 small radicchio (150g), trimmed, leaves separated
½ cup (40g) flaked almonds, roasted
½ cup (65g) dried cranberries
cranberry dressing
¼ cup (60m) olive oil
¼ cup (60ml) red wine vinegar
2 tablespoons cranberry juice
2 teaspoons dijon mustard
1 clove garlic, crushed
2 tablespoons cranberry sauce
½ small red onion (50g), chopped finely

1 Make cranberry dressing.
2 Combine lettuce, rocket and radicchio in large bowl; sprinkle with nuts and cranberries, drizzle with dressing.
cranberry dressing Blend oil, vinegar, juice, mustard, garlic and sauce until combined; stir in onion.

prep time 15 minutes **serves** 8
nutritional count per serving 10.1g total fat (1.2g saturated fat); 619kJ (148 cal); 10.7g carbohydrate; 2.8g protein; 2.4g fibre

from grandma's kitchen

Take yourself back in time with these old-fashioned classic recipes.

This old favourite is pure comfort food in a bowl — it's just the thing to relieve winter chills.

cream of chicken soup

2 litres (8 cups) water
1 litre (4 cups) chicken stock
1.8kg whole chicken
1 medium carrot (120g), chopped coarsely
1 stalk celery (150g), trimmed, chopped coarsely
1 medium brown onion (150g), chopped coarsely
40g butter
⅓ cup (50g) plain flour
2 tablespoons lemon juice
½ cup (125ml) cream
¼ cup finely chopped fresh flat-leaf parsley

1 Place the water and stock in large saucepan with chicken, carrot, celery and onion; bring to the boil. Reduce heat; simmer, covered, 1½ hours. Remove chicken from pan; simmer broth, covered, 30 minutes.
2 Strain broth through muslin-lined sieve or colander into large heatproof bowl; discard solids.
3 Melt butter in large saucepan, add flour; cook, stirring, until mixture thickens and bubbles. Gradually stir in broth and juice; stir over heat until mixture boils and thickens slightly. Add cream, reduce heat; simmer, uncovered, about 25 minutes, stirring occasionally.
4 Meanwhile, remove and discard skin and bones from chicken; shred meat coarsely. Add chicken to soup; stir over medium heat until hot.
5 Sprinkle soup with parsley; serve with crusty bread, if you like.

prep & cook time 3 hours **serves** 4
nutritional count per serving 59.2g total fat (26.2g saturated fat); 3327kJ (796 cal); 15.7g carbohydrate; 50.7g protein; 2.5g fibre

scotch broth

1kg lamb neck chops
2 litres (8 cups) water
½ cup (100g) pearl barley
1 medium brown onion (150g), chopped finely
1 medium carrot (120g), chopped finely
1 medium turnip (230g), chopped finely
1 stalk celery (150g), trimmed, chopped finely
2 cups (160g) finely shredded cabbage
½ cup (60g) frozen peas
¼ cup coarsely chopped fresh flat-leaf parsley

1 Bring lamb, the water and barley to the boil in large saucepan. Reduce heat; simmer, covered, 1 hour, skimming fat from surface occasionally.

2 Add onion, carrot, turnip and celery; simmer, covered, 30 minutes or until vegetables are tender.

3 Remove lamb from pan. When cool enough to handle, remove and discard bones; shred meat coarsely.

4 Return meat to soup with cabbage and peas; simmer, uncovered, about 10 minutes or until cabbage is just tender. Stir in parsley.

prep & cook time 2 hours 15 minutes **serves** 4
nutritional count per serving 23.9g total fat (10.6g saturated fat); 2036kJ (487 cal); 22.6g carbohydrate; 41.4g protein; 8.5g fibre

pea and ham soup

1 medium brown onion (150g), chopped coarsely

2 stalks celery (300g), trimmed, chopped coarsely

2 bay leaves

1.5kg ham hocks

2.5 litres (10 cups) water

1 teaspoon cracked black pepper

2 cups (375g) split green peas

1 Bring onion, celery, bay leaves, hocks, the water and pepper to the boil in large saucepan. Reduce heat; simmer, covered, about 1½ hours. Add peas; simmer, covered, 30 minutes or until peas are tender.

2 Remove hocks from pan; when cool enough to handle, remove meat from hocks. Shred meat finely. Discard bones, fat and skin; remove and discard bay leaves.

3 Blend or process half the soup mixture, in batches, until smooth. Return to pan with remaining soup mixture and ham; stir soup until heated through.

prep & cook time 2 hours 15 minutes **serves** 6
nutritional count per serving 4.9g total fat (1.4g saturated fat); 1162kJ (278 cal); 31g carbohydrate; 23.5g protein; 7.3g fibre

irish stew

750g lamb neck chops
2 large brown onions (400g), chopped coarsely
1 large carrot (180g), chopped coarsely
1 large parsnip (350g), chopped coarsely
1kg potatoes, chopped coarsely
3½ cups (625ml) beef stock
2 tablespoons tomato paste
1 tablespoon worcestershire sauce
2 sprigs thyme
¼ cup coarsely chopped fresh flat-leaf parsley

1 Preheat oven to 160°C/140°C fan-forced.
2 Layer chops and vegetables in large ovenproof dish; pour over combined stock, paste and sauce. Add thyme.
3 Cook, covered, 2 hours. Uncover; cook 30 minutes or until lamb and vegetables are tender. Serve stew sprinkled with parsley.

prep & cook time 3 hours **serves** 4
nutritional count per serving 19.3g total fat (8.6g saturated fat); 2249kJ (538 cal); 46.8g carbohydrate; 39.7g protein; 8.5g fibre

rabbit stew

2 tablespoons oil
1kg rabbit pieces
3 medium brown onions (450g), sliced thickly
4 cloves garlic, crushed
1 cup (250ml) water
1 litre (4 cups) chicken stock
410g can diced tomatoes
5 medium potatoes (1kg), chopped coarsely
2 medium carrots (240g), sliced thickly
1 tablespoon balsamic vinegar
3 bay leaves
1 teaspoon dried chilli flakes
⅓ cup coarsely chopped fresh mint
1 cup (120g) frozen peas

1 Heat half the oil in large saucepan; cook rabbit, in batches, until browned.
2 Heat remaining oil in same pan; cook onion and garlic, stirring, until onion softens.
3 Add the water, stock, undrained tomatoes, potato, carrot, vinegar, bay leaves, chilli and mint to pan. Return rabbit to pan; bring to the boil. Reduce heat; simmer, uncovered, 1¼ hours. Add peas; simmer, uncovered, 5 minutes.

prep & cook time 2 hours **serves** 4
nutritional count per serving 19.4g total fat (5.1g saturated fat); 2750kJ (658 cal); 44.4g carbohydrate; 70.7g protein; 10.6g fibre

irish stew

rabbit stew

serving idea If you've got some little baking dishes you could make this pie in individual servings and present each diner with their own dish. You can also make this recipe with cooked lamb mince if you prefer.

This combination of rich, saucy meat and creamy mash is a timeless classic.

shepherd's pie

30g butter
1 medium brown onion (150g), chopped finely
1 medium carrot (120g), chopped finely
½ teaspoon dried mixed herbs
4 cups (750g) finely chopped cooked lamb
¼ cup (70g) tomato paste
¼ cup (60ml) tomato sauce
2 tablespoons worcestershire sauce
2 cups (500ml) beef stock
2 tablespoons plain flour
⅓ cup (80ml) water
potato topping
5 medium potatoes (1kg), chopped coarsely
60g butter
¼ cup (60ml) milk

1 Preheat oven to 200°C/180°C fan-forced. Oil shallow 2.5-litre (10-cup) ovenproof dish.
2 Make potato topping.
3 Meanwhile, heat butter in large saucepan; cook onion and carrot, stirring, until tender. Add mixed herbs and lamb; cook, stirring, 2 minutes. Stir in paste, sauces and stock, then blended flour and water; stir over heat until mixture boils and thickens. Pour mixture into dish.
4 Drop heaped tablespoons of potato topping onto lamb mixture. Bake in oven about 20 minutes or until browned and heated through.
potato topping Boil, steam or microwave potato until tender; drain. Mash with butter and milk until smooth.

prep & cook time 1 hour **serves** 4
nutritional count per serving 36.2g total fat (20.2g saturated fat); 2976kJ (712 cal); 44.7g carbohydrate; 48.8g protein; 6g fibre

corned beef with parsley sauce

1.5kg whole piece beef corned silverside
2 bay leaves
6 black peppercorns
1 large brown onion (200g), quartered
1 large carrot (180g), chopped coarsely
1 tablespoon brown malt vinegar
¼ cup (50g) firmly packed brown sugar
parsley sauce
30g butter
¼ cup (35g) plain flour
2½ cups (625ml) milk
⅓ cup (40g) grated cheddar cheese
⅓ cup finely chopped fresh flat-leaf parsley
1 tablespoon mild mustard

1 Place beef, bay leaves, peppercorns, onion, carrot, vinegar and half of the sugar in large saucepan. Add enough water to just cover beef; simmer, covered, about 2 hours or until beef is tender. Cool beef 1 hour in liquid in pan.
2 Remove beef from pan; discard liquid. Sprinkle sheet of foil with remaining sugar, wrap beef in foil; stand 20 minutes before serving.
3 Make parsley sauce.
4 Serve sliced corned beef with parsley sauce.
parsley sauce Melt butter in small saucepan, add flour; cook, stirring, until bubbling. Gradually stir in milk; cook, stirring, until sauce boils and thickens. Remove from heat; stir in cheese, parsley and mustard.

prep & cook time 2 hours 30 minutes
(+ cooling & standing) **serves** 4
nutritional count per serving 35.8g total fat (19.3g saturated fat); 3520kJ (842 cal); 31g carbohydrate; 97g protein; 2.5g fibre

savoury glazed meatloaf

750g beef mince
1 cup (70g) stale breadcrumbs
1 medium brown onion (150g), chopped finely
1 egg
2 tablespoons tomato sauce
1 tablespoon worcestershire sauce
185g can evaporated milk
2 teaspoons mustard powder
1 tablespoon brown sugar
½ teaspoon mustard powder, extra
¼ cup (60ml) tomato sauce, extra

1 Preheat oven to 180°C/160°C fan-forced. Oil 14cm x 21cm loaf pan.
2 Combine beef, breadcrumbs, onion, egg, sauces, milk and mustard in medium bowl. Press mixture into pan. Turn pan upside-down onto a foil-lined oven tray. Leave pan in place. Cook 15 minutes.
3 Meanwhile, combine sugar, extra mustard and extra tomato sauce in small bowl.
4 Remove loaf from oven; remove pan. Brush loaf well with glaze, return loaf to oven; cook 45 minutes or until well browned and cooked through.
5 Serve slices of meatloaf with rocket leaves and tomato wedges.

prep & cook time 1 hour **serves** 4
nutritional count per serving 19.9g total fat (10g saturated fat); 1986kJ (475 cal); 29.1g carbohydrate; 45.8g protein; 1.8g fibre

corned beef with parsley sauce

savoury glazed meatloaf

beef and vegetable pie

1 tablespoon olive oil

1.5kg gravy beef, cut into 2cm pieces

60g butter

1 medium brown onion (150g), chopped finely

1 clove garlic, crushed

¼ cup (35g) plain flour

1 cup (250ml) dry white wine

3 cups (750ml) hot beef stock

2 tablespoons tomato paste

2 stalks celery (300g), trimmed, cut into 2cm pieces

2 medium potatoes (400g), cut into 2cm pieces

1 large carrot (180g), cut into 2cm pieces

1 large zucchini (150g), cut into 2cm pieces

150g mushrooms, quartered

1 cup (120g) frozen peas

½ cup finely chopped fresh flat-leaf parsley

2 sheets puff pastry

1 egg, beaten lightly

1 Heat oil in large saucepan; cook beef, in batches, until browned all over.

2 Melt butter in same pan; cook onion and garlic, stirring, until onion softens. Add flour; cook, stirring, until mixture thickens and bubbles. Gradually stir in wine and stock; stir until it boils and thickens slightly.

3 Return beef to pan with paste, celery, potato and carrot; bring to the boil. Reduce heat; simmer, covered, 1 hour.

4 Add zucchini and mushrooms; simmer, uncovered, about 30 minutes or until beef is tender. Add peas, stir until heated through. Remove from heat; stir in parsley.

5 Preheat oven to 220°C/200°C fan-forced.

6 Divide warm beef mixture between two deep 25cm pie dishes; brush outside edge of dishes with a little egg. Top each pie with a pastry sheet; pressing edges to seal. Trim pastry; brush pastry with egg.

7 Bake pies about 20 minutes or until browned.

prep & cook time 2 hours 40 minutes **serves** 8
nutritional count per serving 27.6g total fat (13.3g saturated fat); 2412kJ (577 cal); 28.6g carbohydrate; 46.4g protein; 4.9g fibre

quiche lorraine

country-style beef and potato casserole

quiche lorraine

1 medium brown onion (150g), chopped finely
3 rindless bacon rashers (195g), chopped finely
3 eggs
300ml cream
½ cup (125ml) milk
¾ cup (120g) coarsely grated gruyère cheese
pastry
1¾ cups (260g) plain flour
150g cold butter, chopped coarsely
1 egg yolk
2 teaspoons lemon juice
⅓ cup (80ml) iced water, approximately

1 Make pastry.
2 Preheat oven to 200°C/180°C fan-forced.
3 Roll pastry between sheets of baking paper large
enough to line a deep 23cm loose-based flan tin.
Lift pastry into tin; gently press pastry around side.
Trim edge, place tin on oven tray. Cover pastry with
baking paper; fill with dried beans or rice. Bake
10 minutes; remove paper and beans. Bake pastry
a further 10 minutes or until golden brown; cool.
4 Reduce oven to 180°C/160°C fan-forced.
5 Cook onion and bacon in heated oiled small frying
pan until onion is soft; drain on absorbent paper, cool.
Sprinkle bacon mixture over pastry case.
6 Whisk eggs in medium bowl then whisk in cream,
milk and cheese; pour into pastry case.
7 Bake quiche about 35 minutes or until filling is set.
Stand 5 minutes before removing from tin.
pastry Sift flour into bowl; rub in butter. Add egg yolk,
juice and enough water to make ingredients cling
together. Knead gently on lightly floured surface until
smooth; cover, refrigerate 30 minutes.

prep & cook time 1 hour 30 minutes (+ refrigeration)
serves 6
nutritional count per serving 51.8g total fat (35.4g
saturated fat); 3139kJ (751 cal); 35.4g carbohydrate;
22.1g protein; 2g fibre

country-style beef and potato casserole

1kg beef chuck steak, cut into 2cm pieces
½ cup (75g) plain flour, approximately
2 tablespoons olive oil
3 small brown onion (450g), halved
2 cloves garlic, crushed
2 rindless bacon rashers (130g), chopped coarsely
2 tablespoons tomato paste
3 cups (750ml) beef stock
410g can crushed tomatoes
¼ cup (60ml) worcestershire sauce
2 medium potatoes (400g), chopped coarsely
1 medium kumara (400g), chopped coarsely
1 large red capsicum (350g), chopped coarsely
1 tablespoon coarsely chopped fresh thyme

1 Coat beef in flour, shake away excess. Heat oil in
large saucepan; cook beef, in batches, until browned.
2 Cook onion, garlic and bacon in same pan, stirring,
until bacon crisps. Add paste; cook, stirring, 1 minute.
3 Return beef to pan with stock, undrained tomatoes
and sauce; bring to the boil. Reduce heat; simmer,
covered, 1 hour, stirring occasionally.
4 Add potato, kumara and capsicum to pan; simmer,
uncovered, stirring occasionally, about 30 minutes or
until beef is tender.
5 Serve casserole sprinkled with thyme.

prep & cook time 2 hours 35 minutes **serves** 6
nutritional count per serving 17.3g total fat (5.2g
saturated fat); 2036kJ (487 cal); 34.5g carbohydrate;
45.5g protein; 4.8g fibre

Grandma's kitchen is a loving haven of warmth and comfort, and there are always irresistible homemade goodies around.

apple pie

10 medium apples (1.5kg)
½ cup (125ml) water
¼ cup (55g) caster sugar
1 teaspoon finely grated lemon rind
¼ teaspoon ground cinnamon
1 egg white
1 tablespoon caster sugar, extra
pastry
1 cup (150g) plain flour
½ cup (75g) self-raising flour
¼ cup (35g) cornflour
¼ cup (30g) custard powder
1 tablespoon caster sugar
100g cold butter, chopped coarsely
1 egg yolk
¼ cup (60ml) iced water

1 Make pastry.

2 Peel, core and slice apple thickly. Place apples and the water in large saucepan; bring to the boil. Reduce heat; simmer, covered, about 10 minutes or until apples soften. Drain; stir in sugar, rind and cinnamon. Cool.

3 Preheat oven to 220°C/200°C fan-forced. Grease deep 25cm pie dish.

4 Divide pastry in half. Roll one half between sheets of baking paper until large enough to line dish. Lift pastry into dish; press into base and side. Spoon apple mixture into pastry case; brush edge with egg white.

5 Roll remaining pastry large enough to cover filling; lift onto filling. Press edges together; trim away excess pastry. Brush pastry with egg white; sprinkle with extra sugar. Bake 20 minutes.

6 Reduce oven to 180°C/160°C fan-forced; bake pie a further 25 minutes or until golden brown. Serve with vanilla custard or ice-cream.

pastry Process dry ingredients with the butter until crumbly. Add egg yolk and the water; process until combined. Knead on floured surface until smooth. Cover; refrigerate 30 minutes.

prep + cook time 1 hour 45 minutes (+ refrigeration)
serves 8
nutritional count per serving 11.4g total fat (7g saturated fat); 1438kJ (344 cal); 53.9g carbohydrate; 4.3g protein; 3.7g fibre

tip Golden Delicious apples are the best variety to bake with as they hold their shape well and develop a lovely mellow, sweet flavour when cooked.

classic trifle

pavlova

classic trifle

85g packet raspberry jelly crystals
250g sponge cake, cut into 3cm pieces
¼ cup (60ml) sweet sherry
¼ cup (30g) custard powder
¼ cup (55g) caster sugar
½ teaspoon vanilla extract
1½ cups (375ml) milk
825g can sliced peaches, drained
300ml thickened cream
2 tablespoons flaked almonds, roasted

1 Make jelly according to directions on packet; pour into shallow container. Refrigerate 20 minutes or until jelly is almost set.
2 Arrange cake in 3-litre (12-cup) bowl; sprinkle with sherry.
3 Blend custard powder, sugar and extract with a little of the milk in small saucepan; stir in remaining milk. Stir over heat until mixture boils and thickens. Cover surface with plastic wrap; cool.
4 Pour jelly over cake; refrigerate 15 minutes. Top with peaches. Stir a third of the cream into custard; pour over peaches.
5 Whip remaining cream; spread over custard, sprinkle with nuts. Refrigerate 3 hours or overnight.

prep & cook time 40 minutes (+ refrigeration)
serves 8
nutritional count per serving 18.3g total fat (10.7g saturated fat); 1643kJ (393 cal); 49g carbohydrate; 6.9g protein; 2.1g fibre

pavlova

4 egg whites
1 cup (220g) caster sugar
½ teaspoon vanilla extract
¾ teaspoon white vinegar
300ml thickened cream, whipped
250g strawberries, halved
¼ cup (60ml) passionfruit pulp

1 Preheat oven to 120°C/100°C fan-forced. Line oven tray with foil; grease foil, dust with cornflour, shake away excess. Mark 18cm-circle on foil.
2 Beat egg whites in small bowl with electric mixer until soft peaks form; gradually add sugar, beating until sugar dissolves. Add extract and vinegar; beat until combined.
3 Spread meringue into circle on foil, building up at the side to 8cm in height. Smooth side and top of pavlova gently. Using spatula blade, mark decorative grooves around side of pavlova; smooth top again
4 Bake pavlova about 1½ hours. Turn oven off; cool pavlova in oven with door ajar.
5 Cut around top edge of pavlova (the crisp meringue top will fall on top of the marshmallow centre). Serve pavlova topped with whipped cream, strawberries and passionfruit.

prep & cook time 1 hour 50 minutes (+ cooling)
serves 8
nutritional count per serving 14g total fat (9.2g saturated fat); 1095kJ (262 cal); 30g carbohydrate; 3.3g protein; 1.7g fibre

scones

4 cups (600g) self-raising flour
2 tablespoons icing sugar
60g butter
1½ cups (375ml) milk
¾ cup (180ml) water, approximately

1 Preheat oven to 220°C/ 200°C fan-forced. Grease 20cm x 30cm lamington pan.
2 Sift flour and sugar into large bowl; rub in butter with fingertips.
3 Make a well in centre of flour mixture; add milk and almost all the water. Use knife to "cut" the milk and water through the flour mixture, mixing to a soft, sticky dough. Knead dough on floured surface until smooth.

4 Press dough out to 2cm thickness. Dip 4.5cm round cutter in flour; cut as many rounds as you can from piece of dough. Place scones, side by side, just touching, in pan.
5 Gently knead scraps of dough together; repeat pressing and cutting of dough, place in same pan. Brush tops with a little extra milk; bake 15 minutes or until scones are just browned and sound hollow when tapped firmly on the top with fingers.

prep & cook time 45 minutes **makes** 20
nutritional count per scone 3.6g total fat (2.2g saturated fat); 606kJ (145 cal); 23.6g carbohydrate; 3.9g protein; 1.1g fibre

baked custard

6 eggs
1 teaspoon vanilla extract
⅓ cup (75g) caster sugar
1 litre (4 cups) hot milk
¼ teaspoon ground nutmeg

1 Preheat oven to 160°C/140°C fan-forced. Grease shallow 1.5-litre (6-cup) ovenproof dish.
2 Whisk eggs, extract and sugar in large bowl; gradually whisk in hot milk. Pour custard mixture into dish; sprinkle with nutmeg.
3 Place dish in larger baking dish; add enough boiling water to come halfway up sides of dish. Bake, uncovered, about 45 minutes. Remove custard from large dish; stand 5 minutes before serving.

prep & cook time 50 minutes **serves** 6
nutritional count per serving 12.5g total fat (6.1g saturated fat); 1016kJ (243 cal); 20.7g carbohydrate; 13.2g protein; 0g fibre

serving idea Homemade custard is always better than store-bought. Serve this baked custard with fresh seasonal fruit like berries, which are particularly nice with it.

featherlight sponge

4 eggs
¾ cup (165g) caster sugar
⅔ cup (100g) wheaten cornflour
¼ cup (30g) custard powder
1 teaspoon cream of tartar
½ teaspoon bicarbonate of soda
⅓ cup (110g) apricot jam
300ml thickened cream, whipped

1 Preheat oven to 180°C/160°C fan-forced. Grease and flour two deep 22cm-round cake pans; shake away excess flour.
2 Beat eggs and sugar in small bowl with electric mixer until mixture is thick and creamy and sugar is dissolved; transfer to large bowl.
3 Triple-sift dry ingredients; fold into egg mixture. Divide sponge mixture between pans; bake about 20 minutes. Turn sponges, top-side up, onto baking-paper-covered wire rack to cool.
4 Sandwich sponges with jam and cream.

prep & cook time 40 minutes **serves** 10
nutritional count per serving 14.8g total fat (8.9g saturated fat); 1191kJ (285 cal); 35.5g carbohydrate; 3.6g protein; 0.2g fibre

boiled fruit cake

2¾ cups (500g) mixed dried fruit
1 cup (220g) firmly packed brown sugar
125g butter, chopped
1 teaspoon mixed spice
½ teaspoon bicarbonate of soda
½ cup (125ml) water
½ cup (125ml) sweet sherry
1 egg
1 cup (150g) plain flour
1 cup (150g) self-raising flour
⅓ cup (55g) blanched almonds
2 tablespoons sweet sherry, extra

1 Combine fruit, sugar, butter, spice, soda and the water in large saucepan; stir over low heat, without boiling, until sugar dissolves and butter melts. Bring to the boil. Reduce heat; simmer, covered, 5 minutes. Remove pan from heat; stir in sherry. Cool mixture to room temperature.

2 Preheat oven to 160°C/140°C fan-forced. Grease deep 20cm-round cake pan; line base and side with two layers of baking paper, extending paper 5cm above side.

3 Stir egg and sifted flours into fruit mixture. Spread mixture into pan; decorate with almonds. Bake about 1½ hours. Brush top of hot cake with extra sherry. Cover cake with foil, cool in pan.

prep & cook time 1 hour 45 minutes (+ cooling)
serves 12
nutritional count per serving 12g total fat (6g saturated fat); 1651kJ (395 cal); 62.6g carbohydrate; 5.5g protein; 4.5g fibre

Take yourself back to those rainy Sunday afternoons at Grandma's house with this steamed pudding.

serving idea Serve this proper steamed pudding with ice cream and a spoon not a fork, you'll need it to scrape up all the gingery goodness.

steamed ginger pudding

60g butter
¼ cup (90g) golden syrup
½ teaspoon bicarbonate of soda
1 cup (150g) self raising flour
2 teaspoons ground ginger
½ cup (125ml) milk
1 egg
syrup
⅓ cup (115g) golden syrup
2 tablespoons water
30g butter

1 Grease 1.25-litre (5-cup) pudding steamer.
2 Combine butter and syrup in small saucepan; stir over low heat until smooth. Remove from heat, stir in soda; transfer mixture to medium bowl. Stir in sifted dry ingredients then combined milk and egg, in two batches.
3 Spread mixture into steamer. Cover with pleated baking paper and foil; secure with lid.
4 Place pudding steamer in large saucepan with enough boiling water to come halfway up side of steamer; cover pan with tight-fitting lid. Boil 1 hour, replenishing water as necessary to maintain level. Stand pudding 5 minutes before turning onto plate.
5 Meanwhile, make syrup.
6 Serve pudding topped with syrup and cream.
syrup Stir ingredients in small saucepan over heat until smooth; bring to the boil. Reduce heat; simmer, uncovered, 2 minutes.

prep & cook time 1 hour 15 minutes **serves** 6
nutritional count per serving 14.4g total fat (9g saturated fat); 1342kJ (321 cal); 44.3g carbohydrate; 4.6g protein; 1g fibre

serving idea Try substituting brioche or croissants instead of sliced bread for an even more luxurious version of this classic dessert. Berries, especially raspberries, also make a delicious addition

One of the most comforting puddings, it has just the right amount of custard to soak through its layers of bread.

bread and butter pudding

6 slices white bread (270g)
40g butter, softened
½ cup (80g) sultanas
¼ teaspoon ground nutmeg
custard
1½ cups (375ml) milk
2 cups (500ml) cream
⅓ cup (75g) caster sugar
1 teaspoon vanilla extract
4 eggs

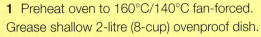

1 Preheat oven to 160°C/140°C fan-forced. Grease shallow 2-litre (8-cup) ovenproof dish.
2 Make custard.
3 Trim crusts from bread. Spread each slice with butter; cut into four triangles. Layer bread, overlapping, in dish; sprinkle with sultanas. Pour custard over bread; sprinkle with nutmeg.
4 Place ovenproof dish in large baking dish; add enough boiling water to come halfway up side of ovenproof dish. Bake about 45 minutes or until pudding is set. Remove pudding from baking dish; stand 5 minutes before serving. Serve dusted with sifted icing sugar.
custard Bring milk, cream, sugar and extract to the boil in medium saucepan. Whisk eggs in large bowl; whisking constantly, gradually add hot milk mixture to egg mixture.

prep & cook time 1 hour 15 minutes **serves** 6
nutritional count per serving 48.6g total fat (30.4g saturated fat); 2859kJ (684 cal); 49.3g carbohydrate; 12.4g protein; 1.8g fibre

hedgehog slice

¾ cup (180ml) sweetened condensed milk
60g butter
125g dark eating chocolate, chopped coarsely
150g plain sweet biscuits
⅓ cup (45g) roasted unsalted peanuts
⅓ cup (55g) sultanas

1 Grease 8cm x 26cm bar pan; line base with baking paper, extending paper 5cm over long sides.
2 Combine condensed milk and butter in small saucepan; stir over low heat until smooth. Remove from heat; add chocolate, stir until smooth.
3 Break biscuits into small pieces; place in large bowl with nuts and sultanas. Add chocolate mixture; stir to combine.
4 Spread mixture into pan; cover, refrigerate 4 hours or until firm. Remove from pan; cut into slices.

prep & cook time 20 minutes (+ refrigeration)
makes 12
nutritional count per slice 12.7g total fat (6.8g saturated fat); 1028kJ (246 cal); 29.9g carbohydrate; 4g protein; 0.9g fibre

kisses

125g butter, softened
½ cup (110g) caster sugar
1 egg
⅓ cup (50g) plain flour
¼ cup (35g) self-raising flour
⅔ cup (100g) cornflour
¼ cup (30g) custard powder
vienna cream
60g butter, softened
¾ cup (120g) icing sugar
2 teaspoons milk

1 Preheat oven to 180°C/160°C fan-forced. Grease two oven trays.
2 Beat butter and sugar in small bowl with electric mixer until smooth and creamy; beat in egg. Stir in sifted dry ingredients in two batches.
3 Spoon mixture into piping bag fitted with 1cm tube. Pipe 3cm-diameter rounds of mixture, about 3cm apart, onto trays. Bake about 10 minutes or until browned lightly. Loosen cakes; cool on trays.
4 Meanwhile, make vienna cream.
5 Sandwich cold cakes with vienna cream; dust with a little extra sifted icing sugar.
vienna cream Beat butter until as white as possible. Gradually beat in half the sifted icing sugar; beat in milk. Gradually beat in remaining icing sugar.

prep & cook time 40 minutes **makes about** 40
nutritional count per kiss 4g total fat (2.6g saturated fat); 322kJ (77 cal); 10g carbohydrate; 0.5g protein; 0.1g fibre

hedgehog slice

kisses

gingernuts

90g butter
⅓ cup (75g) firmly packed brown sugar
⅓ cup (115g) golden syrup
1⅓ cups (200g) plain flour
¾ teaspoon bicarbonate of soda
1 tablespoon ground ginger
1 teaspoon ground cinnamon
¼ teaspoon ground clove

1 Preheat oven to 180°C/160°C fan-forced. Grease oven trays.
2 Stir butter, sugar and syrup in medium saucepan over low heat until smooth. Remove from heat; stir in sifted dry ingredients. Cool 10 minutes.
3 Roll rounded teaspoons of mixture into balls. Place about 3cm apart on trays; flatten slightly. Bake about 10 minutes; cool on trays.

prep & cook time 25 minutes (+ cooling) **makes** 32 **nutritional count per biscuit** 2.4g total fat (1.5g saturated fat); 259kJ (62 cal); 9.5g carbohydrate; 0.7g protein; 0.2g fibre

anzac biscuits

1 cup (90g) rolled oats
1 cup (150g) plain flour
1 cup (220g) firmly packed brown sugar
½ cup (40g) desiccated coconut
125g butter
2 tablespoons golden syrup
1 tablespoon water
½ teaspoon bicarbonate of soda

1 Preheat oven to 160°C/140°C fan-forced. Grease oven trays; line with baking paper.

2 Combine oats, sifted flour, sugar and coconut in large bowl. Combine butter, syrup and the water in small saucepan, stir over low heat until smooth; stir in soda. Stir into dry ingredients.

3 Roll level tablespoons of mixture into balls; place about 5cm apart on trays, flatten slightly. Bake about 20 minutes; cool on trays.

prep & cook time 35 minutes (+ cooling) **makes** 25
nutritional count per biscuit 5.5g total fat (3.7g saturated fat); 506kJ (121 cal); 16.8g carbohydrate; 1.2g protein; 0.7g fibre

world food

Let these exotic flavours from around the world seduce you to the table.

This traditional Spanish dish varies from region to region, and each one claims theirs as the best and most authentic.

paella

500g clams
1 tablespoon coarse cooking salt
500g uncooked medium prawns
500g small black mussels
2 tablespoons olive oil
3 cups (750ml) chicken stock
pinch saffron threads
220g chicken thigh fillets, chopped coarsely
1 chorizo sausage (170g), sliced thickly
1 large red onion (300g), chopped finely
1 medium red capsicum (200g), chopped finely
2 cloves garlic, crushed
2 teaspoons smoked paprika
2 medium tomatoes (300g), peeled, seeded, chopped finely
1½ cups (300g) calasparra rice
1 cup (120g) frozen peas
2 tablespoons finely chopped fresh flat-leaf parsley

1 Rinse clams under cold water, place in large bowl with salt; cover with cold water, stand 2 hours. Drain then rinse.

2 Shell and devein prawns, leaving tails intact. Reserve shells. Scrub mussels and remove beards.

3 Heat 2 teaspoons of the oil in large saucepan, add prawn shells; cook, stirring, until red. Add stock; bring to the boil. Reduce heat; simmer, uncovered, 20 minutes. Strain through fine sieve into jug or bowl; add saffron to the liquid. Discard prawn shells.

4 Heat another 2 teaspoons of the oil in 45cm paella pan or large frying pan, add chicken; cook until browned all over, remove from pan. Add chorizo to same pan; cook until browned all over. Remove chorizo from pan; drain on absorbent paper.

5 Heat remaining oil in pan, add onion, capsicum, garlic, paprika and tomato; cook, stirring, until soft. Add rice; stir to coat in mixture.

6 Add chicken, chorizo and stock to pan; stir until combined. Bring mixture to the boil; reduce heat, simmer, uncovered, about 15 minutes or until rice is almost tender.

7 Sprinkle peas over rice; place clams, prawns and mussels evenly over surface of paella. Cover pan with a lid or large sheets of foil; simmer about 5 minutes or until prawns are cooked and mussels and clams have opened (discard any that do not). Sprinkle with parsley; serve immediately.

prep & cook time 2 hours (+ standing) **serves** 6
nutritional count per serving 18.9g total fat (5.2g saturated fat); 2128kJ (509 cal); 49.1g carbohydrate; 33.6g protein; 3.7g fibre

tortilla de patata

20g butter
¼ cup (60ml) olive oil
3 medium potatoes (600g), chopped finely
1 medium brown onion (150g), chopped finely
8 eggs
½ teaspoon chilli powder

1 Preheat oven to 180°C/160°C fan-forced.
2 Melt butter with oil in 22cm-base ovenproof frying pan; cook potato and onion, stirring occasionally, until potato is tender.

3 Meanwhile, whisk eggs and chilli powder in medium jug.
4 Add egg mixture to pan. Cook, uncovered, over low heat, about 5 minutes or until just set.
5 Place pan in oven; cook, uncovered, 10 minutes or until browned lightly. Carefully turn tortilla onto plate. Cut into wedges; serve with a side salad.

prep & cook time 40 minutes **serves** 4
nutritional count per serving 28.4g total fat (7.8g saturated fat); 1747kJ (418 cal); 22g carbohydrate; 17.5g protein; 28.4g fibre

beef carpaccio

400g piece beef eye fillet

2 tablespoons olive oil

2 teaspoons finely grated lemon rind

2 tablespoons lemon juice

1 clove garlic, crushed

⅓ cup finely chopped fresh flat-leaf parsley

2 tablespoons finely chopped fresh oregano

⅓ cup finely chopped baby rocket leaves

⅓ cup (25g) flaked parmesan cheese

1 Tightly wrap beef fillet in plastic wrap; freeze 1 hour or until firm. Unwrap beef; slice as thinly as possible. Arrange slices on platter.

2 Combine oil, rind, juice, garlic, parsley, oregano and rocket in small bowl. Serve beef sprinkled with herb mixture and cheese.

prep time 30 minutes (+ freezing) **serves** 8
nutritional count per serving 7.8g total fat (2.3g saturated fat); 506kJ (121 cal); 0.3g carbohydrate; 12.3g protein; 0.3g fibre

minestrone

1 cup (200g) dried borlotti beans
1 tablespoon olive oil
1 medium brown onion (150g), chopped coarsely
1 clove garlic, crushed
¼ cup (70g) tomato paste
1.5 litres (6 cups) water
2 cups (500ml) vegetable stock
700g bottled tomato pasta sauce
1 stalk celery (150g), trimmed, chopped finely
1 medium carrot (120g), chopped finely
1 medium zucchini (120g), chopped finely
80g green beans, trimmed, chopped finely
¾ cup (135g) macaroni
⅓ cup coarsely chopped fresh basil

1 Place borlotti beans in medium bowl, cover with water; stand overnight, drain. Rinse under cold water; drain.
2 Heat oil in large saucepan; cook onion and garlic, stirring, until onion softens. Add paste; cook, stirring, 2 minutes. Add borlotti beans to pan with the water, stock and pasta sauce; bring to the boil. Reduce heat; simmer, uncovered, about 1 hour or until beans are tender.
3 Add celery; simmer, uncovered, 10 minutes. Add carrot, zucchini and green beans; simmer, uncovered, about 20 minutes or until carrot is tender. Add pasta; simmer until pasta is tender.
4 Serve bowls of soup sprinkled with basil.

prep & cook time 2 hours 30 minutes (+ standing)
serves 6
nutritional count per serving 5.5g total fat (1g saturated fat); 1095kJ (262 cal); 39.9g carbohydrate; 9.4g protein; 6.5g fibre

gazpacho

1kg ripe tomatoes, peeled, chopped coarsely
2 lebanese cucumbers (260g), seeded, chopped coarsely
2 large red capsicums (700g), chopped coarsely
1 large green capsicum (350g), chopped coarsely
1 large red onion (200g), chopped coarsely
2 cloves garlic, chopped coarsely
415ml can tomato juice
2 tablespoons red wine vinegar
1 tablespoon olive oil
2 teaspoons Tabasco
1 medium avocado (250g), chopped finely
1 small yellow capsicum (150g), chopped finely
¼ cup finely chopped fresh coriander

1 Blend or process tomatoes, cucumber, capsicums, onion, garlic, juice, vinegar, oil and Tabasco, in batches, until smooth. Pour into large jug. Cover; refrigerate 3 hours.
2 Stir soup; pour into serving bowls, top with remaining ingredients. Serve gazpacho sprinkled with extra Tabasco, if you like.

prep time 25 minutes (+ refrigeration) **serves** 6
nutritional count per serving 10.4g total fat (1.9g saturated fat); 786kJ (188 cal); 14.5g carbohydrate; 6.2g protein; 6.3g fibre

minestrone

gazpacho

In Italian cuisine cheese and seafood are never, ever mixed, so let the seafood shine and don't be tempted to sprinkle parmesan on this spectacular dish.

seafood risotto

1.5 litres (6 cups) chicken stock
2 cups (500ml) water
2 tablespoons olive oil
1 medium leek (350g), sliced thinly
1 fresh small red thai chilli, chopped finely
3 cups (600g) arborio rice
pinch saffron threads
1 cup (250ml) dry white wine
2 tablespoons tomato paste
1.5kg marinara mix
1 cup (120g) frozen peas
2 teaspoons finely grated lemon rind
1 cup loosely packed fresh flat-leaf parsley leaves

1 Combine stock and the water in medium saucepan; bring to the boil. Simmer, covered.
2 Heat oil in large saucepan; cook leek and chilli, stirring, until leek softens. Add rice and saffron; stir to coat in leek mixture. Add wine and paste; cook, stirring, until wine has almost evaporated.
3 Add ½ cup simmering stock to the rice mixture. Cook, stirring, over low heat, until liquid is absorbed. Continue adding stock mixture, in ½-cup batches, stirring until liquid is absorbed after each addition. Total cooking time should be about 30 minutes.
4 Add marinara mix and peas; mix gently. Simmer, covered, 5 minutes. Uncover; simmer until all stock has been absorbed and seafood is tender.
5 Stir in rind and parsley.

prep & cook time 1 hour 15 minutes **serves** 8
nutritional count per serving 5.9g total fat (1.1g saturated fat); 1547kJ (370 cal); 63.2g carbohydrate; 8.9g protein; 2.9g fibre

serving idea This risotto looks so appealing in a large saucepan, especially with some parsley sprinkled on top, so bring the whole pan to the table and dish it up from there.

mushroom fettuccine boscaiola

spinach and herb cannelloni

mushroom fettuccine boscaiola

10g dried porcini mushrooms
¼ cup (60ml) boiling water
375g fettuccine
1 tablespoon olive oil
200g pancetta, chopped coarsely
100g button mushrooms, sliced thinly
100g swiss brown mushrooms, sliced thinly
1 flat mushroom (80g), sliced thinly
2 cloves garlic, crushed
¼ cup (60ml) dry white wine
300ml cream
1 tablespoon lemon juice
½ cup (40g) finely grated parmesan cheese
2 tablespoons coarsely chopped fresh chives
2 tablespoons finely grated parmesan cheese, extra

1 Combine porcini mushrooms and the water in small heatproof bowl; cover, stand 15 minutes or until mushrooms are tender. Drain; reserve soaking liquid, chop mushrooms coarsely.
2 Cook pasta in large saucepan of boiling water until tender; drain.
3 Meanwhile, heat oil in large frying pan; cook pancetta until crisp. Add all mushrooms and garlic; cook, stirring, until mushrooms are browned lightly. Add wine; bring to the boil. Boil, uncovered, until liquid has almost evaporated. Add cream, juice and reserved soaking liquid; simmer, uncovered, until sauce reduces by half and thickens slightly. Stir in cheese and chives.
4 Combine pasta and sauce in large bowl. Serve bowls of pasta sprinkled with extra parmesan cheese.

prep & cook time 40 minutes (+ standing) **serves** 4
nutritional count per serving 45.5g total fat (26.1g saturated fat); 3390kJ (811 cal); 66.9g carbohydrate; 28.9g protein; 5.3g fibre

spinach and herb cannelloni

1kg spinach, trimmed, chopped coarsely
500g ricotta cheese
2 eggs
1½ cups (120g) coarsely grated parmesan cheese
¼ cup finely chopped fresh mint
3 teaspoons finely chopped fresh thyme
2 teaspoons finely chopped fresh rosemary
250g cannelloni tubes
creamy tomato sauce
1 tablespoon olive oil
1 medium brown onion (150g), chopped finely
4 cloves garlic, crushed
4 x 400g cans diced tomatoes
½ cup (125ml) cream
1 teaspoon white sugar

1 Make creamy tomato sauce.
2 Meanwhile, preheat oven to 180°C/160°C fan-forced.
3 Cook washed, drained (not dried) spinach in heated large saucepan, stirring, until wilted. Drain; when cool enough to handle, squeeze out excess moisture.
4 Combine spinach in large bowl with ricotta, eggs, ½ cup of the parmesan cheese and the herbs. Using a large piping bag, fill pasta with spinach mixture.
5 Spread a third of the sauce into shallow 25cm x 35cm ovenproof dish; top with pasta, in single layer, then top with remaining sauce. Cook, covered, in oven, 20 minutes. Uncover, sprinkle pasta with remaining parmesan; cook about 15 minutes or until pasta is tender and cheese is browned lightly.
creamy tomato sauce Heat oil in large saucepan; cook onion, stirring, until softened. Add garlic; cook, stirring, until fragrant. Add undrained tomatoes; bring to the boil. Reduce heat; simmer, uncovered, stirring occasionally, about 20 minutes or until sauce thickens slightly. Cool 10 minutes; blend or process sauce with cream and sugar until smooth.

prep & cook time 1 hour **serves** 6
nutritional count per serving 31g total fat (17.1g saturated fat); 2412kJ (577 cal); 41.8g carbohydrate; 28.7g protein; 8.3g fibre

Osso buco originates from Milan and is traditionally served on risotto alla milanese (saffron risotto) with a good sprinkle of gremolata. Here we've served it on polenta.

osso buco

6 pieces veal osso buco (1.8kg)

½ cup (75g) plain flour

40g butter

2 tablespoons olive oil

3 stalks celery (450g), trimmed, chopped coarsely

6 drained anchovy fillets, chopped coarsely

¾ cup (180ml) dry white wine

2 x 400g cans diced tomatoes

½ cup (125ml) chicken stock

5 cloves garlic, crushed

3 bay leaves

10 fresh thyme sprigs

gremolata

½ cup finely chopped fresh flat-leaf parsley

2 cloves garlic, chopped finely

1 teaspoon finely grated lemon rind

1 Preheat oven to 160°C/140°C fan-forced.

2 Coat veal in flour, shake off any excess. Heat butter and oil in large frying pan; cook veal, in batches, until browned both sides. Transfer veal to large ovenproof dish.

3 Cook celery and anchovy in same pan, stirring, until celery softens. Add wine; bring to the boil. Stir in undrained tomatoes, stock, garlic, bay leaves and thyme; return to the boil.

4 Pour tomato mixture over veal. Cook, covered, in oven about 1½ hours or until veal starts to fall from the bone.

5 Meanwhile, make gremolata.

6 Serve osso buco sprinkled with gremolata.

gremolata Combine ingredients in small bowl.

prep & cook time 2 hours **serves** 6

nutritional count per serving 13.2g total fat (4.8g saturated fat); 1626kJ (389 cal); 14.4g carbohydrate; 46.1g protein; 3.8g fibre

veal saltimbocca

chicken wonton soup

veal saltimbocca

8 veal schnitzels (800g)
8 slices prosciutto (120g)
4 bocconcini cheese (240g), sliced thinly
⅓ cup (100g) drained semi-dried tomatoes
16 fresh sage leaves
40g butter
1 cup (250ml) dry white wine
1 tablespoon lemon juice
2 tablespoons coarsely chopped fresh sage

1 Top each piece of veal with prosciutto, cheese, tomatoes and sage leaves. Fold in half to secure filling; secure with toothpicks or small skewers.
2 Melt half the butter in medium frying pan; cook veal, in batches, until cooked as desired. Cover to keep warm.
3 Add wine to same pan; bring to the boil. Boil, uncovered, until wine reduces by half. Stir in remaining butter, juice and sage.
4 Serve saltimbocca drizzled with sauce.

prep & cook time 35 minutes **serves** 4
nutritional count per serving 24g total fat (13.1g saturated fat); 2312kJ (553 cal); 9g carbohydrate; 63.3g protein; 3.6g fibre

chicken wonton soup

1 tablespoon olive oil
1 medium brown onion (150g), chopped coarsely
1 clove garlic, sliced thinly
2cm piece fresh ginger (10g), sliced thinly
1.5 litres (6 cups) water
2 cups (500ml) chicken stock
1kg chicken bones
1 medium carrot (120g), chopped coarsely
1 stalk celery (150g), trimmed, chopped coarsely
1 tablespoon light soy sauce
4 green onions, sliced thinly
chicken wontons
150g chicken mince
1 fresh small red thai chilli, chopped finely
1 clove garlic, crushed
1cm piece fresh ginger (5g), grated
2 teaspoons light soy sauce
1 green onion, sliced thinly
16 x 8cm round wonton wrappers

1 Heat oil in large saucepan; cook brown onion, garlic and ginger, stirring, until onion softens. Add the water, stock, bones, carrot and celery; bring to the boil. Reduce heat; simmer, covered, 2 hours.
2 Strain broth through muslin-lined sieve or colander into large heatproof bowl; discard solids. Cool; cover, refrigerate overnight.
3 Make chicken wontons.
4 Skim and discard fat from surface of broth. Return broth to large saucepan with sauce; bring to the boil. Add wontons, reduce heat; cook about 5 minutes.
5 Divide wontons among bowls; ladle broth into bowls and sprinkle with green onion.
chicken wontons Combine chicken, chilli, garlic, ginger, sauce and onion in small bowl. Place a rounded teaspoon of chicken mixture in centre of each wonton wrapper; brush around edges with a little water, gather edges around filling, pinch together to seal.

prep & cook time 3 hours (+ refrigeration) **serves** 4
nutritional count per serving 5.5g total fat (2g saturated fat); 560kJ (134 cal); 4.7g carbohydrate; 16.6g protein; 0.2g fibre

sang choy bow

2 teaspoons sesame oil
1 small brown onion (80g), chopped finely
2 cloves garlic, crushed
2cm piece fresh ginger (10g), grated
500g lean pork mince
2 tablespoons water
100g shiitake mushrooms, chopped finely
2 tablespoons light soy sauce
2 tablespoons oyster sauce
1 tablespoon lime juice
2 cups bean sprouts
4 green onions, sliced thinly
¼ cup coarsely chopped fresh coriander
12 large butter lettuce leaves

1 Heat oil in wok; stir-fry brown onion, garlic and ginger until onion softens. Add pork; stir-fry until changed in colour.
2 Add the water, mushrooms, sauces and juice; stir-fry until mushrooms are tender. Remove from heat. Add sprouts, green onion and coriander; toss to combine.
3 Spoon sang choy bow into lettuce leaves to serve.

prep & cook time 30 minutes **serves** 4
nutritional count per serving 11.5g total fat (3.6g saturated fat); 1112kJ (266 cal); 8.9g carbohydrate; 29.3g protein; 4.1g fibre

pho bo

2 litres (8 cups) water
1 litre (4 cups) beef stock
1kg beef chuck steak
2 star anise
8cm piece fresh ginger (40g), grated
⅓ cup (80ml) japanese soy sauce
200g bean thread noodles
1½ cups (120g) bean sprouts
¼ cup loosely packed fresh coriander leaves
⅓ cup loosely packed fresh mint leaves
4 green onions, sliced thinly
2 fresh long red chillies, sliced thinly
¼ cup (60ml) fish sauce
1 lime, cut into wedges

1 Place the water and stock in large saucepan with beef, star anise, ginger and soy sauce; bring to the boil. Reduce heat; simmer, covered, 30 minutes. Uncover; simmer about 30 minutes or until beef is tender.
2 Meanwhile, place noodles in medium heatproof bowl, cover with boiling water; stand until just tender, drain.
3 Combine sprouts, herbs, onion and chilli in medium bowl.
4 Remove beef from pan. Strain broth through muslin-lined sieve or colander into large heatproof bowl; discard solids. When beef is cool enough to handle, remove and discard fat and sinew. Slice beef thinly, return to same cleaned pan with broth; bring to the boil. Stir in fish sauce.
5 Divide noodles among soup bowls; ladle hot beef broth into bowls, sprinkle with sprout mixture and serve with lime wedges.

prep & cook time 1 hour 40 minutes **serves** 6
nutritional count per serving 13.8g total fat (6.2g saturated fat); 1601kJ (383 cal); 21g carbohydrate; 41.3g protein; 4.1g fibre

sang choy bow

pho bo

serving idea Like many Asian noodle soups, this laksa is best served with both a spoon and chopsticks.

This popular spicy noodle soup originates in Malaysia and Singapore and is a favourite all over the world.

prawn laksa

1 tablespoon vegetable oil

2 x 400ml cans coconut milk

1 litre (4 cups) chicken stock

1 tablespoon brown sugar

2 teaspoons fish sauce

6 fresh kaffir lime leaves, shredded finely

1kg uncooked medium king prawns

250g fresh thin egg noodles

125g dried thin rice noodles

1 cup (80g) bean sprouts

¼ cup loosely packed fresh coriander leaves

1 lime, quartered

laksa paste

1 medium brown onion (150g), chopped coarsely

⅓ cup (80ml) coconut milk

2 tablespoons lime juice

1 tablespoon shrimp paste

2cm piece fresh ginger (10g), grated

1 tablespoon macadamias (10g), halved

10cm stick fresh lemon grass (20g), chopped finely

4 cloves garlic, quartered

2 fresh small red thai chillies, chopped coarsely

2 teaspoons ground coriander

2 teaspoons ground cumin

1 teaspoon ground turmeric

1 Make laksa paste.

2 Heat oil in large saucepan; cook laksa paste, stirring, about 5 minutes or until fragrant. Add coconut milk, stock, sugar, sauce and lime leaves; bring to the boil. Reduce heat; simmer, covered, 30 minutes.

3 Meanwhile, shell and devein prawns, leaving tails intact.

4 Place egg noodles in medium heatproof bowl, cover with boiling water; separate with fork, drain. Place rice noodles in same bowl, cover with boiling water; stand until just tender, drain.

5 Add prawns to laksa; cook, uncovered, until just changed in colour.

6 Divide noodles among serving bowls; ladle hot laksa into bowls. Top with sprouts and coriander; serve with lime.

laksa paste Blend or process ingredients until mixture forms a smooth paste.

prep & cook time 1 hour 15 minutes **serves** 4
nutritional count per serving 55.2g total fat (41.6g saturated fat); 3775kJ (903 cal); 56.6g carbohydrate; 42g protein; 7.6g fibre

sesame chicken stir-fry

350g bean thread vermicelli noodles
1 tablespoon peanut oil
2 chicken breast fillets (400g), sliced thinly
1 medium brown onion (150g), sliced thinly
1 clove garlic, crushed
300g broccolini, chopped coarsely
2 tablespoons fish sauce
1 tablespoon hot chilli sauce
2 tablespoons dark soy sauce
1 tablespoon toasted sesame seeds
1 fresh long red chilli, chopped finely
4 green onions, sliced thinly
1 cup (80g) bean sprouts

1 Place vermicelli in medium heatproof bowl, cover with boiling water; stand until just tender, drain.
2 Meanwhile, heat half the oil in wok; stir-fry chicken, in batches, until browned.
3 Heat remaining oil in wok; stir-fry brown onion, garlic and broccolini until onion softens.
4 Return chicken to wok with vermicelli, combined sauces, sesame seeds and half the chilli, half the green onion and half the sprouts; stir-fry just until hot.
5 Serve stir-fry topped with remaining chilli, green onion and sprouts.

prep & cook time 40 minutes **serves** 4
nutritional count per serving 9.3g total fat (1.6g saturated fat); 1325kJ (317 cal); 23.9g carbohydrate; 31.3g protein; 5.6g fibre.

hokkien mee

300g hokkien noodles
1 tablespoon peanut oil
700g beef rump steak, sliced thinly
1 medium brown onion (150g), sliced thinly
3cm piece fresh ginger (15g), grated
2 cloves garlic, crushed
2 fresh small red thai chillies, sliced thinly
1 small red capsicum (150g), sliced thinly
1 small green capsicum (150g), sliced thinly
200g mushrooms, quartered
2 tablespoons hoisin sauce
1 tablespoon dark soy sauce

1 Place noodles in medium heatproof bowl, cover with boiling water; separate with fork, drain.
2 Heat half the oil in wok; stir-fry beef, in batches, until browned.
3 Heat remaining oil in wok; stir-fry onion until soft. Add ginger, garlic and chilli; stir-fry until fragrant. Add capsicums and mushrooms; stir-fry until tender.
4 Return beef to wok with noodles and sauces; stir-fry until hot.

prep & cook time 30 minutes **serves** 4
nutritional count per serving 17.4g total fat (6.2g saturated fat); 1927kJ (461 cal); 27.2g carbohydrate; 46.1g protein; 5.3g fibre

sesame chicken stir-fry

hokkien mee

Nasi goreng literally means 'fried rice', but it's no ordinary fried rice — the addition of egg and prawns, as well as many spices and garnishes, make it something quite special.

nasi goreng

720g cooked medium king prawns

1 tablespoon peanut oil

175g dried chinese sausages, sliced thickly

1 medium brown onion (150g), sliced thinly

1 medium red capsicum (200g), sliced thinly

2 fresh long red chillies, sliced thinly

2 cloves garlic, crushed

2cm piece fresh ginger (10g), grated

1 teaspoon shrimp paste

4 cups (600g) cold cooked white long-grain rice

2 tablespoons kecap manis

1 tablespoon light soy sauce

4 green onions, sliced thinly

1 tablespoon peanut oil, extra

4 eggs

1 Shell and devein prawns.

2 Heat half the oil in wok; stir-fry sausage, in batches, until browned.

3 Heat remaining oil in wok; stir-fry onion, capsicum, chilli, garlic, ginger and paste, until vegetables soften. Add prawns and rice; stir-fry 2 minutes. Return sausage to wok with sauces and half the green onion; stir-fry until combined.

4 Heat extra oil in large frying pan; fry eggs, one side only, until just set. Divide nasi goreng among serving plates, top each with an egg; sprinkle with remaining green onion.

prep & cook time 40 minutes **serves** 4

nutritional count per serving 25.7g total fat (7.4g saturated fat); 2730kJ (653 cal); 48.5g carbohydrate; 54.7g protein; 3.3g fibre

The green colour in the curry paste comes from fresh green chillies, coriander and thai basil.

chicken green curry

1 tablespoon peanut oil
¼ cup (75g) green curry paste
3 long green chillies, chopped finely
1kg chicken thigh fillets, cut into 3cm pieces
2 x 400ml cans coconut milk
2 tablespoons fish sauce
2 tablespoons lime juice
1 tablespoon grated palm sugar
150g pea eggplants
1 large zucchini (150g), sliced thinly
⅓ cup loosely packed fresh thai basil leaves
¼ cup loosely packed fresh coriander leaves
2 green onions, chopped coarsely

1 Heat oil in large saucepan; cook paste and about two-thirds of the chilli, stirring, about 2 minutes or until fragrant. Add chicken; cook, stirring, until browned.
2 Add coconut milk, sauce, juice, sugar and eggplants; simmer, uncovered, about 10 minutes or until eggplants are just tender.
3 Add zucchini, basil and coriander; simmer, uncovered, until zucchini is just tender.
4 Serve curry sprinkled with remaining chilli and green onion.

prep & cook time 35 minutes **serves** 4
nutritional count per serving 67.3g total fat (43.2g saturated fat); 3716kJ (889 cal); 17g carbohydrate; 52.9g protein; 6g fibre

vietnamese prawn rolls

combination fried rice

vietnamese prawn rolls

50g rice vermicelli, soaked, drained
¼ small wombok (175g), shredded finely
½ cup loosely packed fresh mint leaves, torn
2 teaspoons brown sugar
2 tablespoons lime juice
500g cooked medium king prawns
12 x 21cm rice paper rounds
hoisin dipping sauce
½ cup (125ml) hoisin sauce
2 tablespoons rice vinegar

1 Combine chopped vermicelli in medium bowl with wombok, mint, sugar and juice.
2 Shell and devein prawns; chop meat finely.
3 Meanwhile, make hoisin dipping sauce.
4 Dip 1 rice paper round into bowl of warm water until soft; place on board covered with tea towel. Top with a little of the prawn meat and noodle filling. Fold and roll to enclose filling. Repeat with remaining rounds, prawn meat and noodle filling.
5 Serve with hoisin dipping sauce.
hoisin dipping sauce Combine ingredients in bowl.

prep & cook time 20 minutes **makes** 12
nutritional count per roll 0.9g total fat (0.1g saturated fat); 326kJ (78 cal); 10.8g carbohydrate; 5.5g protein; 1.7g fibre

combination fried rice

300g uncooked small king prawns
¼ cup (60ml) peanut oil
400g chicken breast fillets, sliced thinly
3 eggs, beaten lightly
4 rindless bacon rashers (260g), chopped coarsely
1 medium brown onion (150g), chopped finely
1 medium red capsicum (200g), chopped finely
2 cloves garlic, crushed
3cm piece fresh ginger (15g), grated
3 cups cooked white long-grain rice
2 tablespoons light soy sauce
¾ cup (90g) frozen peas
3 green onions, sliced thinly

1 Shell and devein prawns, leaving tails intact.
2 Heat 1 tablespoon of the oil in wok; stir-fry chicken, in batches, until cooked. Stir-fry prawns, in batches, until changed in colour.
3 Heat half the remaining oil in wok; stir-fry egg until just set then remove from wok.
4 Heat remaining oil in wok; stir-fry bacon, brown onion, capsicum, garlic and ginger until bacon is crisp. Return chicken, prawns and egg to wok with remaining ingredients; stir-fry until hot.

prep & cook time 40 minutes **serves** 4
nutritional count per serving 35.1g total fat (9.4g saturated fat); 3001kJ (718 cal); 46.5g carbohydrate; 52.3g protein; 3.9g fibre

Pad thai is a contrast of salty, sweet, sour and spicy flavours. Its garnish of roasted peanuts, crisp beansprouts and fried shallots add a crunch to the soft noodles, and the coriander and lime gives it a bit more bite.

pad thai

540g uncooked medium king prawns
¼ cup (85g) tamarind concentrate
⅓ cup (80ml) sweet chilli sauce
2 tablespoons fish sauce
⅓ cup firmly packed fresh coriander leaves
¼ cup (35g) roasted unsalted peanuts
¼ cup (20g) fried shallots
2 cups (160g) bean sprouts
4 green onions, sliced thinly
375g dried rice stick noodles
1 tablespoon peanut oil
2 cloves garlic, crushed
4cm piece fresh ginger (20g), grated
3 fresh small red thai chillies, chopped finely
250g pork mince
2 eggs, beaten lightly
1 lime, quartered

1 Shell and devein prawns, leaving tails intact.
2 Combine tamarind and sauces in small jug.
3 Combine coriander, nuts, shallots, half the sprouts and half the onion in medium bowl.
4 Place noodles in large heatproof bowl, cover with boiling water; stand until just tender, drain.
5 Meanwhile, heat oil in wok; stir-fry garlic, ginger and chilli until fragrant. Add pork; stir-fry until cooked. Add prawns; stir-fry 1 minute. Add egg; stir-fry until set. Add tamarind mixture, remaining sprouts and onion, and noodles; stir-fry until combined.
6 Divide mixture among serving bowls; sprinkle with coriander mixture, serve with lime wedges.

prep & cook time 35 minutes **serves** 4
nutritional count per serving 17.5g total fat (3.9g saturated fat); 1827kJ (437 cal); 30.3g carbohydrate; 36.8g protein; 4.9g fibre

thai beef salad

seafood and vegetable tempura

thai beef salad

800g piece beef rump steak
1 teaspoon peanut oil
250g bean thread vermicelli
1 telegraph cucumber (400g), halved lengthways,
   sliced thinly
1 large red capsicum (350g), sliced thinly
1 small red onion (100g), sliced thinly
1 fresh long red chilli, sliced thinly
1 cup firmly packed fresh mint leaves
1 cup firmly packed fresh coriander leaves

lime dressing
1 tablespoon coarsely chopped fresh
   coriander root and stem mixture
5 cloves garlic, chopped coarsely
1 teaspoon black peppercorns
½ cup (125ml) lime juice
1 tablespoon fish sauce
1 tablespoon grated palm sugar
2 x 10cm sticks fresh lemon grass (40g),
   chopped coarsely

1 Brush beef, both sides, with oil; cook on heated
grill plate (or grill or barbecue) until cooked as desired.
Cover beef; stand 5 minutes.
2 Place vermicelli in large heatproof bowl, cover with
boiling water; stand until tender, drain. Cut vermicelli
into random lengths into same bowl.
3 Meanwhile, make lime dressing.
4 Slice beef thinly; combine in large bowl with half the
dressing and remaining ingredients. Drizzle remaining
dressing over vermicelli. Divide vermicelli among
shallow serving bowls; top with salad.
lime dressing Blend ingredients until chopped finely.

prep & cook time 30 minutes **serves** 6
nutritional count per serving 10.6g total fat (4.2g
saturated fat); 1597kJ (382 cal); 34g carbohydrate;
35.3g protein; 3.4g fibre

seafood and vegetable tempura

840g uncooked medium king prawns
1 medium brown onion (150g)
peanut oil, for deep-frying
450g ocean trout fillets, cut into 3cm pieces
1 large red capsicum (350g), cut into 3cm pieces
1 small kumara (250g), sliced thinly
8 baby zucchini with flowers attached (160g),
   stamens removed
1 cup (150g) plain flour
1 lemon, cut into wedges

tempura batter
1 egg white
2 cups (500ml) cold soda water
1¼ cups (185g) plain flour
1¼ cups (185g) cornflour

lemon dipping sauce
½ cup (125ml) rice vinegar
¼ cup (55g) caster sugar
1 teaspoon light soy sauce
¼ teaspoon finely grated lemon rind
1 green onion (green part only), sliced thinly

1 Shell and devein prawns, leaving tails intact. Make
three small cuts on the underside of each prawn,
halfway through flesh, to prevent curling when cooked.
2 Halve onion from root end. Push 4 toothpicks, at
regular intervals, through each onion half to hold rings
together; cut in between toothpicks.
3 Make tempura batter. Make lemon dipping sauce.
4 Heat oil in wok. Dust prawns, onion, fish, capsicum,
kumara and zucchini in flour; shake off excess. Dip,
piece by piece, in batter; deep-fry until crisp. Drain on
absorbent paper. Serve tempura with dipping sauce.
tempura batter Whisk egg white in large bowl until
soft peaks form; add soda water, whisk to combine.
Add sifted flours, whisk to combine (should be lumpy).
lemon dipping sauce Heat vinegar, sugar and sauce
in small saucepan, stirring, until sugar dissolves. Remove
from heat, add rind; stand 10 minutes. Strain sauce
into serving dish; discard rind. Sprinkle with onion.

prep & cook time 1 hour **serves** 6
nutritional count per serving 16.6g total fat (3.1g
saturated fat); 1831kJ (438 cal); 40.2g carbohydrate;
16.6g protein; 3.5g fibre

An Indian biryani differs from most rice dishes in that the rice and other ingredients are cooked separately. They're then layered, alternately and topped with fruit and nuts.

lamb biryani

1kg lamb shoulder, cut into 3cm pieces
3cm piece fresh ginger (15g), grated
2 cloves garlic, crushed
2 fresh small red thai chillies, chopped finely
2 teaspoons garam masala
1 tablespoon finely chopped fresh coriander
¼ teaspoon ground turmeric
½ cup (140g) yogurt
2 tablespoons ghee
½ cup (40g) flaked almonds
¼ cup (40g) sultanas
2 medium brown onions (300g), sliced thickly
½ cup (125ml) water
pinch saffron threads
1 tablespoon hot milk
1½ cups (300g) basmati rice
¼ cup firmly packed fresh coriander leaves

1 Combine lamb, ginger, garlic, chilli, garam masala, chopped coriander, turmeric and yogurt in medium bowl, cover; refrigerate overnight.
2 Heat half the ghee in large saucepan; cook nuts and sultanas, stirring, until nuts brown lightly. Remove from pan.
3 Heat remaining ghee in same pan; cook onion, covered, 5 minutes. Uncover; cook, stirring occasionally, about 5 minutes or until browned lightly. Reserve half of the onion.

4 Add lamb mixture to pan; cook, stirring, until browned. Add the water; bring to the boil. Reduce heat; simmer, covered, 1 hour. Uncover; simmer about 30 minutes or until lamb is tender and sauce is thickened.
5 Meanwhile, combine saffron and milk in small bowl; stand 15 minutes.
6 Cook rice in medium saucepan of boiling water, uncovered, 5 minutes; drain.
7 Preheat oven to 180°C/160°C fan-forced.
8 Spread half the lamb mixture into oiled deep 2-litre (8-cup) ovenproof dish. Layer with half the rice; top with remaining lamb mixture then remaining rice. Drizzle milk mixture over rice; cover tightly with greased foil and lid. Bake about 30 minutes or until rice is tender.
9 Serve biryani topped with reserved onion, nut and sultana mixture and coriander leaves.

prep & cook time 2 hours 35 minutes (+ refrigeration)
serves 4
nutritional count per serving 38.6g total fat (17.4g saturated fat); 3703kJ (886 cal); 73.8g carbohydrate; 58.7g protein; 3.4g fibre

caesar salad

1 small french bread stick (150g)

¼ cup (60ml) olive oil

1 clove garlic, crushed

4 rindless bacon rashers (260g)

1 large cos lettuce, trimmed, chopped coarsely

3 green onions, sliced thinly

1 cup (80g) flaked parmesan cheese

4 hard-boiled eggs, quartered

caesar dressing

2 egg yolks

1 clove garlic, quartered

1 anchovy fillet

1 tablespoon lemon juice

1 tablespoon worcestershire sauce

2 teaspoons dijon mustard

½ cup (125ml) olive oil

1 Preheat oven to 180°C/160°C fan-forced.

2 Make caesar dressing.

3 Halve bread lengthways; slice halves thinly. Combine oil and garlic in large bowl with bread; place bread on oven tray. Toast bread in oven until croûtons are brown.

4 Meanwhile, cook bacon in heated large frying pan until crisp; drain on absorbent paper. Chop coarsely.

5 Combine lettuce, half the croûtons, half the bacon, half the onion, half the cheese and half the dressing in large bowl.

6 Divide salad among serving bowls; top with egg and remaining ingredients. Drizzle with remaining dressing.

caesar dressing Blend or process egg yolks, garlic, anchovy, juice, sauce and mustard until smooth. With motor operating, gradually add oil in a thin, steady stream; process until mixture thickens. Stir in about a tablespoon of warm water to make dressing pourable.

prep & cook time 30 minutes **serves** 4
nutritional count per serving 62.4g total fat (14g saturated fat); 3394kJ (812 cal); 25.4g carbohydrate; 36.2g protein; 5.7g fibre

waldorf salad

¾ cup (225g) mayonnaise
¼ cup (60ml) lemon juice
8 stalks celery (750g), trimmed, sliced thickly
2 medium red apples (300g), sliced thinly
1 small red onion (100g), sliced thinly
1 cup (100g) roasted walnuts
1 cup loosely packed fresh flat-leaf parsley leaves

1 Combine mayonnaise and juice in large bowl;
mix in remaining ingredients.

prep time 20 minutes **serves** 4
nutritional count per serving 35.7g total fat (3.1g
saturated fat); 1852kJ (443 cal); 22.4g carbohydrate;
5.8g protein; 6.3g fibre

note This classic dish literally means 'chilli with meat'. Feel free to pep it up with more chilli or tone it down by reducing the cayenne and jalapeño chillies. It is also excellent served on a jacket potato, on couscous or with a good chunk of crusty bread.

chilli con carne

1 cup (200g) dried kidney beans
1.5kg beef chuck steak
2 litres (8 cups) water
1 tablespoon olive oil
2 medium brown onions (300g), chopped coarsely
2 cloves garlic, crushed
2 teaspoons ground cumin
2 teaspoons ground coriander
½ teaspoon cayenne pepper
2 teaspoons sweet paprika
2 x 400g cans crushed tomatoes
1 tablespoon tomato paste
4 green onions, chopped coarsely
2 tablespoons coarsely chopped fresh coriander
⅓ cup (65g) finely chopped bottled jalapeño chillies

1 Place beans in medium bowl, cover with water; stand overnight, drain.
2 Combine beef with the water in large saucepan; bring to the boil. Reduce heat, simmer, covered, 1½ hours.
3 Drain beef in large muslin-lined strainer over bowl; reserve 3½ cups (875ml) of the cooking liquid. Using two forks, shred beef.
4 Heat oil in same pan; cook brown onion and garlic, stirring, until onion is soft. Add spices; cook, stirring, until fragrant. Add beans, undrained tomatoes, paste and 2 cups of the reserved liquid; bring to the boil. Reduce heat, simmer, covered, 1 hour.
5 Add beef and remaining reserved liquid to pan; simmer, covered, about 30 minutes or until beans are tender. Remove from heat; stir in green onions, coriander and chilli. Serve chilli con carne with steamed rice, if you like.

prep & cook time 3 hours 45 minutes (+ standing)
serves 8
nutritional count per serving 11.4g total fat (3.9g saturated fat); 1496kJ (358 cal); 14.7g carbohydrate; 45.1g protein; 7.6g fibre

tip Mexe-beans are kidney beans with some spices already added. Look for them in the international section of your supermarket with other Mexican-style ingredients, or try refried beans instead.

How fiery a chilli is can be judged by how wide the 'shoulders' on it are. The wider the area that joins the chilli to the stem, the milder it is.

bean and coriander quesadillas

2 x 425g cans mexe-beans, drained, mashed
8 large (20cm) flour tortillas (300g)
2 large tomatoes (440g), seeded, chopped finely
2 fresh long red chillies, chopped finely
½ cup finely chopped fresh coriander
1¼ cups (150g) coarsely grated cheddar cheese

1 Preheat sandwich press.
2 Spread beans over four tortillas. Sprinkle with tomato, chilli, coriander and cheese. Top with remaining tortillas.
3 Cook quesadillas in sandwich press until browned both sides and heated through; cut into wedges. Serve accompanied with sour cream, if you like.

prep & cook time 15 minutes **serves** 4
nutritional count per serving 15g total fat (8.4g saturated fat); 1898kJ (454 cal); 49.5g carbohydrate; 23.3g protein; 13.4g fibre

tabbouleh

¼ cup (40g) burghul
3 medium tomatoes (450g)
3 cups coarsely chopped fresh flat-leaf parsley
3 green onions, chopped finely
½ cup coarsely chopped fresh mint
1 clove garlic, crushed
¼ cup (60ml) lemon juice
¼ cup (60ml) olive oil

1 Place burghul in shallow medium bowl. Halve tomatoes, scoop pulp from tomato over burghul. Chop tomato flesh finely; spread over burghul. Cover; refrigerate 1 hour.
2 Combine burghul mixture in large bowl with remaining ingredients.

prep time 30 minutes (+ refrigeration) **serves** 4
nutritional count per serving 14.2g total fat (2g saturated fat); 790kJ (189 cal); 9.4g carbohydrate; 3.6g protein; 5.9g fibre

greek salad with grilled lamb

¼ cup (70g) yogurt
⅓ cup (80ml) lemon juice
¼ cup (60ml) olive oil
2 cloves garlic, crushed
600g lamb fillets
3 medium tomatoes (450g), cut into thin wedges
1 small red onion (100g), sliced thinly
2 medium red capsicums (400g), chopped coarsely
2 lebanese cucumbers (260g), chopped coarsely
½ cup (75g) seeded kalamata olives
400g can chickpeas, rinsed, drained
1 cup firmly packed fresh flat-leaf parsley leaves
100g fetta cheese, crumbled

1 Combine yogurt, 1 tablespoon of the juice, 1 tablespoon of the oil and half the garlic in medium bowl, add lamb; mix well. Cover; refrigerate until needed.
2 Meanwhile, place remaining juice, oil and garlic in screw-top jar; shake well.
3 Drain lamb; discard marinade. Cook lamb on heated oiled grill plate (or grill or barbecue) until cooked as desired. Cover; stand 5 minutes then slice thickly.
4 Combine remaining ingredients in large bowl with lemon dressing. Serve salad topped with lamb.

prep & cook time 25 minutes (+ refrigeration)
serves 6
nutritional count per serving 27.5g total fat (8.8g saturated fat); 2215kJ (530 cal); 23.1g carbohydrate; 44g protein; 7.8g fibre

tabbouleh

greek salad with grilled lamb

felafel

2 x 400g cans chickpeas, rinsed, drained

1 clove garlic, chopped coarsely

1 small brown onion (80g), chopped coarsely

1 tablespoon olive oil

1 egg

2 teaspoons ground cumin

½ teaspoon bicarbonate of soda

2 tablespoons plain flour

vegetable oil, for shallow-frying

4 large pitta breads (320g), warmed

yogurt sauce

1 cup (280g) yogurt

½ clove garlic, crushed

1 tablespoon lemon juice

½ teaspoon cayenne pepper

1 Process chickpeas, garlic, onion and olive oil until ingredients begin to combine; transfer mixture to medium bowl. Stir in egg, cumin, soda and flour until combined. Shape mixture into 12 patties.

2 Heat vegetable oil in large frying pan; cook felafel, in batches, until browned. Drain on absorbent paper.

3 Meanwhile, make yogurt sauce.

4 Serve felafel on pitta, topped with yogurt sauce. You can serve the felafel with a rocket and tomato salad.

yogurt sauce Combine ingredients in small bowl.

prep & cook time 30 minutes **serves** 4

nutritional count per serving 21.8g total fat (4.3g saturated fat); 2416kJ (575 cal); 68.3g carbohydrate; 21.7g protein; 9.1g fibre

If you like hummus then you'll love this Middle-Eastern vegetarian specialty, which is also made from chickpeas.

coq au vin

boeuf bourguignon

coq au vin

800g spring onions
¼ cup (60ml) olive oil
6 rindless bacon rashers (390g), chopped coarsely
300g button mushrooms
2 cloves garlic, crushed
8 chicken thigh fillets (880g)
¼ cup (35g) plain flour
2 cups (500ml) dry red wine
1½ cups (375ml) chicken stock
2 tablespoons tomato paste
3 bay leaves
4 sprigs fresh thyme
2 sprigs fresh rosemary

1 Trim green ends from onions, leaving about 4cm of stem attached; trim roots. Heat 1 tablespoon of the oil in large frying pan; cook onions, stirring, until browned all over; remove from pan.
2 Add bacon, mushrooms and garlic to pan; cook, stirring, until bacon is crisp, remove from pan.
3 Coat chicken in flour; shake off excess. Heat remaining oil in same pan. Cook chicken, in batches, until browned all over; drain on absorbent paper.
4 Return chicken to pan with wine, stock, paste, bay leaves, herbs, onions and bacon mixture. Bring to the boil; reduce heat, simmer, uncovered, about 35 minutes or until chicken is tender and sauce has thickened slightly.

prep & cook time 1 hour 30 minutes **serves** 4
nutritional count per serving 43.6g total fat (11.8g saturated fat); 3428kJ (820 cal); 16.3g carbohydrate; 67.8g protein; 6.4g fibre

boeuf bourguignon

300g baby brown onions
2 tablespoons olive oil
2kg gravy beef, trimmed, chopped coarsely
30g butter
4 rindless bacon rashers (260g), chopped coarsely
400g button mushrooms, halved
2 cloves garlic, crushed
¼ cup (35g) plain flour
1¼ cups (310ml) beef stock
2½ cups (625ml) dry red wine
2 bay leaves
2 sprigs fresh thyme
½ cup coarsely chopped fresh flat-leaf parsley

1 Peel onions, leaving root end intact so onion remains whole during cooking.
2 Heat oil in large flameproof dish; cook beef, in batches, until browned.
3 Add butter to dish; cook onions, bacon, mushrooms and garlic, stirring, until onions are browned lightly.
4 Sprinkle flour over onion mixture; cook, stirring, until flour mixture thickens and bubbles. Gradually add stock and wine; stir over heat until mixture boils and thickens. Return beef and any juices to dish, add bay leaves and thyme; bring to the boil. Reduce heat; simmer, covered, about 2 hours or until beef is tender, stirring every 30 minutes.
5 Remove pan from heat; discard bay leaves. Stir in parsley.

prep & cook time 2 hours 45 minutes **serves** 6
nutritional count per serving 31.4g total fat (12.1g saturated fat); 2658kJ (636 cal); 6.6g carbohydrate; 80.3g protein; 2.8g fibre

pecan pie

1 cup (120g) pecans, chopped coarsely
2 tablespoons cornflour
1 cup (220g) firmly packed brown sugar
60g butter, melted
2 tablespoons cream
1 teaspoon vanilla extract
3 eggs
⅓ cup (40g) pecans, extra
2 tablespoons apricot jam, warmed, sieved
pastry
1¼ cups (185g) plain flour
⅓ cup (55g) icing sugar
125g cold butter, chopped
1 egg yolk
1 teaspoon water

1 Make pastry.
2 Grease 24cm-round loose-based flan tin. Roll pastry between sheets of baking paper until large enough to line tin. Ease pastry into tin, press into base and side; trim edge. Cover; refrigerate 30 minutes.
3 Preheat oven to 180°C/160°C fan-forced.
4 Place tin on oven tray. Line pastry case with baking paper, fill with dried beans or rice. Bake 10 minutes; remove paper and beans carefully from pie shell. Bake about 5 minutes; cool.
5 Reduce oven temperature to 160°C/140°C fan-forced.
6 Combine chopped nuts and cornflour in medium bowl. Add sugar, butter, cream, extract and eggs; stir until combined. Pour mixture into shell, sprinkle with extra nuts.
7 Bake pie about 45 minutes. Cool; brush with jam.
pastry Process flour, icing sugar and butter until crumbly. Add egg yolk and the water; process until ingredients just come together. Knead dough on floured surface until smooth. Cover; refrigerate 30 minutes.

prep & cook time 1 hour 25 minutes (+ refrigeration)
serves 10
nutritional count per serving 30.8g total fat (12.5g saturated fat); 2023kJ (484 cal); 46.5g carbohydrate; 6.3g protein; 2.1g fibre

This sticky sweet-textured pie is a specialty of America's South.

This upside-down tart is a French classic. The traditional recipe uses apples but you could easily replace them with pears or even bananas.

tarte tatin

2 tablespoons orange juice
⅔ cup (150g) caster sugar
70g butter
3 medium apples (450g), peeled
pastry
1 cup (150g) plain flour
80g cold butter, chopped
1 tablespoon caster sugar
1 tablespoon cold water, approximately

1 Combine juice, sugar and butter in 23cm heavy-based ovenproof frying pan; stir over heat, without boiling, until sugar is dissolved. Simmer, stirring occasionally, until mixture becomes a thick, light golden caramel. Remove from heat.

2 Halve apples; cut each half into 3 wedges, remove cores. Pack apple wedges tightly into pan over caramel, return to heat; simmer, uncovered, about 15 minutes or until most of the liquid is evaporated and caramel is dark golden brown. Remove from heat; cool 1 hour.

3 Preheat oven to 180°C/160°C fan-forced.

4 Roll pastry into circle a little larger than the pan. Lift pastry, without stretching it, on top of apples, tuck inside edge of pan. Bake in oven about 25 minutes or until pastry is golden brown and crisp. Remove tart from oven, stand 5 minutes. Carefully invert tart onto plate. Serve warm with cream, if desired.

pastry Blend or process flour, butter and sugar until mixture resembles fine breadcrumbs. Add just enough water to make ingredients just cling together. Knead dough on floured surface until smooth. Cover; refrigerate 1 hour.

prep & cook time 1 hour 15 minutes (+ refrigeration & cooling) **serves** 6
nutritional count per serving 20.9g total fat (13.6g saturated fat); 1705kJ (408 cal); 53.1g carbohydrate; 3.1g protein; 2g fibre

panna cotta with fresh figs

new york cheesecake

panna cotta with fresh figs

1 teaspoon whole cloves
300ml thickened cream
⅔ cup (160ml) milk
2 teaspoons gelatine
2 tablespoons caster sugar
½ teaspoon vanilla extract
4 medium fresh figs (240g)
2 tablespoons honey

1 Grease four ½-cup (125ml) moulds.
2 Place cloves, cream and milk in small saucepan; stand 10 minutes. Sprinkle gelatine and sugar over cream mixture; stir over low heat, without boiling, until gelatine and sugar dissolve. Stir in extract. Strain into medium jug; cool to room temperature.
3 Divide mixture among prepared moulds, cover; refrigerate 3 hours or until set.
4 Quarter figs; stir honey in small saucepan until warm.
5 Turn panna cotta onto serving plates; serve with figs drizzled with honey.

prep & cook time 30 minutes
(+ cooling & refrigeration) **serves** 4
nutritional count per serving 29.3g total fat (19.2g saturated fat); 1639kJ (392 cal); 29.1g carbohydrate; 5.1g protein; 1.3g fibre

new york cheesecake

250g plain sweet biscuits
125g butter, melted
750g cream cheese, softened
2 teaspoons finely grated orange rind
1 teaspoon finely grated lemon rind
1 cup (220g) caster sugar
3 eggs
¾ cup (180g) sour cream
¼ cup (60ml) lemon juice
sour cream topping
1 cup (240g) sour cream
2 tablespoons caster sugar
2 teaspoons lemon juice

1 Process biscuits until fine. Add butter, process until combined. Press mixture over base and side of 24cm springform tin. Place tin on oven tray; refrigerate 30 minutes.
2 Preheat oven to 180°C/160°C fan forced.
3 Beat cream cheese, rinds and sugar in medium bowl with electric mixer until smooth. Beat in eggs, one at a time, then sour cream and juice.
4 Pour filling into tin; bake 1¼ hours. Remove from oven; cool 15 minutes.
5 Make sour cream topping; spread over cheesecake. Bake cheesecake 20 minutes; cool in oven with door ajar. Refrigerate cheesecake 3 hours or overnight.
sour cream topping Combine ingredients in small bowl.

prep & cook time 2 hours 30 minutes
(+ refrigeration & cooling) **serves** 12
nutritional count per serving 47.8g total fat (30.1g saturated fat); 2587kJ (619 cal); 39g carbohydrate; 9.2g protein; 0.4g fibre

crème caramel

¾ cup (165g) caster sugar
½ cup (125ml) water
6 eggs
1 teaspoon vanilla extract
⅓ cup (75g) caster sugar, extra
300ml cream
1¾ cups (430ml) milk

1 Preheat oven to 160°C/140°C fan-forced.
2 Combine sugar and the water in medium heavy-based frying pan; stir over heat, without boiling, until sugar dissolves. Bring to the boil; boil, uncovered, without stirring, until mixture is a deep caramel colour. Remove from heat; allow bubbles to subside. Pour toffee into deep 20cm-round cake pan.
3 Whisk eggs, extract and extra sugar in large bowl.
4 Combine cream and milk in medium saucepan; bring to the boil. Whisking constantly, pour hot milk mixture into egg mixture. Strain mixture into cake pan.
5 Place pan in baking dish; add enough boiling water to come half way up side of pan. Bake about 40 minutes or until set. Remove custard from baking dish, cover; refrigerate overnight.
6 Gently ease crème caramel from side of pan; invert onto deep-sided serving plate.

prep & cook time 1 hour (+ refrigeration) **serves** 8
nutritional count per serving 22.3g total fat (13.3g saturated fat); 1526kJ (365 cal); 33.8g carbohydrate; 7.5g protein; 0g fibre

Plain old custard gets all grown-up in this classic French dessert. The rich custard is topped with a layer of soft caramel.

kids in the kitchen

Your kids will become young chefs with these easy-to-make recipes.

turkey on toasted turkish

1 small turkish bread roll (160g)
1 tablespoon cranberry sauce
30g shaved turkey
10g shaved reduced-fat jarlsberg cheese
10g baby spinach leaves

1 Split bread in half. Spread sauce onto cut sides then sandwich turkey, cheese and spinach between pieces.
2 Toast in sandwich press until golden brown.

prep & cook time 10 minutes **makes** 1
nutritional count per serving 9.5g total fat (2.8g saturated fat); 2207kJ (528 cal); 80.9g carbohydrate; 26.2g protein; 4.4g fibre

Turkey is tasty and full of lean protein, making it a healthy option for growing little ones.

chicken noodle soup

3 cups (750ml) chicken stock
1 litre (4 cups) water
3 chicken breast fillets (600g), cut into 1cm strips
310g can corn kernels, drained
2 teaspoons soy sauce
2 x 85g packets chicken-flavoured 2-minute noodles
1 tablespoon chopped fresh chives

1 Combine stock and the water in large saucepan, bring to the boil; add chicken, corn, sauce, the chicken-flavour sachet from the noodles and the noodles to the pan.

2 Bring soup back to the boil, turn the heat to medium and cook about 5 minutes or until chicken is cooked through.

3 Serve soup sprinkled with chives.

prep & cook time 20 minutes **serves** 4
nutritional count per serving 10.3g total fat (3.1g saturated fat); 1852kJ (443 cal); 43.5g carbohydrate; 41.8g protein; 3.2g fibre

hoisin and barbecued chicken rolls

½ lebanese cucumber (65g)

½ medium carrot (60g)

12 x 17cm square rice paper sheets

2 tablespoons hoisin sauce

1¼ cups (200g) finely shredded barbecued
chicken meat

50g snow peas, trimmed, sliced thinly

1 Using vegetable peeler, slice cucumber and carrot into ribbons.

2 To assemble rolls, place one sheet of rice paper in medium bowl of warm water until just softened; lift sheet carefully from water, placing it on a tea-towel-covered board with a corner point facing towards you. Place a little of the sauce and chicken vertically along centre of sheet; top with a little of the cucumber, carrot and snow peas. Fold corner point facing you up over filling; roll rice paper sheet side to side to enclose filling. Repeat with remaining rice paper sheets and filling ingredients.

prep & cook time 20 minutes **makes** 12
nutritional count per serving 1.1g total fat (0.3g saturated fat); 184kJ (44 cal); 5g carbohydrate; 3.1g protein; 0.8g fibre

Bring a rainbow of colour to the kitchen and inspire your budding young chefs.

The kids will love creating their own Mexican fiesta with these taco treats.

beef tacos

2 teaspoons olive oil
500g beef mince
1 clove garlic, crushed
1½ cups (375ml) water
2 tablespoons tomato paste
35g packet taco seasoning
12 taco shells
8 lettuce leaves, shredded finely
2 medium tomatoes (300g), chopped finely
1 cup (120g) grated cheddar cheese
½ cup bottled mild chunky salsa

1 Preheat oven to 180°C/160°C fan-forced.
2 Heat oil in large frying pan; cook beef and garlic, stirring, about 5 minutes or until beef is browned all over. Add the water, paste and taco seasoning; stir until well combined, bring to the boil. Reduce heat; simmer, uncovered, about 10 minutes or until most of the liquid is evaporated.
3 Meanwhile, place taco shells, upside down, on oven tray. Heat shells in oven, uncovered, about 5 minutes or until heated through. Using oven mitts, remove tray from oven, place on a wooden board.
4 Divide beef mixture among taco shells; top with lettuce, tomato and cheese, drizzle with salsa

prep & cook time 40 minutes **makes** 12
nutritional count per taco 10.9g total fat (3.9g saturated fat); 874kJ (209 cal); 12.7g carbohydrate; 13.6g protein; 2.9g fibre

meat pie scrolls

1 tablespoon olive oil
1 small brown onion (80g), chopped finely
1 clove garlic, crushed
3 rindless bacon rashers (195g), chopped finely
300g beef mince
400g can diced tomatoes
1 tablespoon tomato paste
2 tablespoons worcestershire sauce
½ cup (125ml) beef stock
¼ cup coarsely chopped fresh flat-leaf parsley
2 cups (300g) self-raising flour
1 tablespoon caster sugar
50g butter, chopped coarsely
¾ cup (180ml) milk
1 cup (110g) pizza cheese

1 Heat oil in large frying pan; cook onion, garlic and bacon, stirring, until onion softens. Add beef; cook, stirring, until beef changes colour. Add undrained tomatoes, paste, sauce and stock; bring to the boil. Reduce heat; simmer, uncovered, about 20 minutes or until sauce thickens. Remove from heat; stir in parsley. Cool.
2 Preheat oven to 180°C/160°C fan-forced. Grease two six-hole (¾-cup/180ml) texas muffin pans.
3 Sift flour and sugar into medium bowl; rub in butter with fingers. Stir in milk; mix to a soft, sticky dough. Knead dough on floured surface; roll dough out to 30cm x 40cm rectangle.
4 Spread beef mixture over dough; sprinkle with cheese. Roll dough tightly from one long side; trim ends. Cut roll into 12 slices; place one slice in each pan hole.
5 Bake scrolls about 25 minutes. Serve top-side up.

prep & cook time 1 hour 15 minutes **makes** 12
nutritional count per scroll 11g total fat (5.4g saturated fat); 1024kJ (245 cal); 22.3g carbohydrate; 13.3g protein; 1.6g fibre

chicken sausage rolls

1kg chicken mince
1 medium brown onion (150g), chopped finely
½ cup (35g) stale breadcrumbs
1 egg
¼ cup finely chopped fresh basil
½ cup (75g) drained semi-dried tomatoes in oil, chopped finely
2 tablespoons tomato paste
5 sheets puff pastry
1 egg, extra

1 Preheat oven to 220°C/200°C fan-forced. Line oven trays with baking paper.
2 Combine mince, onion, breadcrumbs, egg, basil, semi-dried tomato and paste in large bowl.
3 Cut pastry sheets in half lengthways. Place equal amounts of chicken filling mixture lengthways along centre of each pastry piece; roll pastry to enclose filling. Cut each roll into six pieces; place, seam-side down, on trays. Brush with extra egg.
4 Bake rolls about 30 minutes. Serve hot, with tomato sauce.

prep & cook time 45 minutes **makes** 60
nutritional count per serving 4.8g total fat (2.2g saturated fat); 359kJ (86 cal); 6g carbohydrate; 4.5g protein; 0.5g fibre

meat pie scrolls

chicken sausage rolls

serving idea This is a clever way to make sure your kids get their vegies. You could also use other vegetables in here too – try grated carrot, zucchini or capsicum.

cheesy-vegie pasta bake

375g penne
300g broccoli, cut into florets
500g cauliflower, cut into florets
2 teaspoons vegetable oil
1 large brown onion (200g), chopped finely
1 teaspoon mustard powder
1 teaspoon sweet paprika
¼ cup (35g) plain flour
1½ cups (375ml) low-fat milk
420g can tomato soup
400g can diced tomatoes
1½ cups (180g) coarsely grated reduced-fat
  cheddar cheese
2 tablespoons finely chopped fresh flat-leaf parsley

1 Cook pasta in large saucepan of boiling water until just tender; drain. Cover to keep warm.
2 Meanwhile, boil, steam or microwave broccoli and cauliflower until tender; drain. Cover to keep warm.
3 Heat oil in same large saucepan; cook onion, stirring, until softened. Add mustard, paprika and flour; cook, stirring, over low heat, 2 minutes. Gradually stir in milk and soup; stir over heat until mixture boils and thickens. Add undrained tomatoes; cook, stirring, until mixture is hot.
4 Preheat grill.
5 Stir pasta, broccoli, cauliflower and 1 cup of the cheese into tomato mixture. Divide pasta mixture among six 1-cup (250ml) flameproof dishes, sprinkle with remaining cheese; grill until cheese melts and is browned lightly. Sprinkle pasta bake with parsley just before serving.

prep & cook time 35 minutes **serves** 6
nutritional count per serving 10.9g total fat (5.4g saturated fat); 1952kJ (467 cal); 62.3g carbohydrate; 25.5g protein; 7.4g fibre

honey, soy and sesame chicken wings

1kg chicken wings
¼ cup (60ml) japanese soy sauce
2 tablespoons honey
1 clove garlic, crushed
2cm piece fresh ginger (10g), grated
2 teaspoons sesame seeds
1 teaspoon sesame oil
2 green onions, sliced thinly

1 Cut chicken wings into three pieces at joints; discard tips. Combine sauce, honey, garlic, ginger, seeds and oil in large bowl with chicken. Cover; refrigerate 3 hours or overnight.
2 Preheat oven to 220°C/200°C fan-forced.
3 Place chicken, in single layer, on oiled wire rack over shallow large baking dish; brush remaining marinade over chicken. Roast about 30 minutes or until chicken is cooked.
4 Serve chicken wings sprinkled with onion.

prep & cook time 45 minutes (+ refrigeration)
serves 4
nutritional count per serving 10.3g total fat (3g saturated fat); 1233kJ (295 cal); 12.6g carbohydrate; 37.4g protein; 0.4g fibre

oven-baked fish and chips

1kg potatoes, peeled
cooking-oil spray
8 firm white fish fillets (750g)
¼ cup (35g) plain flour
3 egg whites, beaten lightly
1 tablespoon milk
2¼ cups (155g) stale breadcrumbs
¾ cup (120g) cornflake crumbs

1 Preheat oven to 200°C/180°C fan-forced.
2 Cut potatoes into 1.5cm slices; cut slices into 1cm chips. Place chips, in single layer, on greased oven tray; spray lightly with cooking-oil spray. Bake, uncovered, about 35 minutes or until brown.
3 Meanwhile, working with one fish fillet at a time, toss fish in flour, shake off excess; dip fish into combined egg white and milk, then combined crumbs. Place on oiled oven tray; repeat with remaining fish.
4 Bake fish, uncovered, for the final 20 minutes of chip baking time.
5 Serve fish and chips with tartare sauce.

prep & cook time 1 hour 10 minutes **serves** 4
nutritional count per serving 6.8g total fat (1.8g saturated fat); 2696kJ (645 cal); 86.3g carbohydrate; 54.6g protein; 6.3g fibre

honey, soy and sesame chicken wings

oven-baked fish and chips

chocolate sundaes

2 litres vanilla ice-cream
½ cup (70g) crushed nuts
12 ice-cream wafers
100g marshmallows
hot chocolate sauce
200g dark eating chocolate, chopped coarsely
½ cup (125ml) thickened cream

1 Make hot chocolate sauce.
2 Place a little of the hot chocolate sauce in the bottom of six ¾-cup (180ml) serving glasses; top with ice-cream, more chocolate sauce, nuts, wafers and marshmallows.
hot chocolate sauce Stir chocolate and cream in small saucepan over low heat until chocolate is melted and sauce is smooth; do not overheat.

prep & cook time 10 minutes **serves** 6
nutritional count per serving 41.4g total fat (23.5g saturated fat); 2863kJ (685 cal); 72.1g carbohydrate; 11.8g protein; 1.4g fibre

tropical fruit skewers with orange glaze

strawberry jelly cakes

tropical fruit skewers with orange glaze

1 teaspoon finely grated orange rind
¼ cup (60ml) orange juice
2 tablespoons brown sugar
2 medium bananas (400g)
250g strawberries
600g piece pineapple
1 star fruit (160g)
200g low-fat vanilla yogurt

1 Stir rind, juice and sugar in small saucepan over low heat until sugar dissolves. Cool.
2 Preheat grill.
3 Peel bananas; slice thickly crossways. Hull and halve strawberries. Peel pineapple; cut into chunks. Slice star fruit thickly.
4 Thread fruits, alternately, onto skewers. Place skewers on oven tray lined with baking paper; pour orange mixture over skewers.
5 Grill skewers, turning occasionally, 10 minutes or until browned lightly. Serve with yogurt.

prep & cook time 35 minutes **serves** 4
nutritional count per serving 0.5g total fat (0.1g saturated fat); 974kJ (233 cal); 45.9g carbohydrate; 7.1g protein; 7.3g fibre

strawberry jelly cakes

125g butter, softened
½ teaspoon vanilla extract
½ cup (110g) caster sugar
2 eggs
1½ cups (225g) self-raising flour
⅓ cup (80ml) low-fat milk
1¾ cups (430ml) boiling water
85g packet strawberry jelly crystals
2 tablespoons passionfruit pulp
3 cups (225g) shredded coconut

1 Preheat oven to 180°C/160°C fan-forced. Grease deep 23cm-square cake pan; line base with baking paper.
2 Beat butter, extract and sugar in small bowl with electric mixer until light and fluffy. Add eggs, one at a time; beat until just combined. Stir in flour and milk until smooth; spread mixture into pan.
3 Bake about 25 minutes. Stand 5 minutes; turn, top-side up, onto wire rack to cool.
4 Meanwhile, stir the water and jelly in medium heatproof jug until crystals dissolve; stir pulp into jelly. Pour into 19cm x 29cm slice pan; refrigerate, stirring occasionally, until set to the consistency of unbeaten egg white.
5 Cut cake into 36 squares; dip each square into jelly then toss in coconut. Stand jelly cakes on tray; cover, refrigerate 30 minutes.

prep & cook time 1 hour 10 minutes (+ refrigeration)
makes 36
nutritional count per cake 6.7g total fat (5g saturated fat); 456kJ (109 cal); 10.2g carbohydrate; 1g protein; 1.2g fibre

serving Idea Serve this deliciously gooey pudding with ice-cream, and drizzle the chocolate sauce over the ice-cream as well.

chocolate self-saucing pudding

60g butter

½ cup (125ml) milk

½ teaspoon vanilla extract

¾ cup (165g) caster sugar

1 cup (150g) self-raising flour

1 tablespoon cocoa powder

¾ cup (165g) firmly packed brown sugar

1 tablespoon cocoa powder, extra

2 cups (500ml) boiling water

1 Preheat oven to 180°C/160°C fan-forced. Grease 1.5-litre (6-cup) ovenproof dish.

2 Melt butter with milk in medium saucepan. Remove from heat; stir in extract and caster sugar then sifted flour and cocoa. Spread mixture into dish.

3 Sift brown sugar and extra cocoa over mixture; gently pour boiling water over mixture.

4 Bake pudding 40 minutes or until centre is firm. Stand 5 minutes before serving.

prep & cook time 1 hour **serves** 6
nutritional count per serving 9.7g total fat (6.2g saturated fat); 1618kJ (387 cal); 73.4g carbohydrate; 3.8g protein; 1.1g fibre

apple berry crumbles

2 medium apples (300g)
¾ cup (115g) frozen mixed berries
2 tablespoons lemon juice
2 tablespoons brown sugar
2 tablespoons plain flour
¼ cup (20g) rolled oats
20g butter
¼ cup (30g) finely chopped roasted hazelnuts

1 Preheat oven to 200°C/180°C fan-forced. Grease four ¾-cup (180ml) ovenproof dishes, place on oven tray.
2 Peel and core apples; chop coarsely. Combine apple, berries, juice and half the sugar in medium bowl; divide mixture among dishes.
3 Combine remaining sugar, flour and oats in small bowl. Rub butter into flour mixture; stir in nuts. Divide crumble over fruit mixture, pressing down firmly.
4 Bake crumbles 30 minutes or until browned lightly. Dust with sifted icing sugar and serve with yogurt.

prep & cook time 45 minutes **serves** 4
nutritional count per serving 9.3g total fat (3g saturated fat); 803kJ (192 cal); 22.3g carbohydrate; 3.1g protein; 3.1g fibre

after-school snacks

Being at school all day is tiring – your little learners will be ravenous.

bruschetta fingers

1 small turkish bread roll (160g)
2 teaspoons sun-dried tomato pesto
6 cherry tomatoes, quartered
30g cherry bocconcini cheese, sliced thinly
1 tablespoon finely chopped fresh flat-leaf parsley

1 Split bread in half; toast, cut-side up, then cut into fingers.
2 Spread toasted sides with pesto; top with tomato and cheese then sprinkle with parsley.

prep & cook time 10 minutes **serves** 1
nutritional count per serving 14.5g total fat (4.7g saturated fat); 2358kJ (569 cal); 81.9g carbohydrate; 22.5g protein; 6.1g fibre

baked beans, bacon and tomato on toast

1 medium tomato (150g), chopped coarsely
2 teaspoons finely chopped chives
½ x 420g can baked beans in tomato sauce
2 rindless bacon rashers (1130g), chopped coarsely
¼ large loaf turkish bread (105g), halved

1 Preheat grill.
2 Combine tomato and chives in small bowl.
3 Heat beans in small saucepan.
4 Meanwhile, cook bacon in heated small frying pan, stirring, until crisp; drain on absorbent paper.
5 Cut bread pieces horizontally; toast cut sides. Top toast with beans, bacon and tomato mixture; grill about 2 minutes or until hot.

prep & cook time 10 minutes **serves** 2
nutritional count per serving 10.4g total fat (3.2g saturated fat); 1450kJ (347 cal); 37.5g carbohydrate; 22g protein; 7.4g fibre

banana smoothie

1 cups (250ml) skim milk
1 medium banana (230g), chopped coarsely
2 tablespoons low-fat yogurt
1 teaspoon honey
1 teaspoon wheat germ
pinch ground cinnamon

1 Blend or process ingredients until smooth.

prep time 5 minutes **serves** 1
nutritional count per serving 0.4g total fat (0.2g saturated fat); 648kJ (155 cal); 28.3g carbohydrate; 8.3g protein; 1.8g fibre

apple and pear juice

1 medium apple (150g)
1 medium pear (230g)

1 Cut apple and pear into wedges.
2 Push fruit through juice extractor into glass; stir to combine.

prep & cook time 5 minutes **serves** 1
nutritional count per serving 0.4g total fat (0g saturated fat); 853kJ (204 cal); 51.3g carbohydrate; 1.1g protein; 9g fibre

These healthy snacks are fun to eat. And kids always love to eat things where they can break the 'don't play with your food' rule.

noodle and vegetable rolls

60g rice vermicelli noodles
½ medium carrot (60g), grated coarsely
½ small wombok (350g), shredded finely
1 tablespoon fish sauce
1 tablespoon brown sugar
¼ cup (60ml) lemon juice
12 x 17cm-square rice paper sheets
12 large fresh mint leaves
sweet chilli dipping sauce
¼ cup (60ml) sweet chilli sauce
1 tablespoon fish sauce
1 tablespoon lime juice

1 Place noodles in medium heatproof bowl, cover with boiling water; stand until just tender, drain. Using kitchen scissors, cut noodles into random lengths.
2 Place noodles in medium bowl with carrot, wombok, sauce, sugar and juice; toss gently to combine.
3 To assemble rolls, place one sheet of rice paper in medium bowl of warm water until just softened; lift sheet carefully from water, placing it on a tea-towel-covered board with a corner point facing towards you. Place a little of the vegetable filling and one mint leaf vertically along centre of sheet; fold top and bottom corners over filling then roll sheet from side to side to enclose filling. Repeat with remaining rice paper sheets, vegetable filling and mint leaves.
4 Combine ingredients for sweet chilli dipping sauce in small bowl.
5 Serve rolls with dipping sauce.

prep & cook time 25 minutes **makes** 12 rolls
nutritional count per roll 0.2g total fat (0g saturated fat); 188kJ (45 cal); 9g carbohydrate; 1.4g protein; 0.8g fibre
nutritional count per tablespoon dipping sauce 0.4g total fat (0.1g saturated fat); 71kJ (17 cal); 2.7g carbohydrate; 0.4g protein; 0.6g fibre

tip If sweet chilli sauce is too spicy for your kids, try plum sauce instead.

tomato, spinach and cheese melts

barbecued chicken pizza

tomato, spinach
and cheese melts

30g baby spinach leaves
1 medium tomatoes (150g), sliced thinly
⅔ cup (60g) grated cheddar cheese
4 english muffins or crumpets

1 Preheat grill.
2 Layer spinach leaves, tomato and cheese
between muffins.
3 Place under grill 5 minutes or until cheese melts.

prep & cook time 15 minutes **makes** 2
nutritional count per serving 7.8g total fat (4.5g
saturated fat); 949kJ (227 cal); 24.9g carbohydrate;
12.5g protein; 3.2g fibre

barbecued
chicken pizza

1 sheet puff pastry
2 tablespoons barbecue sauce
½ cup (80g) shredded barbecued chicken
20g drained, coarsely chopped roasted
   red capsicum
½ green onion, sliced thinly
½ cup (50g) pizza cheese

1 Preheat oven to 200ºC/180ºC fan-forced.
Oil oven tray.
2 Cut four 11.5cm rounds from pastry; place on tray.
3 Spread rounds with sauce; top with chicken,
capsicum, onion and cheese.
4 Bake pizzas about 15 minutes or until browned.

prep & cook time 30 minutes **makes** 4
nutritional count per pizza 14.7g total fat (3.1g
saturated fat); 1074kJ (257 cal); 20.3g carbohydrate;
10.7g protein; 0.8g fibre

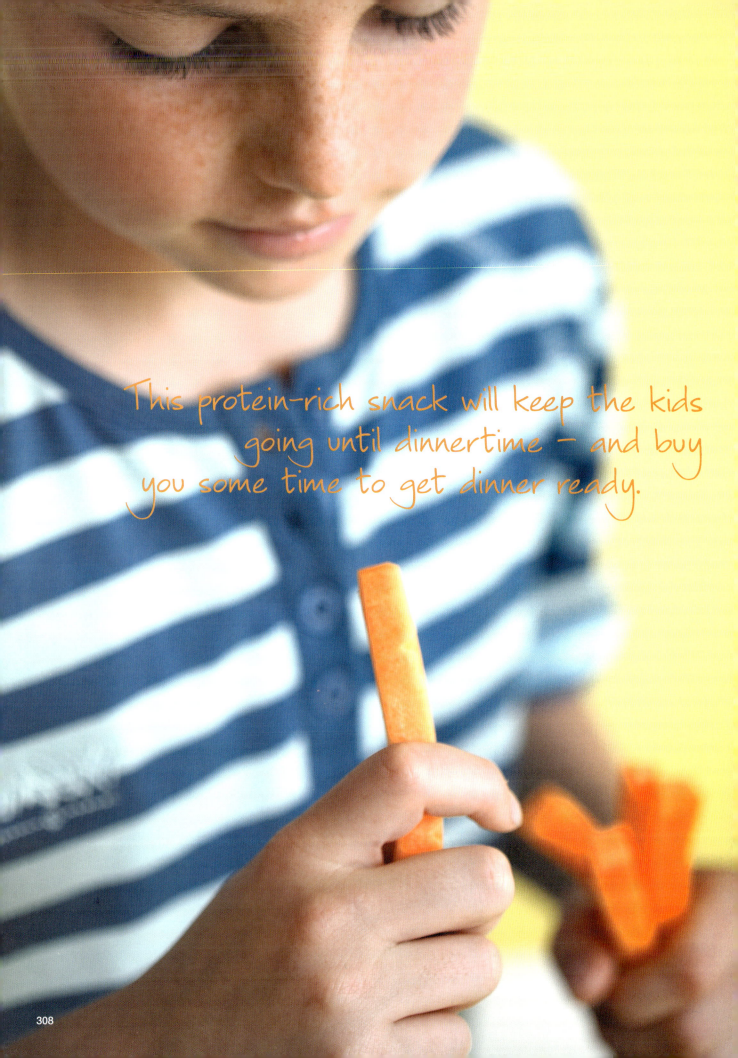

This protein-rich snack will keep the kids
going until dinnertime – and buy
you some time to get dinner ready.

ham, egg and cheese toastie

2 slices wholemeal bread (90g)
1 tablespoon barbecue sauce
30g shaved ham
1 hard-boiled egg, sliced thinly
¼ cup (30g) coarsely grated reduced-fat
   cheddar cheese

1 Spread bread with sauce; sandwich ham, egg and cheese between bread slices.
2 Toast in sandwich press until golden brown.

prep & cook time 10 minutes **makes** 1
nutritional count per toastie 16.1g total fat (6.9g saturated fat); 1898kJ (454 cal), 44.3g carbohydrate; 29.7g protein; 5.9g fibre

frozen fruit yogurt blocks

rhubarb, muesli and yogurt cups

frozen fruit yogurt blocks

1½ cups (420g) vanilla yogurt
1 cup (150g) frozen mixed berries
1 tablespoon honey

1 Combine yogurt, berries and honey in medium bowl.
2 Spoon mixture into six ¼-cup (60ml) ice-block moulds. Press lids on firmly; freeze 6 hours or overnight.

prep time 5 minutes (+ freezing) **makes** 6
nutritional count per block 2.5g total fat (1.5g saturated fat); 389kJ (93 cal); 12.6g carbohydrate; 3.8g protein; 1.5g fibre

rhubarb, muesli and yogurt cups

2 cups (220g) coarsely chopped fresh
  rhubarb stalks
¼ cup (55g) caster sugar
½ cup (125ml) water
½ teaspoon ground cinnamon
1⅓ cups (375g) low-fat vanilla yogurt
½ cup (45g) toasted muesli

1 Place rhubarb, sugar, the water and cinnamon in medium saucepan; bring to the boil. Reduce heat; simmer, uncovered, stirring occasionally, 10 minutes or until rhubarb is tender. Transfer to medium heatproof bowl; cover, refrigerate 1 hour.
2 Divide rhubarb mixture among four ¾-cup (180ml) serving glasses; top with yogurt then muesli.

prep & cook time 20 minutes (+ refrigeration)
serves 4
nutritional count per serving 1.5g total fat (0.5g saturated fat); 782kJ (187 cal); 33.9g carbohydrate; 7.4g protein; 2.9g fibre

apple and raisin french toast

1 small apple (130g)
1 tablespoon water
2 tablespoons coarsely chopped raisins
¼ loaf unsliced white bread (160g)
2 eggs
¼ cup (60ml) low-fat milk
2 teaspoons honey
pinch ground cinnamon
10g butter
1 tablespoon icing sugar

1 Peel, core then thinly slice apple.
2 Place apple and the water in small saucepan; bring to the boil. Reduce heat; simmer, covered, about 5 minutes or until apple is just tender. Remove from heat; stir in raisins. Cool 15 minutes.
3 Meanwhile, slice bread into quarters; cut each piece three-quarters of the way through. Divide apple mixture among bread pockets.
4 Whisk eggs in medium bowl; whisk in milk, honey and cinnamon.
5 Heat half the butter in large frying pan. Dip two bread pockets into egg mixture, one at a time; cook, uncovered, until browned both sides.
6 Remove from pan; cover to keep warm. Repeat with remaining butter and bread. Cut pockets into quarters; serve sprinkled with sifted icing sugar.

prep & cook time 30 minutes (+ cooling) **serves** 2
nutritional count per serving 10.3g total fat (4.3g saturated fat); 1668kJ (399 cal); 60.6g carbohydrate; 13.6g protein; 3.5g fibre

chocolate-dipped fruit

2½ cups (375g) milk chocolate Melts
2 medium bananas (400g), sliced thickly
250g strawberries
¾ cup (110g) dried apricots

1 Grease oven tray; line with baking paper.
2 Place chocolate in microwave-safe bowl; cook on medium-low (30%) in microwave oven for 1 minute. Using oven mitts, remove bowl from microwave oven; stir chocolate. If it's not completely melted, return bowl to microwave oven briefly.
3 Using hand, dip fruit, one piece at a time, into melted chocolate to coat three-quarters of each piece of fruit. Place fruit, in single layer, on tray; refrigerate until set.

prep & cook time 15 minutes (+ refrigeration) **serves** 4
nutritional count per serving 25.9g total fat (15.8g saturated fat); 2646kJ (633 cal); 88.9g carbohydrate; 11.5g protein; 6.5g fibre

serving idea You can use any fruit you like here. Try rockmelon, honeydew melon, pineapple, orange or apples as well.

These delicious fruity snacks also make
a great dessert for both kids and adults.
Make an extra batch at the same time and
refrigerate them until dessert time.

pears on fruit toast

lemonade ice-blocks

pears on fruit toast

2 slices fruit bread
½ small pear (180g), sliced thinly
1 teaspoon brown sugar

1 Preheat grill.
2 Toast fruit bread.
3 Place pear slices on each slice of toast.
4 Sprinkle pear with sugar. Toast under grill about
2 minutes or until browned lightly.

prep & cook time 10 minutes **makes** 2
nutritional count per toast 1.3g total fat (0.2g
saturated fat); 518kJ (124 cal); 25.2g carbohydrate;
2.8g protein; 2.4g fibre

lemonade ice-blocks

¼ cup (60ml) lemon juice
⅔ cup (110g) icing sugar
1 cup (250ml) sparkling mineral water

1 Stir juice and icing sugar in medium jug until
sugar dissolves. Stir in mineral water.
2 Pour mixture into four ⅓-cup (80ml) ice-block
moulds. Press lids on firmly; freeze 6 hours or
overnight.

prep time 5 minutes (+ freezing) **makes** 4
nutritional count per ice-block 0g total fat (0g
saturated fat); 305kJ (73 cal); 18.6g carbohydrate;
0.1g protein; 0g fibre

the great outdoors

Change the scenery and head outside with these easy-to-transport meals.

tomato, olive and ricotta tart

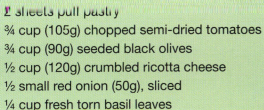

2 sheets puff pastry
¾ cup (105g) chopped semi-dried tomatoes
¾ cup (90g) seeded black olives
½ cup (120g) crumbled ricotta cheese
½ small red onion (50g), sliced
¼ cup fresh torn basil leaves
1 egg, beaten lightly

1 Preheat oven to 200°C/180°C fan-forced. Line an oven tray with baking paper.
2 Cut a 16cm x 24cm rectangle from one sheet pastry; place on oven tray. Top with tomatoes, olives, cheese, onion and basil leaves.
3 Cut a 18cm x 24cm rectangle from remaining pastry; score pastry in a diamond pattern then place on top of pastry on oven tray, press edges to seal.
4 Brush with egg; bake about 20 minutes.

prep & cook time 35 minutes **serves** 4
nutritional count per serving 25.1g total fat (12.5g saturated fat); 1965kJ (470 cal); 46.9g carbohydrate; 11.5g protein; 5.8g fibre

moroccan carrot dip

4 medium carrots (480g), chopped coarsely
2 cloves garlic, peeled
1 teaspoon ground cumin
1 tablespoon honey
2 tablespoons lemon juice
¼ cup (70g) greek-style yogurt
1 tablespoon coarsely chopped fresh
   coriander leaves

1 Cover carrots and garlic with water in small
saucepan; bring to the boil. Reduce heat; simmer,
covered, 20 minutes or until carrots are soft. Drain.
2 Blend or process carrot mixture with cumin,
honey and juice until smooth. Add yogurt; blend
until smooth.
3 Serve dip sprinkled with coriander.

prep & cook time 30 minutes **makes** 2 cups
nutritional count per tablespoon 0.2g total fat
(0.1g saturated fat); 46kJ (11 cal); 1.9g carbohydrate;
0.3g protein; 0.5g fibre

artichoke spinach dip

340g jar marinated artichokes, rinsed, drained
250g frozen chopped spinach, thawed
½ cup (120g) sour cream
¼ cup (75g) mayonnaise
¾ cup (60g) coarsely grated parmesan cheese
1 clove garlic, crushed

1 Preheat oven to 200°C/180°C fan-forced.
2 Chop artichokes coarsely; combine with remaining
ingredients in medium bowl.
3 Transfer dip mixture to 2-cup (500ml) ovenproof
dish; cook, covered, 20 minutes.

prep & cook time 30 minutes **makes** 2 cups
nutritional count per tablespoon 2.7g total fat (1.3g
saturated fat); 130kJ (31 cal); 0.7g carbohydrate;
1.1g protein; 0.4g fibre

From back to front moroccan carrot dip, artichoke spinach dip

serving idea This yummy chicken mixture is also great for party nibbles. Dollop a spoonful on blini for a sophisticated party snack.

The roasted almonds add a lovely crunch to these picture-perfect rolls.

chicken, almond and tarragon mini rolls

200g cooked chicken breast fillet, shredded finely
⅓ cup finely chopped fresh tarragon
¼ cup (35g) roasted slivered almonds
1 stalk celery (150g), trimmed, chopped finely
3 green onions, chopped finely
⅓ cup (100g) mayonnaise
12 mini bread rolls

1 Combine chicken, tarragon, almonds, celery, onion and mayonnaise in medium bowl.
2 Make a cut in tops of bread rolls. Spoon chicken mixture into bread rolls.

prep time 20 minutes **makes** 12
nutritional count per roll 5.7g total fat (0.7g saturated fat); 660kJ (158 cal); 17.5g carbohydrate; 8.2g protein; 1.7g fibre

tomato, fetta and pancetta frittata

6 slices pancetta (100g), chopped coarsely
100g fetta cheese, crumbled
¼ cup (20g) finely grated parmesan cheese
⅓ cup coarsely chopped fresh basil
6 eggs
⅔ cup (160ml) cream
9 mini roma tomatoes (150g), halved lengthways

1 Preheat oven to 180°C/160°C fan-forced. Grease six-hole (¾-cup/180ml) texas muffin pan; line bases with baking paper.
2 Layer pancetta, cheeses and basil in pan holes. Whisk eggs and cream in medium bowl; pour into pan holes. Top each frittata with three tomato halves.
3 Bake frittatas about 25 minutes. Stand in pan 5 minutes before turning out.

prep & cook time 35 minutes **makes** 6
nutritional count per frittata 24.1g total fat (13.3g saturated fat); 1170kJ (280 cal); 1.6g carbohydrate; 14.9g protein; 0.4g fibre

crab, fennel and herb quiche

3 sheets shortcrust pastry
1 tablespoon olive oil
1 medium fennel bulb (300g), sliced thinly
250g crab meat
2 tablespoons finely chopped fennel fronds
2 tablespoons finely chopped fresh flat-leaf parsley
½ cup (60g) coarsely grated cheddar cheese
quiche filling
300ml cream
¼ cup (60ml) milk
3 eggs

1 Preheat oven to 200°C/180°C fan-forced. Grease 12-hole (⅓-cup/80ml) muffin pan.
2 Cut twelve 9cm rounds from pastry; press into pan holes.
3 Heat oil in large frying pan; cook fennel, stirring, about 5 minutes or until fennel softens and browns slightly. Divide fennel among pastry cases; top with combined crab, fronds, parsley and cheese.
4 Make quiche filling; pour into pastry cases.
5 Bake quiches about 25 minutes. Stand in pan 5 minutes before serving with lime wedges.
quiche filling Whisk ingredients in large jug.

prep & cook time 50 minutes **makes** 12
nutritional count per quiche 27.1g total fat (15g saturated fat); 1509kJ (361 cal); 20.3g carbohydrate; 9g protein; 1.3g fibre

tomato, fetta and pancetta frittata

crab, fennel and herb quiche

picnic cottage loaf

1 large red capsicum (350g)
1 large zucchini (150g), sliced thinly lengthways
1 medium eggplant (300g), sliced thinly
cooking-oil spray
1 tablespoon olive oil
1 large red onion (300g), sliced thinly
1 tablespoon brown sugar
1 tablespoon red wine vinegar
1 round cob loaf (450g)
1 cup (240g) ricotta cheese
200g thinly sliced rare roast beef
20g baby rocket leaves
rocket pesto
20g baby rocket leaves
¼ cup (40g) roasted pine nuts
¼ cup (20g) coarsely grated parmesan cheese
1 clove garlic, quartered
1 tablespoon lemon juice
2 tablespoons olive oil

1 Make rocket pesto.
2 Preheat oven to 220°C/200°C fan-forced.
3 Quarter capsicum; discard seeds and membranes. Roast or grill, skin-side up, until skin blisters and blackens. Cover capsicum pieces with plastic or paper for 5 minutes; peel away skin.
4 Place zucchini and eggplant on oiled oven tray; spray with oil. Roast about 15 minutes; cool.
5 Meanwhile, heat oil in medium frying pan; cook onion, stirring, until soft. Add sugar and vinegar; cook, stirring, until onion caramelises.
6 Cut shallow lid from top of loaf; remove soft bread inside, leaving 2cm-thick shell.
7 Spread pesto inside bread shell and lid. Layer eggplant, cheese, onion mixture, zucchini, capsicum, beef and rocket inside bread shell, pressing layers down firmly. Replace lid; press down firmly.
8 Wrap loaf tightly with kitchen string and plastic wrap; refrigerate about 2 hours or until required.
rocket pesto Blend or process rocket, nuts, cheese, garlic and juice until coarsely chopped. With motor operating, gradually add oil in a thin steady stream; process until thick.

prep & cook time 55 minutes (+ refrigeration)
serves 6
nutritional count per serving 24g total fat (6.2g saturated fat); 2069kJ (495 cal); 43.1g carbohydrate; 23.8g protein; 5.4g fibre

This bright and colourful loaf will never fail to impress. For an extra bite you could replace the ricotta with spreadable goats cheese.

antipasto ciabatta rolls

1 medium eggplant (300g), sliced thinly
1 tablespoon ground cumin
4 ciabatta bread rolls
½ cup (130g) hummus
⅔ cup (100g) drained sun-dried tomatoes
40g baby rocket leaves

1 Cook eggplant, in batches, on heated oiled grill plate.
2 Split and toast cut sides of bread rolls.
3 Spread rolls with hummus, then sandwich eggplant, tomatoes and rocket leaves among rolls.

prep & cook time 30 minutes **serves** 4
nutritional count per serving 8.3g total fat (1.4g saturated fat); 966kJ (231 cal); 25.9g carbohydrate; 8.9g protein; 8.4g fibre

These Mediterranean flavours perfectly complement each other in this healthy vegetarian roll.

Head outside for a change of scenery and an alfresco feast, then lie back, relax and enjoy the fresh air and sunshine.

smoked trout, brie and cranberry salad

350g trimmed watercress
200g smoked trout, flaked coarsely
110g brie cheese, sliced thinly
cranberry dressing
2 tablespoons olive oil
2 tablespoons cranberry juice
1 tablespoon lemon juice

1 Divide watercress, trout and cheese among serving plates.
2 Make cranberry dressing.
3 Drizzle dressing over salad.
cranberry dressing Place ingredients in screw-top jar; shake well.

prep & cook time 15 minutes **serves** 4
nutritional count per serving 19.8g total fat (7g saturated fat); 1095kJ (262 cal); 1.4g carbohydrate; 19.3g protein; 0.7g fibre

smoked chicken, spinach and almond salad

350g smoked chicken breast fillets, sliced thinly
3 stalks celery (450g), trimmed, sliced thinly
3 small tomatoes (270g), quartered, seeded
100g baby spinach leaves
4 hard-boiled eggs, quartered
2 green onions, sliced thinly
½ cup (70g) slivered almonds, roasted
cumin mayonnaise
2 teaspoons cumin seeds, toasted
½ cup (150g) mayonnaise
¼ cup (60ml) lemon juice

1 Make cumin mayonnaise.
2 Combine chicken, celery, tomato, spinach, egg, onion and nuts in large bowl.
3 Divide salad among serving plates; drizzle over mayonnaise.
cumin mayonnaise Using mortar and pestle, crush seeds finely; combine with mayonnaise and juice in small bowl.

prep & cook time 30 minutes **serves** 4
nutritional count per serving 33.5g total fat (5.3g saturated fat); 2044kJ (489 cal); 11.3g carbohydrate; 34g protein; 4.7g fibre

smoked trout, brie and cranberry salad

smoked chicken, spinach and almond salad

peanut butter cookies

125g butter, softened
¼ cup (70g) crunchy peanut butter
¾ cup (165g) firmly packed brown sugar
1 egg
1½ cups (225g) plain flour
½ teaspoon bicarbonate of soda
½ cup (70g) roasted unsalted peanuts,
   chopped coarsely

1 Preheat oven to 180°C/160°C fan-forced. Grease oven trays; line with baking paper.
2 Beat butter, peanut butter, sugar and egg in small bowl with electric mixer until smooth; do not over-mix. Transfer mixture to medium bowl; stir in sifted flour and soda, then nuts.
3 Roll level tablespoons of mixture into balls; place 5cm apart on trays, flatten with floured fork.
4 Bake cookies about 12 minutes; cool on trays.

prep & cook time 25 minutes **makes** 30
nutritional count per cookie 6g total fat (2.7g saturated fat); 451kJ (108 cal); 11.2g carbohydrate; 2.3g protein; 0.7g fibre

apple slice

1 cup (150g) self-raising flour
½ cup (75g) plain flour
80g cold butter, chopped coarsely
¼ cup (55g) caster sugar
1 egg, beaten lightly
¼ cup (60ml) milk, approximately
1 tablespoon milk, extra
1 tablespoon caster sugar, extra
apple filling
6 medium apples (900g), peeled, cored,
   cut into 1cm pieces
¼ cup (55g) caster sugar
¼ cup (60ml) water
¾ cup (120g) sultanas
1 teaspoon mixed spice
2 teaspoons finely grated lemon rind

1 Make apple filling.
2 Grease 20cm x 30cm lamington pan; line base with baking paper, extending paper 5cm over long sides.
3 Sift flours into medium bowl, rub in butter. Stir in sugar, egg and enough milk to make a firm dough. Knead on floured surface until smooth. Cover; refrigerate 30 minutes.
4 Preheat oven to 200°C/180°C fan-forced.
5 Divide dough in half. Roll one half large enough to cover base of pan; press firmly into pan. Spread apple filling over dough. Roll remaining dough large enough to cover filling and place over the top. Brush with extra milk; sprinkle with extra sugar.
6 Bake slice about 25 minutes; stand in pan 5 minutes.
apple filling Cook apple, sugar and the water in large saucepan, uncovered, stirring occasionally, about 10 minutes or until apple softens. Remove from heat; stir in sultanas, spice and rind. Cool.

prep & cook time 45 minutes (+ refrigeration)
serves 8
nutritional count per serving 9.7g total fat (5.9g saturated fat); 1463kJ (350 cal); 58.6g carbohydrate; 4.8g protein; 3.4g fibre

For a beautiful finish sift a little
icing sugar over the top of this
wonderful dessert.

tip Granny Smith or Golden Delicious
apples are the best variety to use in
this slice. For a twist you could use
chopped dates instead of sultanas.

hazelnut brownies

125g butter
200g dark eating chocolate
½ cup (110g) caster sugar
2 eggs, beaten lightly
1¼ cups (185g) plain flour
½ cup (70g) roasted hazelnuts, chopped coarsely
1 cup (190g) white Choc Bits

1 Preheat oven to 180°C/160°C fan-forced. Grease deep 19cm-square cake pan; line base and two opposite sides with baking paper, extending paper 5cm above sides.
2 Melt butter and chocolate in medium saucepan over low heat. Stir in sugar; cook, stirring, 5 minutes. Cool 10 minutes.
3 Stir in egg and sifted flour then nuts and Choc Bits. Spread mixture into pan.
4 Bake brownies about 30 minutes; cool in pan, cut into squares. Serve dusted with icing sugar.

prep & cook time 40 minutes **makes** 9
nutritional count per brownie 30g total fat (15.5g saturated fat); 2174kJ (520 cal); 54.7g carbohydrate; 7.2g protein; 2.1g fibre

rock cakes

2 cups (300g) self-raising flour
¼ teaspoon ground cinnamon
⅓ cup (75g) caster sugar
90g butter, chopped
1 cup (160g) sultanas
1 egg, beaten lightly
½ cup (125ml) milk
1 tablespoon caster sugar, extra

1 Preheat oven to 200°C/180°C fan-forced.
Grease oven trays.
2 Sift flour, cinnamon and sugar into medium
bowl; rub in butter. Stir in sultanas, egg and milk.
Do not over-mix.
3 Drop rounded tablespoons of mixture about
5cm apart onto trays; sprinkle with extra sugar.
4 Bake cakes about 15 minutes; cool on trays.

prep & cook time 30 minutes **makes** 18
nutritional count per cake 4.9g total fat (3g
saturated fat); 631kJ (151 cal); 23.9g carbohydrate;
2.6g protein; 1g fibre

serving idea These hard, crunchy biscuits are traditionally enjoyed at the end of a meal, dipped in Vin Santo, an Italian dessert wine, to soften them. Dipping them in coffee is also delicious.

pistachio and cranberry biscotti

60g unsalted butter, softened
1 teaspoon vanilla extract
1 cup (220g) caster sugar
2 eggs
1¾ cups (260g) plain flour
½ teaspoon bicarbonate of soda
1 cup (130g) dried cranberries
¾ cup (110g) coarsely chopped roasted pistachios
1 egg, extra
1 tablespoon water
2 tablespoons caster sugar, extra

1 Beat butter, extract and sugar in medium bowl until combined. Beat in eggs, one at a time. Stir in sifted flour and soda then cranberries and nuts. Cover dough; refrigerate 1 hour.
2 Preheat oven to 180°C/160°C fan-forced. Grease oven tray.
3 Knead dough on floured surface until smooth but still sticky. Halve dough; shape each half into 30cm log. Place logs on oven tray.
4 Combine extra egg with the water in small bowl. Brush egg mixture over logs; sprinkle with extra sugar.
5 Bake biscotti about 20 minutes or until firm; cool 3 hours or overnight.
6 Preheat oven to 150°C/130°C fan-forced.
7 Using serrated knife, cut logs diagonally into 1cm slices. Place slices on ungreased oven trays.
8 Bake about 15 minutes or until dry and crisp, turning halfway through baking; cool on wire racks.

prep & cook time 1 hour (+ refrigeration & cooling)
makes 60
nutritional count per piece 2.1g total fat (0.7g saturated fat); 259kJ (62 cal); 9.2g carbohydrate; 1.2g protein; 0.4g fibre

chocolate caramel slice

½ cup (75g) self-raising flour
½ cup (75g) plain flour
1 cup (80g) desiccated coconut
1 cup (220g) firmly packed brown sugar
125g butter, melted
caramel filling
395g can sweetened condensed milk
30g butter
2 tablespoons golden syrup
chocolate topping
200g dark eating chocolate, chopped coarsely
2 teaspoons vegetable oil

1 Preheat oven to 180°C/160°C fan forced. Grease 20cm x 30cm lamington pan; line with baking paper, extending paper 5cm over long sides.
2 Combine sifted flours, coconut, sugar and butter in medium bowl; press mixture evenly over base of pan. Bake about 15 minutes or until browned lightly.
3 Meanwhile, make caramel filling.
4 Pour filling over base; bake 10 minutes. Cool.
5 Make chocolate topping.
6 Pour warm topping over caramel. Refrigerate slice 3 hours or overnight. Serve cut into squares.
caramel filling Stir ingredients in small saucepan over medium heat about 15 minutes or until mixture is golden brown.
chocolate topping Stir ingredients in small saucepan over low heat until smooth.

prep & cook time 45 minutes (+ cooling & refrigeration)
makes 16
nutritional count per piece 17.7g total fat (11.8g saturated fat); 1450kJ (347 cal); 44.4g carbohydrate; 4.1g protein; 1.2g fibre

celebrations

Pop open the bubbly and get the party started with a bang.

champagne side car

Place 20ml brandy, 20ml cointreau, 20ml lemon juice and 15ml sugar syrup (see recipe below) in chilled 230ml champagne flute glass; stir gently. Top with 150ml chilled dry white sparkling wine. Garnish with strawberry slices.

prep time 5 minutes **serves** 1
nutritional count per serving 0.1g total fat (0g saturated fat); 1095kJ (262 cal); 20g carbohydrate; 0.5g protein; 0g fibre

sugar syrup Stir 1 cup (220g) caster sugar with 1 cup (250ml) water in small saucepan over low heat, until sugar dissolves; bring to the boil. Reduce heat; simmer, uncovered, 5 minutes. Cool. Refrigerate in an airtight container for up to 1 month.
prep & cook time 10 minutes **makes** 350ml

margarita

Rub lime slice around rim of 150ml margarita glass; turn glass upside-down and dip wet rim into saucer of salt. Place 1 cup ice cubes, 45ml dark tequila, 30ml cointreau, 30ml lime juice and 30ml sugar syrup (see recipe below) in cocktail shaker; shake vigorously. Strain into glass. Garnish with lime slice and curl of lime rind made using a zester.

prep time 5 minutes **serves** 1
nutritional count per serving 0.3g total fat (0g saturated fat); 1647kJ (394 cal); 53g carbohydrate; 0.3g protein; 0.1g fibre

manhattan

Place 1 maraschino cherry into chilled 120ml martini glass; rub the cut edge of an orange over the rim of the glass. Place ½ cup ice cubes, 45ml whiskey, 15ml sweet vermouth and dash of angostura bitters in a mixing glass; stir gently. Strain into glass.

prep time 5 minutes **serves** 1
nutritional count per serving 0.1g total fat (0g saturated fat); 610kJ (146 cal); 7g carbohydrate; 0.1g protein; 0.1g fibre

caipiroska

Cut 1 lime into eight wedges; place into cocktail shaker. Using muddler, crush lime wedges with 2 teaspoons caster sugar. Add 45ml vodka and ½ cup crushed ice; shake vigorously. Pour into 260ml old-fashioned glass. Garnish with a curl of lime rind made using a zester.

prep time 5 minutes **serves** 1
nutritional count per serving 0.2g total fat (0g saturated fat); 869kJ (208 cal); 19.8g carbohydrate; 0.7g protein; 1.2g fibre

serving idea You could also serve these as part of a mezze platter with other bite-size Greek nibbles like grilled haloumi, olives or the oregano-baked fetta on page 363.

dolmades

2 tablespoons olive oil
2 medium brown onions (300g), chopped finely
150g lean lamb mince
¾ cup (150g) white long-grain rice
2 tablespoons pine nuts
½ cup finely chopped fresh flat-leaf parsley
2 tablespoons finely chopped fresh dill
2 tablespoons finely chopped fresh mint
2 tablespoons lemon juice
1 cup (250ml) water
500g preserved vine leaves
1 cup (250ml) water, extra
1 tablespoon lemon juice, extra
¾ cup (200g) yogurt

1 Heat oil in large saucepan; cook onion, stirring, until softened. Add mince; cook, stirring, until mince is browned. Stir in rice and pine nuts. Add herbs, juice and the water. Bring to the boil; reduce heat, simmer, covered, about 10 minutes or until water is absorbed and rice is partially cooked. Cool.
2 Rinse vine leaves in cold water. Drop leaves into a large saucepan of boiling water, in batches, for a few seconds, transfer to colander; rinse under cold water, drain well.
3 Place a vine leaf, smooth-side down on bench, trim large stem. Place a heaped teaspoon of rice mixture in centre. Fold stem end and sides over filling; roll up firmly. Line medium heavy-based saucepan with a few vine leaves, place rolls, close together, seam side down on leaves.
4 Pour the extra water over top of rolls; cover rolls with any remaining vine leaves. Place a plate on top of the leaves to keep rolls under the water during cooking. Cover pan tightly, bring to the boil; reduce heat, simmer, over very low heat, 1½ hours. Remove from heat; stand, covered about 2 hours or until all the liquid has been absorbed.
5 Serve with combined extra juice and yogurt.

prep & cook time 3 hours (+ standing) **serves** 10
nutritional count per serving 7.6g total fat (1.6g saturated fat); 690kJ (165 cal); 14.9g carbohydrate; 7.7g protein; 3.2g fibre

haloumi and asparagus bites

eggplant fritters

haloumi and asparagus bites

340g asparagus, trimmed
250g haloumi cheese
lemony dressing
1 tablespoon rinsed drained baby capers,
  chopped finely
1 tablespoon olive oil
2 teaspoons finely grated lemon rind
1 tablespoon lemon juice
½ teaspoon white sugar

1 Make lemony dressing.
2 Cut asparagus into 3cm lengths. Boil, steam or microwave until barely tender; rinse under cold water, drain.
3 Cut haloumi into 1cm slices, then into 1cm x 3cm pieces. Thread one piece of asparagus, one piece of haloumi, then another piece of asparagus close together onto each toothpick.
4 Cook bites in large oiled frying pan over high heat about 30 seconds each side or until browned lightly.
5 Serve bites immediately, drizzled with dressing.
lemony dressing Place ingredients in screw-top jar; shake well.

prep & cook time 55 minutes **makes** 40
nutritional count per serving 1.5g total fat (0.8g saturated fat); 88kJ (21 cal); 0.3g carbohydrate; 1.5g protein; 0.1g fibre

eggplant fritters

2 large eggplants (1kg)
1 cup (100g) coarsely grated mozzarella cheese
½ cup coarsely chopped fresh flat-leaf parsley
2 cloves garlic, crushed
½ cup (50g) packaged breadcrumbs
¼ cup (35g) plain flour
2 eggs
vegetable oil, for shallow-frying

1 Preheat oven to 220°C/200°C fan-forced.
2 Remove and discard stem ends from eggplants; prick eggplants all over with fork. Place on oiled oven tray; roast, uncovered, about 30 minutes or until soft. Cool. Peel eggplants; chop flesh finely.
3 Combine eggplant, cheese, parsley, garlic, breadcrumbs, flour and eggs in large bowl. Using wetted hands, shape level tablespoons of mixture into oval patties.
4 Heat oil in large frying pan; cook fritters, in batches, until browned both sides. Drain on absorbent paper. Serve warm or cold, with lemon wedges.

prep & cook time 1 hour **makes** 36
nutritional count per fritter 5.3g total fat (1g saturated fat); 272kJ (65 cal); 2.4g carbohydrate; 1.7g protein; 0.8g fibre

fennel grissini with prosciutto

2 cups (300g) plain flour
½ teaspoon white sugar
1 teaspoon cooking salt
1 teaspoon dried yeast
2 teaspoons fennel seeds
1 cup (250ml) water, approximately
cooking-oil spray
sea salt
20 slices prosciutto (300g)

1 Sift flour, sugar and cooking salt into medium bowl, stir in yeast, seeds and enough of the water to make a soft dough. Turn dough onto floured surface, knead about 5 minutes or until dough is smooth and elastic.
2 Place dough in large oiled bowl, cover with plastic wrap; stand in warm place about 1 hour or until dough is doubled in size.

3 Preheat oven to 220°C/200°C fan-forced. Oil oven trays.
4 Turn dough onto floured surface, knead until smooth. Divide dough into four portions, cut each portion into 15 pieces; roll each piece into a long thin stick.
5 Place sticks on oven trays, coat lightly with oil spray. Sprinkle with sea salt.
6 Bake grissini about 15 minutes or until crisp.
7 Meanwhile, cut each prosciutto slice lengthways into three. Wrap a strip around each warm grissini. Serve immediately.

prep & cook time 1 hour (+ standing) **makes** 60
nutritional count per grissini 0.4g total fat (0.1g saturated fat); 105kJ (25 cal); 3.7g carbohydrate; 1.5g protein; 0.2g fibre

smoked seafood and mixed vegetable antipasti

onion and kumara pakoras with green chilli yogurt

smoked seafood and mixed vegetable antipasti

⅓ cup (80g) sour cream
2 teaspoons raspberry vinegar
1 tablespoon coarsely chopped fresh chives
1 clove garlic, crushed
1 large yellow zucchini (150g)
1 tablespoon raspberry vinegar, extra
¼ cup (60ml) extra virgin olive oil
⅓ cup (45g) roasted slivered almonds
1 cup (150g) drained semi-dried tomatoes
1 large avocado (320g)
1 tablespoon lemon juice
300g hot-smoked ocean trout portions
200g sliced smoked salmon
16 drained caperberries (80g)
1 lemon, cut into wedges
170g packet roasted garlic bagel crisps

1 Combine sour cream, vinegar, chives and garlic in small bowl, cover; refrigerate until required.
2 Meanwhile, using vegetable peeler, slice zucchini lengthways into ribbons; combine zucchini in small bowl with extra vinegar and 2 tablespoons of the oil.
3 Combine nuts, tomatoes and remaining oil in small bowl. Slice avocado thickly into small bowl; sprinkle with juice. Flake trout into bite-sized pieces.
4 Arrange zucchini mixture, nut mixture, avocado, trout, salmon and caperberries on large platter; serve with sour cream mixture, lemon and bagel crisps.

prep time 35 minutes **serves** 4
nutritional count per serving 54.4g total fat (14.1g saturated fat); 3607kJ (863 cal); 44g carbohydrate; 43.2g protein; 10.9g fibre

onion and kumara pakoras with green chilli yogurt

2 cups (300g) chickpea (besan) flour
1 teaspoon ground turmeric
2 teaspoons ground cumin
½ teaspoon chilli powder
1 teaspoon baking powder
½ teaspoon salt
2 teaspoons kalonji seeds
2 medium brown onions (300g), quartered, sliced thinly
1 small uncooked kumara (250g), grated coarsely
1 fresh long green chilli, chopped finely
½ cup (125ml) water, approximately
vegetable oil, for deep-frying
green chilli yogurt
1½ cups (420g) greek-style yogurt
2 fresh long green chillies, seeded, chopped finely
2 tablespoons finely chopped coriander leaves
½ teaspoon ground cumin

1 Sift flour, turmeric, cumin, chilli, baking powder and salt into large bowl. Stir in seeds, onion, kumara and chilli. Gradually stir in enough water to make a thick batter.
2 Make green chilli yogurt.
3 Heat oil in wok or deep wide saucepan; deep-fry rounded teaspoons of batter mixture, in batches, until browned. Drain on absorbent paper.
4 Serve pakoras hot, with yogurt.
green chilli yogurt Combine ingredients in medium bowl.

prep & cook time 35 minutes **makes** 80
nutritional count per pakora 1.2g total fat (0.4g saturated fat); 121kJ (29 cal); 2g carbohydrate; 2.2g protein; 0.6g fibre

There's no work involved in eating these delicious little crabs — no need to crack, dig and pick to get to the flesh.

tip Don't be put off by the idea of consuming the whole crab – soft-shell crab is considered by many to be one of the greatest seafood delicacies. The shells are paper thin and slightly crunchy, like a potato crisp.

soft-shell crabs with green onion aïoli

½ cup (100g) rice flour
1 teaspoon dried chilli flakes
2 teaspoons sea salt
8 uncooked small soft-shell crabs (500g)
vegetable oil, for deep-frying
1 cup loosely packed fresh basil leaves
green onion aïoli
¾ cup (225g) mayonnaise
2 green onions, sliced finely
1 clove garlic, crushed
1 tablespoon lemon juice

1 Make green onion aïoli.
2 Combine flour, chilli and salt in medium bowl.
3 Clean crabs; pat dry then cut into quarters. Coat crabs with flour mixture; shake away excess.
4 Heat oil in large saucepan; deep-fry basil about 30 seconds or until crisp. Drain on absorbent paper. Deep-fry crabs, in batches, until browned lightly. Drain on absorbent paper. Serve with basil and aïoli.
green onion aïoli Combine ingredients in small bowl.

prep & cook time 30 minutes **serves** 8
nutritional count per serving 13g total fat (1.5g saturated fat); 920kJ (220 cal); 16.7g carbohydrate; 9g protein; 0.6g fibre

These brightly coloured little terrines are just as impressive to eat as they are to look at, and can be made well in advance.

roasted capsicum and goats cheese terrines

3 large red capsicums (1kg)
1½ cups (360g) ricotta cheese, chopped coarsely
250g firm goats cheese, chopped coarsely
¼ cup finely chopped fresh chives
2 tablespoons lemon juice
1 clove garlic, crushed
spinach and walnut pesto
¼ cup (20g) finely grated parmesan cheese
100g baby spinach leaves
¼ cup (25g) roasted walnuts
1 clove garlic, quartered
¼ cup (60ml) olive oil
2 tablespoons lemon juice
1 tablespoon water

1 Preheat oven to 240°C/220°C fan-forced. Grease six holes of eight-hole (½-cup/125ml) petite loaf pan. Line base and two long sides of each hole with a strip of baking paper, extending 5cm over sides.
2 Halve capsicums; discard seeds and membranes. Place on oven tray; roast, skin-side up, 15 minutes or until skin blisters and blackens. Cover with plastic wrap for 5 minutes then peel away skin. Cut capsicum into strips; line base and two long sides of pan holes with capsicum strips, extending 2cm over edges.
3 Combine remaining ingredients in medium bowl; spoon cheese mixture into pan holes, pressing down firmly. Fold capsicum strips over to enclose filling. Cover; refrigerate 1 hour.
4 Meanwhile, make spinach and walnut pesto.
5 Carefully remove terrines from pan holes; serve with spinach and walnut pesto. Sprinkle with chopped fresh chives.
spinach and walnut pesto Process cheese, spinach, nuts and garlic until chopped finely. With motor operating, gradually add combined oil, juice and the water in a thin, steady stream; process until pesto is smooth.

prep & cook time 45 minutes (+ refrigeration)
makes 6
nutritional count per terrine 26.8g total fat (10.8g saturated fat); 1417kJ (339 cal); 7.5g carbohydrate; 16.5g protein; 2.6g fibre

crostini with fetta, artichokes and rocket

olive oil spray

1 small french bread (150g), cut into 8mm-thick slices

1 clove garlic, halved

30g baby rocket leaves

1 teaspoon extra virgin olive oil

1 teaspoon red wine vinegar

5 marinated drained artichoke hearts

100g fetta cheese, crumbled

1 Preheat oven to 180°C/160°C fan-forced.

2 Spray both sides bread slices with oil spray; place on oven tray, toast in oven. Rub one side of each crostini with cut side of garlic clove; place crostini on serving platter.

3 Combine rocket leaves, oil and vinegar in medium bowl. Cut each artichoke heart into six wedges.

4 Top crostini with rocket mixture, then artichokes; sprinkle with fetta and freshly ground black pepper.

prep & cook time 20 minutes **serves** 6
nutritional count per serving 5.7g total fat (2.8g saturated fat); 548kJ (131 cal); 13.6g carbohydrate; 5.6g protein; 1.4g fibre

oregano-baked fetta

200g piece fetta cheese
1 tablespoon extra virgin olive oil
1 tablespoon coarsely chopped fresh
 oregano leaves
¼ teaspoon sweet paprika
¼ teaspoon freshly ground black pepper

1 Preheat oven to 200°C/180°C fan-forced.
2 Place fetta in small ovenproof dish; sprinkle with oil and remaining ingredients.
3 Bake fetta, covered, about 10 minutes or until cheese is heated through.
4 Serve fetta warm from dish, with slices of french bread and seeded black olives, if you like.

prep & cook time 15 minutes **serves** 6
nutritional count per serving 10.8g total fat (5.5g saturated fat); 502kJ (120 cal); 0.1g carbohydrate; 5.9g protein; 0g fibre

roast duck with orange and snow pea salad

4 medium oranges (960g)
½ cup (125ml) oyster sauce
½ cup (125ml) chinese cooking wine
¼ cup (55g) brown sugar
6 star anise
6 x 150g duck breast fillets
2 teaspoons peanut oil
2 teaspoons sesame oil
300g snow peas, trimmed, sliced thinly
150g baby spinach leaves
1 small red onion (100g), sliced thinly
2 teaspoons sesame seeds, toasted

1 Peel 4 thin strips of rind from one of the oranges. Juice this orange (you need ¼ cup juice); refrigerate.
2 Place rind in small saucepan with sauce, cooking wine, sugar and star anise; stir over heat until sugar dissolves. Bring marinade to the boil; remove from heat, cool.
3 Combine marinade with duck in large bowl. Cover; refrigerate 3 hours or overnight.
4 Preheat oven to 220°C/200°C fan-forced. Line oven tray with baking paper.
5 Drain duck; reserve marinade. Heat peanut oil in large frying pan; cook duck, skin-side down, over high heat about 1 minute or until skin is golden brown. Turn duck; cook 1 minute. Place duck, skin-side up, on tray; roast, uncovered, in oven, about 10 minutes or until cooked as desired. Stand duck 5 minutes.
6 Meanwhile, combine ¼ cup of the reserved marinade with 1 tablespoon water in small saucepan; bring to the boil. Reduce heat; simmer, uncovered, 5 minutes. Whisk in orange juice and sesame oil.
7 Segment remaining oranges into medium bowl; add peas, spinach and onion to bowl; toss gently to combine. Divide salad among plates; top with sliced duck, drizzle with warm dressing then sprinkle with sesame seeds.

prep & cook time 35 minutes (+ refrigeration)
serves 6
nutritional count per serving 59.5g total fat (17.3g saturated fat); 3143kJ (752 cal); 26.9g carbohydrate; 23.9g protein; 4.3g fibre

Two of the best things in life are good food and good friends — so bring them together, pour out the bubbly and chink your glasses.

Lamb cutlets are perfect stand-up party food — ready to pick up and eat with their own natural 'handle' to hold.

lamb cutlets with spinach skordalia

2 tablespoons olive oil
2 tablespoons lemon juice
2 cloves garlic, crushed
2 teaspoons dried oregano
18 french-trimmed small lamb cutlets (900g)
spinach skordalia
¾ cup (50g) stale breadcrumbs
⅓ cup (80ml) water
1kg spinach, trimmed, chopped coarsely
¾ cup (75g) roasted walnuts
2 cloves garlic, chopped coarsely
¼ cup (60ml) lemon juice
¼ cup (60ml) olive oil

1 Combine oil, juice, garlic and oregano with lamb in large bowl. Cover; refrigerate 1 hour.
2 Meanwhile, make spinach skordalia.
3 Cook lamb, in batches, on heated oiled grill plate (or grill or barbecue) until browned both sides and cooked as desired.
4 Serve cutlets with skordalia.

spinach skordalia Combine breadcrumbs and the water in small bowl. Drop spinach into large saucepan of boiling water; drain, rinse immediately under cold water, drain. Squeeze spinach to extract any excess water. Blend or process spinach and breadcrumb mixture with nuts, garlic and juice until smooth. With motor operating, gradually add oil in a thin steady stream; process until skordalia thickens.

prep & cook time 30 minutes (+ refrigeration)
serves 6
nutritional count per serving 37.5g total fat (8.6g saturated fat); 1944kJ (465 cal); 7.7g carbohydrate; 22.3g protein; 6g fibre

twice-cooked chicken with asian greens

2.5 litres (10 cups) water

1 litre (4 cups) chicken stock

2 cups (500ml) chinese cooking wine

8 cloves garlic, crushed

10cm piece fresh ginger (50g), sliced thinly

1 teaspoon sesame oil

1.6kg chicken

peanut oil, for deep-frying

1 tablespoon peanut oil

150g snow peas, trimmed

500g choy sum, chopped coarsely

350g gai lan, chopped coarsely

2 green onions, sliced thinly

char siu dressing

2 cloves garlic, crushed

5cm piece fresh ginger (25g), grated finely

¼ cup (60ml) char siu sauce

2 tablespoons soy sauce

1 teaspoon white sugar

1 tablespoon rice vinegar

1 Bring the water, stock, wine, garlic, ginger and sesame oil to the boil in large saucepan. Boil, uncovered, 10 minutes. Add chicken, reduce heat; simmer, uncovered, 15 minutes. Remove from heat, cover; stand chicken in stock 3 hours. Remove chicken; pat dry with absorbent paper. Reserve stock for another use.

2 Using sharp knife, halve chicken lengthways; cut halves crossways through the centre. Cut breasts from wings and thighs from legs to give you eight chicken pieces in total. Cut wings in half; cut breast and thighs into thirds. Place chicken pieces on tray; refrigerate, uncovered, 3 hours or overnight.

3 Make char siu dressing.

4 Heat peanut oil for deep-frying in wok; deep-fry chicken, in batches, until browned. Drain on absorbent paper.

5 Heat the 1 tablespoon of peanut oil in cleaned wok; stir-fry snow peas, choy sum and gai lan until just tender. Add 2 tablespoons of the dressing, stir-fry to combine.

6 Divide vegetables among serving plates; top with chicken, drizzle with remaining dressing, sprinkle with onion.

char siu dressing Stir garlic, ginger, sauces and sugar over heat in small saucepan until mixture comes to the boil. Remove from heat; stir in vinegar.

prep & cook time 1 hour 45 minutes (+ standing & refrigeration) **serves** 4

nutritional count per serving 47.4g total fat (12.5g saturated fat); 3081kJ (737 cal); 17.8g carbohydrate; 43.8g protein; 8.9g fibre

tip There is a lot of confusion between green onions, spring onions and shallots. Green onions are long thin shoots, the white at the bottom changes to a deep green at the top. They are milder in flavour than spring onions and have not formed the round, white bulb.

The trio of mushroom varieties used here gives this dish an earthy depth of flavour and texture.

roasted eye fillet with rösti and mushrooms

2 tablespoons olive oil
800g beef eye fillet
1 large kumara (500g)
2 large russet burbank potatoes (600g)
80g butter
2 tablespoons olive oil, extra
30g butter, extra
200g swiss brown mushrooms, halved
200g enoki mushrooms, trimmed
150g oyster mushrooms, halved
200g crème fraîche
3 green onions, sliced thinly
⅓ cup firmly packed fresh flat-leaf parsley

1 Preheat oven to 220°C/200°C fan-forced.
2 Heat oil in large shallow flameproof baking dish; cook beef, uncovered, until browned all over. Roast, uncovered, about 35 minutes or until cooked as desired. Cover to keep warm.
3 Meanwhile, coarsely grate kumara and potatoes into large bowl. Using hands, squeeze out excess moisture from potato mixture; shape mixture into eight portions. Heat 10g of the butter and 1 teaspoon of the extra oil in medium non-stick frying pan; spread one portion of the potato mixture over base of pan, flatten with spatula to form a firm pancake-like rösti. Cook, uncovered, over medium heat until browned; invert rösti onto large plate then gently slide back into pan to cook other side. Drain on absorbent paper; cover to keep warm. Repeat process with remaining butter, oil and potato mixture.
4 Heat extra butter in same cleaned pan; cook mushrooms, stirring, until just tender. Add crème fraîche; bring to the boil. Reduce heat; simmer, stirring, until sauce thickens slightly. Remove from heat; stir in onion and parsley.
5 Serve sliced beef with rösti and mushrooms.

prep & cook time 1 hour 10 minutes **serves** 4
nutritional count per serving 69.9g total fat (34.1g saturated fat); 4080kJ (976 cal); 34.4g carbohydrate; 54.2g protein; 8.4g fibre

chocolate and raspberry tart

¾ cup (240g) raspberry jam
200g dark eating chocolate, chopped finely
25g unsalted butter, melted
⅔ cup (160ml) cream, warmed
120g raspberries
sweet pastry
1¼ cups (185g) plain flour
½ cup (80g) icing sugar
125g cold unsalted butter, chopped coarsely
¼ cup (60ml) iced water, approximately

1 Make sweet pastry.
2 Grease 12.5cm x 35cm (or 24cm-round) loose-based flan tin. Roll pastry between sheets of baking paper until large enough to line tin. Ease pastry into tin, press into base and side; trim edge, prick base with fork. Cover; refrigerate 30 minutes.
3 Preheat oven to 200°C/180°C fan-forced.

4 Place tin on oven tray; cover pastry with baking paper, fill with dried beans or uncooked rice. Bake 15 minutes; remove paper and beans carefully from pastry case. Bake about 10 minutes. Spread jam over pastry base; return to oven 2 minutes. Cool.
5 Whisk chocolate, butter and cream in medium bowl until smooth. Pour chocolate mixture into pastry case; refrigerate 2 hours. Top tart with raspberries.
sweet pastry Process flour, icing sugar and butter until crumbly; add enough of the water to make ingredients come together. Knead dough gently on floured surface until smooth. Wrap in plastic; refrigerate 30 minutes.

prep & cook time 45 minutes (+ refrigeration)
serves 12
nutritional count per serving 21g total fat (13.4g saturated fat), 1559kJ (373 cal); 42.4g carbohydrate; 3g protein; 1.6g fibre

raspberry brownie ice-cream cake

1 litre vanilla ice-cream, softened

150g frozen raspberries

125g butter, chopped coarsely

200g dark eating chocolate, chopped coarsely

½ cup (110g) caster sugar

2 eggs

1¼ cups (185g) plain flour

150g milk eating chocolate, chopped coarsely

1 tablespoon icing sugar

1 Line deep 23cm-round cake pan with plastic wrap, extending wrap so it will cover pan. Combine ice-cream and raspberries in medium bowl. Spoon ice-cream into pan; smooth surface. Fold plastic wrap over to enclose. Freeze 3 hours or until firm.

2 Preheat oven to 160°C/140°C fan-forced. Remove ice-cream from pan, still wrapped in plastic; place on tray. Return to freezer.

3 Grease same cake pan; line base and side with baking paper.

4 Stir butter, dark chocolate and sugar in medium saucepan over low heat until smooth. Cool 10 minutes.

5 Stir in eggs, sifted flour and milk chocolate. Spread mixture into pan.

6 Bake brownie about 30 minutes; cool in pan.

7 Split brownie in half. Sandwich ice-cream cake between brownie slices; serve immediately, dusted with sifted icing sugar. Serve with fresh raspberries, if you like.

prep & cook time 1 hour (+ freezing) **serves** 12
nutritional count per serving 22.4g total fat (13.8g saturated fat); 1739kJ (416 cal); 48.5g carbohydrate; 6.5g protein; 1.6g fibre

tiramisu

460g double unfilled round sponge cake

2 tablespoons instant coffee granules

¼ cup (60ml) boiling water

⅓ cup (80ml) coffee-flavoured liqueur

1 teaspoon gelatine

1 tablespoon boiling water, extra

¾ cup (180ml) thickened cream

¼ cup (40g) icing sugar

1 teaspoon vanilla extract

1½ cups (375g) mascarpone cheese

ganache

⅔ cup (160ml) cream

180g dark eating chocolate, chopped coarsely

1 Make ganache.

2 Line each hole of a greased six-hole (¾-cup/180ml) texas muffin pan with plastic wrap. Divide half the ganache over the base of each pan hole. Refrigerate 20 minutes.

3 Meanwhile, cut each sponge cake into three slices horizontally. Cut six 8cm rounds from three sponge slices and six 7cm rounds from remaining three sponge slices.

4 Dissolve coffee in the boiling water in small jug; stir in liqueur.

5 Sprinkle gelatine over the extra boiling water in another small jug; stir until gelatine dissolves. Cool.

6 Beat cream, sifted icing sugar and extract in small bowl with electric mixer until soft peaks form; beat in gelatine mixture. Transfer mixture to large bowl; fold in cheese.

7 Brush both sides of sponge rounds with coffee mixture. Spread half the cheese mixture into pan holes; top with small sponge rounds. Spread remaining cheese mixture over sponge layers; top with larger sponge rounds.

8 Spread remaining ganache over sponge layers; refrigerate 3 hours or overnight.

9 Remove tiramisu from pan; turn, top-side down, onto serving plates, remove plastic wrap. Serve dusted with a little sifted cocoa powder.

ganache Bring cream to the boil in small saucepan; remove from heat. Add chocolate; stir until smooth.

prep & cook time 40 minutes (+ refrigeration)
makes 6
nutritional count per tiramisu 70.5g total fat (44.6g saturated fat); 4255kJ (1018 cal); 80.6g carbohydrate; 10.8g protein; 2.1g fibre

Tiramisu in Italian literally means 'pick me up' — an appropriate name for this dessert, loaded with coffee and liqueur.

blackberry parfait

450g fresh blackberries
300ml thickened cream
¼ cup (40g) icing sugar, sifted
⅓ cup (90g) greek-style yogurt
100g vanilla meringues

1 Roughly mash 300g of the blackberries in small bowl; drain and reserve about ¼ cup of juice.
2 Beat cream and sugar in small bowl with electric mixer until soft peaks form; stir in yogurt.

3 Layer cream mixture, berries and crushed meringues in serving glasses; drizzle with reserved juice. Top with remaining blackberries.

prep time 10 minutes **serves** 6
nutritional count per serving 20.1g total fat (13.1g saturated fat); 1329kJ (318 cal); 30.2g carbohydrate; 3.4g protein; 4.6g fibre

orange-poached pears

6 medium pears (1.4kg)

2 cups (500ml) water

2 cups (500ml) dry red wine

2 tablespoons orange-flavoured liqueur

¾ cup (165g) caster sugar

1 teaspoon vanilla bean paste

4 x 5cm strips orange rind

⅓ cup (80ml) orange juice

1 Peel pears, leaving stems intact.

2 Place the remaining ingredients in large saucepan; stir over heat, without boiling, until sugar dissolves. Add pears; bring to the boil. Reduce heat; simmer, covered, about 1 hour or until pears are tender.

3 Transfer pears to serving bowls.

4 Bring syrup in pan to the boil. Boil, uncovered, about 10 minutes or until syrup thickens slightly. Serve pears drizzled with warm syrup.

prep & cook time 1 hour 20 minutes **serves** 6
nutritional count per serving 0.2g total fat (0g saturated fat); 1317kJ (315 cal); 57.1g carbohydrate; 0.8g protein; 3.5g fibre

glossary

allspice also called pimento or jamaican pepper; tastes like a combination of nutmeg, cumin, clove and cinnamon. Available whole or ground.

almonds

blanched brown skins removed.

flaked paper-thin slices.

meal also called ground almonds.

slivered small pieces cut lengthways.

bacon also called bacon slices.

baking powder a raising agent consisting mainly of two parts cream of tartar to one part bicarbonate of soda.

bay leaves aromatic leaves from the bay tree, fresh or dried; adds a strong, slightly peppery flavour.

beans

black-eyed also known as black-eyed peas or cowpea; the dried seed of a variant of the snake or yard-long bean. Not too dissimilar to white beans in flavour; good cooked and used cold in salads.

borlotti also called roman beans or pink beans, can be eaten fresh or dried. Interchangeable with pinto beans due to their similarity in appearance – pale pink or beige with dark red streaks.

broad also called fava, windsor and horse beans; available dried, fresh, canned and frozen. Fresh should be peeled twice (discard the outer long green pod and the beige-green tough inner shell); the frozen beans have had their pods removed but the beige shell still needs removal.

cannellini small white bean similar in appearance and flavour to other *Phaseolus vulgaris* varieties (great northern, navy or haricot). Available dried or canned.

kidney medium-size red bean, slightly floury in texture yet sweet in flavour; sold dried or canned, it's found in bean mixes and is used in chilli con carne.

lima large, flat kidney-shaped, beige dried and canned beans. Also known as butter beans.

pinto similar to borlotti, a plump, kidney-shaped, pinky-beige bean speckled with brown to red streaks; available canned or dried and used in Mexican cooking.

snake long (about 40cm), thin, round, fresh green beans, Asian in origin, with a taste similar to green or french beans. Used most frequently in stir-fries, they are also called yard-long beans because of their (pre-metric) length.

sprouts also called bean shoots; tender new growths of assorted beans and seeds germinated for consumption as sprouts. Sprout mixtures or tendrils are also available.

beef

corned beef also called corned silverside; little fat, cut from the upper leg and cured. Sold cryovac-packed in brine.

eye-fillet tenderloin, fillet; fine texture, most expensive and extremely tender.

beetroot also called red beets; firm, round root vegetable.

bicarbonate of soda also called baking soda.

breadcrumbs

packaged prepared fine-textured but crunchy white breadcrumbs; good for coating foods that are to be fried.

stale crumbs made by grating, blending or processing 1- or 2-day-old bread.

brioche French in origin; a rich, yeast-leavened, cake-like bread made with butter and eggs. Available from cake or specialty bread shops.

broccolini a cross between broccoli and Chinese kale; long asparagus-like stems with a long loose floret, both completely edible. Resembles broccoli but is milder and sweeter in taste.

butter we use salted butter unless stated otherwise; 125g is equal to 1 stick (4 ounces).

butter lettuce small, round, loosely formed heads with a sweet flavour; soft, buttery-textured leaves range from pale green on the outer leaves to pale yellow-green inner leaves.

buttermilk in spite of its name, buttermilk is actually low in fat. Originally the term given to the slightly sour liquid left after butter was churned from cream, today it is intentionally made from no-fat or low-fat milk with specific bacterial cultures added during manufacturing. It is readily available from the dairy department in supermarkets. Because it is low in fat, it's a good substitute for dairy products like cream or sour cream in some baking and salad dressings.

caperberries olive-sized fruit formed after the buds of the caper bush have flowered; they are usually sold pickled in a vinegar brine with stalks intact.

capers grey green buds of a Mediterranean shrub, sold either dried and salted or pickled in a vinegar brine; tiny young ones, called baby capers, are also available both in brine or dried in salt. Their pungent taste adds piquancy to a classic steak tartare, tapenade, sauces and condiments.

capsicum also called pepper or bell pepper. Discard seeds and membranes before use.

caraway seeds the small, half-moon-shaped dried seed from a member of the parsley family; adds a sharp anise flavour when used in both sweet and savoury dishes. Used widely, in foods such as rye bread, harissa and the classic Hungarian fresh cheese, liptauer.

cardamom a spice native to India and used extensively in its cuisine; can be purchased in pod, seed or ground form. Has a distinctive aromatic, sweetly rich flavour and is one of the world's most expensive spices.

cashews plump, kidney-shaped, golden-brown nuts with a

distinctive sweet, buttery flavour; conts about 48 per cent fat. Due to their high fat content, they should be kept, sealed, in the refrigerator to avoid becoming rancid. We use roasted unsalted cashews unless otherwise stated; they're available from health-food stores and most supermarkets. Roasting cashews brings out their intense nutty flavour.

cayenne pepper a thin-fleshed, long, extremely hot dried red chilli, usually purchased ground.

cheese

blue mould-treated cheeses mottled with blue veining. Varieties include firm and crumbly stilton types and mild, creamy brie-like cheeses.

bocconcini from the diminutive of "boccone", meaning mouthful in Italian; walnut-sized, baby mozzarella, a delicate, semi-soft, white cheese traditionally made from buffalo milk. Sold fresh, it spoils rapidly so will only keep, refrigerated in brine, for 1 or 2 days at the most.

fetta Greek in origin; a crumbly textured goat- or sheep-milk cheese having a sharp, salty taste. Ripened and stored in salted whey; particularly good cubed and tossed into salads.

fontina a smooth, firm Italian cow-milk cheese with a creamy, nutty taste and brown or red rind; an ideal melting or grilling cheese.

gorgonzola a creamy Italian blue cheese with a mild, sweet taste;

good as an accompaniment to fruit or used to flavour sauces.

gruyère a hard rind Swiss cheese with small holes and a nutty, slightly salty flavour. A popular cheese for soufflés.

haloumi a Greek Cypriot cheese with a semi-firm, spongy texture and very salty sweet flavour. Ripened and stored in salted whey; best grilled or fried, and holds its shape well on being heated. Eat while still warm as it becomes tough and rubbery on cooling.

mascarpone an Italian fresh cultured-cream product made in much the same way as yogurt. White to creamy yellow in colour, with a buttery-rich, luscious texture. Soft, creamy and spreadable, it is used in Italian desserts and as an accompaniment to fresh fruit.

mozzarella soft, spun-curd cheese; originating in southern Italy where it was traditionally made from water-buffalo milk. Now generally made from cow milk, it is the most popular pizza cheese because of its low melting point and elasticity when heated.

parmesan also called parmigiano; is a hard, grainy cow-milk cheese originating in the Parma region of Italy. The curd for this cheese is salted in brine for a month, then aged for up to 2 years in humid conditions. Reggiano is the best parmesan, aged for a minimum 2 years and made only in the Italian region of Emilia-Romagna.

ricotta a soft, sweet, moist, white cow-milk cheese with a low fat content (8.5 per cent) and a slightly grainy texture. The name roughly translates as "cooked again" and refers to ricotta's manufacture from a whey that is itself a by-product of other cheese making.

chervil also known as cicily; mildly fennel flavoured member of the parsley family with curly dark-green leaves. Available both fresh and dried but, like all herbs, is best used fresh; like coriander and parsley, its delicate flavour diminishes the longer it's cooked.

chicken

barbecued we use cooked whole barbecued chickens about 900g each in our recipes. Skin discarded and bones removed, this size chicken provides about 4 cups (400g) shredded meat or 3 cups (400g) coarsely chopped meat.

breast fillet breast halved, skinned and boned.

thigh skin and bone intact.

thigh cutlet thigh with skin and centre bone intact; sometimes found skinned with bone intact.

thigh fillet thigh with skin and centre bone removed.

chilli

powder the Asian variety is the hottest, made from dried ground thai chillies; can be used instead of fresh in the proportion of ½ teaspoon chilli powder to 1 medium chopped fresh red chilli.

thai also known as "scuds"; tiny, very hot and bright red in colour.

chinese cooking wine Chinese cooking wine also called hao hsing or chinese rice wine; made from fermented rice, wheat, sugar and salt with a 13.5 per cent alcohol content. Inexpensive and found in Asian food shops; if you can't find it, replace with mirin or sherry.

chipolata sausages also known as 'little fingers'; highly spiced, coarse-textured beef sausage.

chocolate

Choc Bits also known as chocolate chips or chocolate morsels; available in milk, white and dark chocolate. Made of cocoa liquor, cocoa butter, sugar and an emulsifier, these hold their shape in baking and are ideal for decorating.

dark eating also called semi-sweet or luxury chocolate; made of a high percentage of cocoa liquor and cocoa butter, and little added sugar. Unless stated otherwise, we use dark eating chocolate as it's ideal for use in desserts and cakes.

milk most popular eating chocolate, mild and very sweet; similar in make-up to dark with the difference being the addition of milk solids.

white contains no cocoa solids but derives its sweet flavour from cocoa butter. Very sensitive to heat.

chocolate hazelnut spread also known as Nutella; made of cocoa powder, hazelnuts, sugar and milk.

chorizo sausage of Spanish origin, made of coarsely ground pork and highly seasoned with garlic and chilli.

choy sum also called pakaukeo or flowering cabbage, a member of the buk choy family; easy to identify with its long stems, light green leaves and yellow flowers. Stems and leaves are both edible, steamed or stir-fried.

cinnamon available both in pieces (called sticks or quills) and ground into powder; one of the world's most common spices, it is used universally as a sweet, fragrant flavouring for both sweet and savoury foods.

cloves dried flower buds of a tropical tree; can be used whole or in ground form. They have a strong scent and taste so should be used sparingly.

cocoa powder also known as unsweetened cocoa.

coconut

desiccated concentrated, dried, unsweetened and finely shredded coconut flesh.

flaked dried flaked coconut flesh.

milk not the liquid found inside the fruit, which is called coconut water, but the diluted liquid from the second pressing of the white flesh of a mature coconut (the first pressing produces coconut cream). Available in cans and cartons at most supermarkets.

shredded unsweetened thin strips of dried coconut flesh.

coffee-flavoured liqueur such as kahlua.

cornflour also called cornstarch. Available made from corn or wheat (wheaten cornflour, gluten-free, gives a lighter texture in cakes); used as a thickening agent in cooking.

cornichon French for gherkin, a very small variety of cucumber. Pickled, they are a traditional accompaniment to pâté; the Swiss always serve them with fondue (or raclette).

cos lettuce also called romaine lettuce; the traditional caesar salad lettuce. Long, with leaves ranging from dark green on the outside to almost white near the core; the leaves have a stiff centre rib giving a slight cupping effect to the leaf on either side.

couscous a fine, grain-like cereal product made from semolina; from the countries of North Africa. A semolina flour and water dough is sieved then dehydrated to produce minuscule even-sized pellets of couscous; it is rehydrated by steaming or with the addition of a warm liquid and swells to three or four times its original size, eaten like rice with a tagine, as a side dish or salad ingredient.

cranberries available fresh and frozen; have a rich, astringent flavour and can be used in cooking sweet and savoury dishes.

dried sweetened and dried cranberries; used in cooking sweet or savoury dishes. Can usually be substituted for or with other dried fruit in most recipes.

cream

pouring also called pure cream. It has no additives, and contains a minimum fat content of 35 per cent.

thickened a whipping cream that contains a thickener; a minimum fat content of 35 per cent.

cream of tartar the acid ingredient in baking powder; added to confectionery mixtures to help prevent sugar from crystallising. Keeps frostings creamy and improves volume when beating egg whites.

crème fraîche a mature, naturally fermented cream (minimum fat content 35 per cent) having a velvety texture and slightly tangy, nutty flavour. Crème fraîche, a French variation of sour cream, can boil without curdling and be used in sweet and savoury dishes.

cumin also known as zeera or comino; resembling caraway in size, cumin is the dried seed of a plant related to the parsley family. Its spicy, almost curry-like flavour is essential to the traditional foods of Mexico, India, North Africa and the Middle East. Available dried as seeds or ground.

custard powder instant mixture used to make pouring custard;

similar to North American instant pudding mixes.

dates fruit of the date palm tree, eaten fresh or dried, on their own or in prepared dishes. About 4cm to 6cm in length, oval and plump, thin-skinned, with a honey-sweet flavour and sticky texture.

dried chinese sausage also called lap cheong; highly spiced, bright red, thin pork sausages. The meat is preserved by the high spice content and can be kept at room temperature.

dried currants tiny, almost black raisins so-named after a grape variety that originated in Corinth, Greece.

duck we use whole ducks in some recipes; available from specialty chicken shops, open-air markets and some supermarkets.

breast fillets boneless whole breasts, with the skin on.

chinese barbecued traditionally cooked in special ovens in China; dipped into and brushed during roasting with a sticky sweet coating made from soy sauce, sherry, ginger, five-spice, star anise and hoisin sauce. Available from Asian food shops as well as dedicated Chinese barbecued meat shops.

eggplant also called aubergine; often thought of as a vegetable but actually a fruit and belongs to the same family as the tomato, chilli and potato. ranging in size from tiny to very large and in colour from pale green to deep purple. can be purchased char-grilled, packed in oil, in jars.

eggs if a recipe calls for raw or barely cooked eggs, exercise caution if there is a salmonella problem in your area, particularly in food eaten by children and pregnant women.

fennel also called finocchio or anise; a crunchy green vegetable slightly resembling celery that's eaten raw in salads; fried as an accompaniment; or used as an ingredient in soups and sauces. Also the name given to the dried seeds of the plant which have a stronger licorice flavour.

flour

buckwheat a herb in the same plant family as rhubarb, not a cereal so it is gluten-free. Available as flour; ground (cracked) into coarse, medium or fine granules (kasha) and used similarly to polenta; or groats, the whole kernel sold roasted as a cereal product.

chickpea (besan) made from ground chickpeas so is gluten-free and high in protein. Used in Indian cooking to make dumplings, noodles and chapati; for a batter coating for deep-frying; and as a sauce thickener.

plain also known as all-purpose; unbleached wheat flour is the best for baking: the gluten content ensures a strong dough, which produces a light result.

rice very fine, almost powdery, gluten-free flour; made from ground white rice. Used in baking, as a thickener, and in some Asian noodles and desserts. Another variety, made from glutinous sweet rice, is used for chinese dumplings and rice paper.

self-raising all-purpose plain or wholemeal flour with baking powder and salt added; make yourself with plain or wholemeal flour sifted with baking powder in the proportion of 1 cup flour to 2 teaspoons baking powder.

gai lan also known as gai larn, chinese broccoli and chinese kale; green vegetable appreciated more for its stems than its coarse leaves. Can be served steamed and stir-fried, in soups and noodle dishes. One of the most popular Asian greens, best known for its appearance on a yum cha trolley, where it's steamed then sprinkled with a mixture of oyster sauce and sesame oil.

gelatine we use dried (powdered) gelatine in this book; it's also available in sheet form known as leaf gelatine. A thickening agent made from either collagen, a protein found in animal connective tissue and bones, or certain algae (agar-agar). Three teaspoons of dried gelatine (8g or one sachet) is about the same as four gelatine leaves. The two types are interchangable but leaf gelatine gives a much clearer mixture than dried gelatine; it's perfect in dishes where appearance matters.

ginger

fresh also called green or root ginger; the thick gnarled root of a tropical plant. Store, peeled, covered with dry sherry in a jar and refrigerated, or frozen in an airtight container.

ground also called powdered ginger; cannot be substituted for fresh ginger.

golden syrup a by-product of refined sugarcane; pure maple syrup or honey can be substituted. Golden syrup and treacle (a thicker, darker syrup not unlike molasses), also known as flavour syrups, are similar sugar products made by partly breaking down sugar into its component parts and adding water. Treacle is more viscous, and has a stronger flavour and aroma than golden syrup (which has been refined further and contains fewer impurities, so is lighter in colour and more fluid).

Both can be use in baking and for making certain confectionery items.

hazelnuts also known as filberts; plump, grape-sized, rich, sweet nut having a brown skin that is removed by rubbing heated nuts together vigorously in a tea-towel.

meal is made by grounding the hazelnuts to a coarse flour texture for use in baking or as a thickening agent.

hazelnut-flavoured liqueur such as frangelico.

honey the variety sold in a squeezable container is not suitable for the recipes in this book.

horseradish a vegetable with edible green leaves but mainly grown for its long, pungent white root. Occasionally found fresh in specialty greengrocers and some Asian food shops, but commonly purchased in bottles at the supermarket in two forms: prepared horseradish and horseradish cream. These cannot be substituted one for the other in cooking but both can be used as table condiments. Horseradish cream is a commercially prepared creamy paste consisting of grated horseradish, vinegar, oil and sugar, while prepared horseradish is the preserved grated root.

kaffir lime leaves also known as bai magrood and looks like two glossy dark green leaves joined end to end, forming a rounded hourglass shape. Used fresh or dried in many South-East Asian dishes, they are used like bay leaves or curry leaves, especially in Thai cooking. Sold fresh, dried or frozen, the dried leaves are less potent so double the number if using them as a substitute for fresh; a strip of fresh lime peel may be substituted for each kaffir lime leaf.

kalonji also called nigella or black onion seeds. Tiny, angular seeds, black on the outside and creamy within, with a sharp nutty flavour that is enhanced by frying briefly in a dry hot pan before use. Typically sprinkled over Turkish bread immediately after baking or as an important spice in Indian cooking, kalonji can be found in most Asian and Middle Eastern food shops. Often erroneously called black cumin seeds.

kecap asin a thick, dark, salty Indonesian soy sauce.

kecap manis a dark, thick sweet soy sauce used in most South-East Asian cuisines. Depending on the manufacturer, the sauces's sweetness is derived from the addition of either molasses or palm sugar when brewed.

kumara the polynesian name of an orange-fleshed sweet potato often confused with yam; good baked, boiled, mashed or fried similarly to other potatoes.

lamb

backstrap also known as eye of loin; the larger fillet from a row of loin chops or cutlets. Tender, best cooked rapidly: barbecued or pan-fried.

shank forequarter leg; sometimes sold as drumsticks or frenched shanks if the gristle and narrow end of the bone are discarded and the remaining meat trimmed.

lebanese cucumbers short, slender and thin-skinned. Probably the most popular variety because of its tender, edible skin, tiny, yielding seeds, and sweet, fresh and flavoursome taste.

leeks a member of the onion family, the leek resembles a green onion but is much larger and more subtle in flavour. Tender baby or pencil leeks can be eaten whole with minimal cooking but adult leeks are usually trimmed of most of the green tops then chopped or sliced and cooked as an ingredient in stews, casseroles and soups.

lemon grass also known as takrai, serai or serah. A tall, clumping, lemon-smelling and tasting, sharp-edged aromatic tropical grass; the white lower part of the stem is used, finely chopped, in much of the cooking of South-East Asia. Can be found, fresh, dried, powdered and frozen, in supermarkets, greengrocers and Asian food shops.

lychees a small fruit from China with a hard shell and sweet, juicy flesh. The white flesh has a gelatinous texture and musky, perfumed taste. Discard the rough skin and seed before using in salads or as a dessert fruit. Also available canned in a sugar syrup.

maple-flavoured syrup is made from sugar cane and is also known as golden or pancake syrup. It is not a substitute for pure maple syrup.

maple syrup distilled from the sap of sugar maple trees found only in Canada and about ten states in the USA. Most often eaten with pancakes or waffles, but also used as an ingredient in baking or in preparing desserts. Maple-flavoured syrup or pancake syrup is not an adequate substitute for the real thing.

mayonnaise, whole-egg high quality commercial mayonnaise made with whole eggs and labelled as such; some mayonnaises substitute emulsifiers such as food starch, cellulose gel or other thickeners to achieve the same thick and creamy consistency but never achieve the same rich flavour. Must be refrigerated once opened

milk we use full-cream homogenised milk unless stated otherwise.

evaporated unsweetened canned milk from which water has been extracted by evaporation. Evaporated skim or low-fat milk has 0.3 per cent fat content.

sweetened condensed a canned milk product consisting of milk with more than half the water content removed and sugar added to the remaining milk.

mixed dried fruit a combination of sultanas, raisins, currants, mixed peel and cherries.

mixed spice a classic spice mixture generally containing caraway, allspice, coriander, cumin, nutmeg and ginger, although cinnamon and other spices can be added. It is used with fruit and in cakes.

mushrooms

button small, cultivated white mushrooms with a mild flavour. When a recipe in this book calls for an unspecified type of mushroom, use button.

enoki also known as enokitake; grown and bought in clumps, these delicately-flavoured mushrooms have small cream caps on long thin stalks. Available from Asian food shops and most supermarkets.

flat large, flat mushrooms with a rich earthy flavour, ideal for filling and barbecuing. They are sometimes misnamed field mushrooms which are wild mushrooms.

oyster also known as abalone; grey-white mushrooms shaped like a fan. Prized for their smooth texture and subtle, oyster-like flavour.

shiitake fresh, are also known as Chinese black, forest or golden oak mushrooms. Although cultivated, they have the earthiness

and taste of wild mushrooms. Large and meaty, they can be used as a substitute for meat in some Asian vegetarian dishes. dried also called donko or dried Chinese mushrooms; have a unique meaty flavour. Sold dried; rehydrate before use.

swiss brown also known as roman or cremini. Light to dark brown mushrooms with full-bodied flavour, suited for use in casseroles or being stuffed and baked.

mustard

dijon also called french. Pale brown, creamy, distinctively flavoured, fairly mild French mustard.

powder finely ground white (yellow) mustard seeds.

wholegrain also known as seeded. A French-style coarse-grain mustard made from crushed mustard seeds and dijon-style french mustard. Works well with cold meats and sausages.

noodles

dried rice noodles also known as rice stick noodles. Made from rice flour and water, available flat and wide or very thin (vermicelli). Must be soaked in boiling water to soften.

fresh rice also called ho fun, khao pun, sen yau, pho or kway tiau, depending on the country of manufacture; the most common form of noodle used in Thailand. Can be purchased in strands of various widths or large sheets weighing about 500g which are to be cut into the desired noodle size. Chewy and pure white, they do not need pre-cooking before use.

hokkien also known as stir-fry noodles; fresh wheat noodles resembling thick, yellow-brown spaghetti needing no pre-cooking before use.

rice stick also known as sen lek, ho fun or kway teow; especially popular South-East Asian dried rice noodles. They come in different widths (thin used in soups, wide in stir-fries), but all should be soaked in hot water to soften. The traditional noodle used in pad thai which, before soaking, measures about 5mm in width.

rice vermicelli also known as sen mee, mei fun or bee hoon. Used throughout Asia in spring rolls and cold salads; similar to bean threads, only longer and made with rice flour instead of mung bean starch. Before using, soak the dried noodles in hot water until softened, boil them briefly then rinse with hot water. Vermicelli can also be deep-fried until crunchy and used in salad or as a garnish or bed for sauces.

nutmeg a strong and pungent spice ground from the dried nut of an evergreen tree native to Indonesia. Usually found ground but the flavour is more intense from a whole nut, available from spice shops, so it's best to grate your own. Used most often in baking and milk-based desserts, but also works nicely in savoury dishes. Found in mixed spice mixtures.

oil

cooking spray we use a cholesterol-free cooking spray made from canola oil.

olive made from ripened olives. Extra virgin and virgin are the first and second press, respectively, of the olives and are therefore considered the best; the "extra light" or "light" name on other types refers to taste not fat levels.

peanut pressed from ground peanuts; the most commonly used oil in Asian cooking because of its

high smoke point (capacity to handle high heat without burning).

sesame made from roasted, crushed, white sesame seeds; a flavouring rather than a cooking medium.

vegetable any number of oils from plant rather than animal fats.

onions

brown and white are interchangeable. Their pungent flesh adds flavour to a vast range of dishes.

green also known as scallion or (incorrectly) shallot; an immature onion picked before the bulb has formed, having a long, bright-green edible stalk.

red also known as spanish, red spanish or bermuda onion; a sweet flavoured, large, purple-red onion.

spring crisp, narrow green-leafed tops and a round sweet white bulb larger than green onions.

orange-flavoured liqueur such as grand marnier and cointreau.

pancetta an Italian unsmoked bacon, pork belly cured in salt and spices then rolled into a sausage shape and dried for several weeks. Used, sliced or chopped, as an ingredient rather than eaten on its own; can also be used to add taste and moisture to tough or dry cuts of meat.

paprika ground dried sweet red capsicum (bell pepper); grades and types available include sweet, hot, mild and smoked.

peanuts also called groundnut, not in fact a nut but the pod of a legume. We use raw (unroasted) or roasted unsalted peanuts.

pecans native to the US and now grown locally; pecans are golden brown, buttery and rich. Good in savoury as well as sweet dishes; walnuts are a good substitute.

pine nuts also known as pignoli; not a nut but a small, cream-coloured kernel from pine cones. They are best roasted before use to bring out the flavour.

pistachios green, delicately flavoured nuts inside hard off-white shells. Available salted or unsalted in their shells; you can also get them shelled.

polenta also known as cornmeal; a flour-like cereal made of dried corn (maize). Also the name of the dish made from it.

potatoes

desiree oval, smooth and pink-skinned, waxy yellow flesh; good in salads, boiled and roasted.

kipfler small, finger-shaped, nutty flavour; great baked and in salads.

new potatoes also known as chats; not a separate variety but an early harvest with very thin skin. Good unpeeled steamed, eaten hot or cold in salads.

russet burbank long and oval, rough white skin with shallow eyes, white flesh; good for baking and frying.

prosciutto a kind of unsmoked Italian ham; salted, air-cured and aged, it is usually eaten uncooked. There are many styles of prosciutto, one of the best being Parma ham, from Italy's Emilia Romagna region, traditionally lightly salted, dried then eaten raw.

puff pastry packaged sheets of frozen puff pastry, available from supermarkets.

radicchio Italian in origin; a member of the chicory family. The dark burgundy leaves and strong, bitter flavour can be cooked or eaten raw in salads.

rhubarb a plant with long, green-red stalks; becomes sweet and edible when cooked.

rice

arborio small, round grain rice well-suited to absorb a large amount of liquid; the high level of starch makes it especially suitable for risottos, giving the dish its classic creaminess.

basmati a white, fragrant long-grained rice; the grains fluff up beautifully when cooked. It should be washed several times before cooking.

calasparra a short-grained rice available from Spanish delicatessens and gourmet-food stores. If you can't find calasparra, any short-graine rice can be substituted.

jasmine or Thai jasmine, is a long-grained white rice recognised around the world as having a perfumed aromatic quality; moist in texture, it clings together after cooking. Sometimes substituted for basmati rice.

koshihikari small, round-grain white rice. Substitute white short-grain rice and cook by the absorption method.

long-grain elongated grains that remain separate when cooked; this is the most popular steaming rice in Asia.

short-grain fat, almost round grain with a high starch content; tends to clump together when cooked.

white is hulled and polished rice, can be short- or long-grained.

rocket also called arugula, rugula and rucola; peppery green leaf eaten raw in salads or used in cooking. Baby rocket leaves are smaller and less peppery.

rolled oats flattened oat grain rolled into flakes and traditionally used for porridge. Instant oats are also available, but use traditional oats for baking

rosewater extract made from crushed rose petals, called gulab in India; used for its aromatic quality in many sweetmeats and desserts.

saffron stigma of a member of the crocus family, available ground or in strands; imparts a yellow-orange colour to food once infused. The quality can vary greatly; the best is the most expensive spice in the world.

sauces

char siu a Chinese barbecue sauce made from sugar, water, salt, fermented soybean paste, honey, soy sauce, malt syrup and spices. It can be found at most supermarkets.

fish called naam pla on the label if it is Thai made; the Vietnamese version, nuoc naam, is almost identical. Made from pulverised salted fermented fish (most often anchovies); has a pungent smell and strong taste. There are many versions of varying intensity, so use according to your taste.

hoisin a thick, sweet and spicy Chinese barbecue sauce made from salted fermented soybeans, onions and garlic; used as a marinade or baste, or to accent stir-fries and barbecued or roasted foods. From Asian food shops and supermarkets.

oyster Asian in origin, this rich, brown sauce is made from oysters and their brine, cooked with salt and soy sauce, and thickened with starches.

plum a thick, sweet and sour dipping sauce made from plums, vinegar, sugar, chillies and spices.

soy also known as sieu; made from fermented soybeans. Several variations are available in supermarkets and Asian food stores; we use Japanese soy sauce unless indicated otherwise.

dark deep brown, almost black in colour; rich, with a thicker consistency than other types. Pungent but not particularly salty; good for marinating. *Japanese* an all-purpose low-sodium soy sauce made with more wheat content than its Chinese counterparts, fermented in barrels and aged. Possibly the best table soy and the one to choose if you only want one variety. *light* fairly thin in consistency and, while paler than the others, the saltiest tasting; used in dishes in which the natural colour of the ingredients is to be maintained. Not to be confused with salt-reduced or low-sodium soy sauces.

worcestershire thin, dark-brown spicy sauce developed by the British when in India; used as a seasoning for meat, gravies and cocktails, and as a condiment.

seafood

balmain bug also called slipper or shovelnose lobster, or southern bay lobster; crustacean, a type of crayfish. Substitute with moreton bay bugs, king prawns or scampi.

blue-eye also called deep sea trevalla or trevally and blue-eye cod; thick, moist white-fleshed fish.

clams also called vongole; we use a small ridge-shelled variety of this bivalve mollusc.

fish fillet use your favourite firm-fleshed white fish fillet.

crab meat flesh of fresh crabs; frozen uncooked flesh is also available. Use canned if neither is available.

marinara mix a mixture of uncooked, chopped seafood available from fishmarkets and fishmongers.

mussels should only be bought from a reliable fish market: they must be tightly closed when bought, indicating they are alive.

Before cooking, scrub shells with a strong brush and remove the beards; do not eat any that do not open after cooking. Varieties include black and green-lip.

octopus usually tenderised before you buy them; both octopus and squid require either long slow cooking (usually for the large molluscs) or quick cooking over high heat (usually for the small molluscs) — anything in between will make the octopus tough and rubbery.

oysters available in many varieties, including pacific, bay/blacklip, and Sydney or New Zealand rock oyster.

prawns also known as shrimp. Varieties include, school, king, royal red, Sydney harbour, tiger. Can be bought uncooked (green) or cooked, with or without shells.

salmon red-pink firm flesh with few bones; moist delicate flavour.

squid also knowns as calamari; a type of mollusc. Buy squid hoods to make preparation and cooking faster.

swordfish also called broadbill. Substitute with yellowfin or bluefin tuna or mahi mahi.

tuna reddish, firm flesh; slightly dry. Varieties include bluefin, yellowfin, skipjack or albacore; substitute with swordfish.

white fish means non-oily fish; includes bream, flathead, whiting, snapper, dhufish, redfish and ling.

sesame seeds black and white are the most common of this small oval seed, however there are also red and brown varieties. The seeds are used as an ingredient and as a condiment. Roast the seeds in a heavy-based frying pan over low heat.

shallots also called french shallots, golden shallots or eschalots. Small

and elongated, with a brown skin, they grow in tight clusters similar to garlic.

shrimp paste also called kapi, trasi and blanchan; a strong-scented, very firm preserved paste made of salted dried shrimp. Used sparingly as a flavouring in many South-East Asian soups, sauces and rice dishes. It should be chopped or sliced thinly then wrapped in foil and roasted before use.

silver beet also known as swiss chard and incorrectly, spinach; has fleshy stalks and large leaves, both of which can be prepared as for spinach.

sour cream thick, commercially-cultured sour cream with a minimum fat content of 35 per cent.

spinach also known as english spinach and incorrectly, silver beet. Baby spinach leaves are best eaten raw in salads; the larger leaves should be added last to soups, stews and stir-fries, and should be cooked until barely wilted.

star anise a dried star-shaped pod whose seeds have an astringent aniseed flavour; commonly used to flavour stocks and marinades.

sugar we use coarse, granulated table sugar, also known as crystal sugar, unless otherwise specified.

brown a soft, finely granulated sugar retaining molasses for its characteristic colour and flavour.

caster also known as superfine or finely granulated table sugar.

demerara small-grained golden-coloured crystal sugar.

icing also called confectioners' sugar or powdered sugar; pulverised granulated sugar crushed together with a small amount of cornflour.

palm also called nam tan pip, jaggery, jawa or gula melaka;

made from the sap of the sugar palm tree. Light brown to black in colour and usually sold in rock-hard cakes; use with brown sugar if unavailable.

pure icing also called confectioners' sugar or powdered sugar.

sumac a purple-red, astringent spice ground from berries growing on shrubs that flourish wild around the Mediterranean; adds a tart, lemony flavour to dips and dressings and goes well with barbecued meat. Can be found in Middle Eastern food stores.

tomatoes

canned whole peeled tomatoes in natural juices; available crushed, chopped or diced, and unsalted or reduced salt. Use undrained.

cherry also called tiny tim or tom thumb tomatoes; small and round.

egg also called plum or roma, these are smallish, oval-shaped tomatoes much used in Italian cooking or salads.

grape small, long oval-shaped tomatoes with a good tomato flavour.

paste triple-concentrated tomato puree used to flavour soups, stews, sauces and casseroles.

puree canned pureed tomatoes (not tomato paste); substitute with fresh peeled and pureed tomatoes.

semi-dried partially dried tomato pieces in olive oil; softer and juicier than sun-dried, these are not a preserve thus do not keep as long as sun-dried.

sun-dried tomato pieces that have been dried with salt; this dehydrates the tomato and concentrates the flavour. We use sun-dried tomatoes packaged in oil, unless otherwise specified.

truss small vine-ripened tomatoes with vine still attached.

tarragon often called the king of herbs by the French, it is used as the essential flavouring for many of their classic sauces (béarnaise, tartare, etc). It is one of the herbs blended with parsley, chives and chervil to make fines herbes, and is the unique, immediately identified taste giving singularity to so many French egg, fish and chicken dishes.

turmeric also called kamin; is a rhizome related to galangal and ginger. Must be grated or pounded to release its acrid aroma and pungent flavour. Known for the golden colour it imparts, fresh turmeric can be substituted with the more commonly found dried powder.

vanilla

bean dried, long, thin pod from a tropical golden orchid; the minuscule black seeds inside the bean are used to impart a luscious vanilla flavour in baking and desserts.

bean paste is made from vanilla pods and contains real seeds. It is highly concentrated and 1 teaspoon replaces a whole vanilla pod without mess or fuss, as you neither have to split or scrape the pod. It can also be used instead of vanilla extract. It is found in most supermarkets in the baking section.

extract obtained from vanilla beans infused in water; a non-alcoholic version of essence.

veal

osso buco another name butchers use for veal shin, usually cut into 3cm to 5cm thick slices and used in the famous Italian slow-cooked casserole of the same name.

rack row of small chops or cutlets.

schnitzel thinly sliced steak.

vinegar

balsamic originally from Modena, Italy, there are now many balsamic vinegars on the market ranging in pungency and quality depending on how, and for how long, they have been aged. Quality can be determined up to a point by price; use the most expensive sparingly.

brown malt made from fermented malt and beech shavings.

cider made from fermented apples.

red wine made from red wine.

rice a colourless vinegar made from fermented rice and flavoured with sugar and salt. Also called seasoned rice vinegar; sherry can be substituted.

white made from distilled grain alcohol.

white wine made from white wine.

vine leaves from early spring, fresh grapevine leaves can be found in most specialist greengrocers. Alternatively, cryovac-packages containing about 60 leaves in brine can be found in Middle Eastern food shops and some delicatessens; these must be well rinsed and dried before using. Used as wrappers for a large of number of savoury fillings in Mediterranean cuisines.

walnuts as well as being a good source of fibre and healthy oils, nuts contain a range of vitamins, minerals and other beneficial plant components called phytochemicals. Each type of nut has a special make-up and walnuts contain the beneficial omega-3 fatty acids.

watercress one of the cress family, a large group of peppery greens used raw in salads, dips and sandwiches, or cooked in soups. Highly perishable, so it must be used as soon as possible after purchase.

witlof also known as belgian endive; related to and confused with chicory. A versatile vegetable, it tastes as good cooked as it does eaten raw. Grown in darkness like white asparagus to prevent it becoming green; looks somewhat like a tightly furled, cream to very light-green cigar. The leaves can be removed and used to hold a canapé filling; the whole vegetable can be opened up, stuffed then baked or casseroled; and the leaves can be tossed in a salad with other vegetables.

wombok also known as chinese cabbage, peking or napa cabbage; elongated in shape with pale green, crinkly leaves, this is the most common cabbage in South-East Asia. Can be shredded or chopped and eaten raw or braised, steamed or stir-fried.

wonton wrappers (and gow gee or spring roll pastry sheets), made of flour, egg and water, are found in the refrigerated or freezer section of Asian food shops and many supermarkets. These come in different thicknesses and shapes. Thin wrappers work best in soups, while the thicker ones are best for frying; and the choice of round or square, small or large is dependent on the recipe.

yeast (dried and fresh), a raising agent used in dough making. Granular (7g sachets) and fresh compressed (20g blocks) yeast can almost always be substituted one for the other when yeast is called for.

yogurt we use plain full-cream yogurt in our recipes unless specifically noted otherwise.

zucchini also called courgette. Harvested when young, its edible flowers can be filled with a mild cheese filling and deep fried.

conversion chart

measures

One Australian metric measuring cup holds approximately 250ml; one Australian metric tablespoon holds 20ml; one Australian metric teaspoon holds 5ml.

The difference between one country's measuring cups and another's is within a two- or three-teaspoon variance, and will not affect your cooking results. North America, New Zealand and the United Kingdom use a 15ml tablespoon.

All cup and spoon measurements are level. The most accurate way of measuring dry ingredients is to weigh them. When measuring liquids, use a clear glass or plastic jug with the metric markings.

We use large eggs with an average weight of 60g.

dry measures

metric	imperial
15g	½oz
30g	1oz
60g	2oz
90g	3oz
125g	4oz (¼lb)
155g	5oz
185g	6oz
220g	7oz
250g	8oz (½lb)
280g	9oz
315g	10oz
345g	11oz
375g	12oz (¾lb)
410g	13oz
440g	14oz
470g	15oz
500g	16oz (1lb)
750g	24oz (1½lb)
1kg	32oz (2lb)

liquid measures

metric	imperial
30ml	1 fluid oz
60ml	2 fluid oz
100ml	3 fluid oz
125ml	4 fluid oz
150ml	5 fluid oz (¼ pint/1 gill)
190ml	6 fluid oz
250ml	8 fluid oz
300ml	10 fluid oz (½ pint)
500ml	16 fluid oz
600ml	20 fluid oz (1 pint)
1000ml (1 litre)	1¾ pints

length measures

metric	imperial
3mm	⅛ in
6mm	¼in
1cm	½in
2cm	¾in
2.5cm	1in
5cm	2in
6cm	2½in
8cm	3in
10cm	4in
13cm	5in
15cm	6in
18cm	7in
20cm	8in
23cm	9in
25cm	10in
28cm	11in
30cm	12in (1ft)

oven temperatures

These oven temperatures are only a guide for conventional ovens. For fan-forced ovens, check the manufacturer's manual.

	°C (Celsius)	°F (Fahrenheit)	Gas Mark
Very slow	120	250	½
Slow	150	275-300	1-2
Moderately slow	160	325	3
Moderate	180	350-375	4-5
Moderately hot	200	400	6
Hot	220	425-450	7-8
Very hot	240	475	9

index